How do we introduce non-fiction to children in an enjoyable way?

This lively and informative text examines children's first experience of non-fiction during the pre-school and foundation years. Its careful consideration of different kinds of quality non-fiction, including books, posters, charts, and computer software will provide a helpful framework from which early years teachers can work. With annotated lists, notes and suggestions for further reading, this is an ideal source of inspiration and stimulation for the busy classroom teacher, placing literacy teaching in a fresh, modern context.

The book offers a rich resource of information, with illustrative case studies and many examples of children's responses to non-fiction, providing:

- coverage of pre-school and foundation years for children up to six years of age;
- references to research findings on the place of non-fiction in early years;
- references to the National Literacy Strategy, Early Learning Goals and the National Curriculum for English;
- an evaluation of the place of e-books, CD-ROMs and video-film in early years;
- a substantial glossary of terms relevant to non-fiction reading and writing.

The author's zest and expertise helps to give this book an infectious enthusiasm that will permeate the classroom, providing the nursery and primary school teacher, student teacher or classroom assistant with an invaluable guide and resource tool.

Margaret Mallett is currently Visiting Tutor in Primary English at Goldsmiths College, London. Her previous book with RoutledgeFalmer, *Young Researchers: Informational Reading and Writing in the Early and Primary Years*, won her the UKRA author award in 2001.

Early Years Non-Fiction

A guide to helping young researchers use
and enjoy information texts

Margaret Mallett

RoutledgeFalmer
Taylor & Francis Group

LONDON AND NEW YORK

First published 2003
by RoutledgeFalmer
11 New Fetter Lane, London EC4P 4EE

Simultaneously published in the USA and Canada
by RoutledgeFalmer
29 West 35th Street, New York, NY 10001

RoutledgeFalmer is an imprint of the Taylor & Francis Group

© 2003 Margaret Mallett

Typeset in Times by
HWA Text and Data Management, Tunbridge Wells
Printed and bound in Great Britain by
TJ International Ltd, Padstow, Cornwall

British Library Cataloguing in Publication Data
A catalogue record for this book is available from the British Library

Library of Congress Cataloging in Publication Data
A catalog record for this book has been requested

ISBN 0–415–32139–5 (hbk)
ISBN 0–415–25337–3 (pbk)

Even very young children will grow into informational sorts of reading, using active problem-solving and interaction with their educators. Through these experiences and processes, they will come to realise that reading for information is just as imaginative and exciting as reading stories.

(Helen Arnold, 1996)

Contents

Illustrations

Figures

Tables

Preface

Non-fiction can engage the interest of children from a young age and encourage them to reflect and ask questions. The best non-fiction or 'informational' texts have imaginative appeal and contribute significantly to children's learning. This book aims to present a coherent notion of how to introduce very young children to these texts and to help them take the first steps in informational reading and writing. I have been particularly aware of the needs of student teachers but I hope the book will also be of interest to teachers and indeed anyone concerned with early years literacy. I have kept three things in mind: how children's language and thinking develops; the importance of the range and quality of the texts we select; and the need to create meaningful contexts for non-fiction reading and writing. These three aspects of non-fiction learning work together throughout the book but each comes into sharper focus when appropriate.

Most of what I have to say about the under-threes is in the early chapters while the later chapters concentrate on the years from three to six, the children in what are now referred to as 'the foundation years'. This transition is signalled by a passage headed 'Moving forward' which nudges us towards the concerns of older nursery, reception and year 1 children.

Chapter 1 provides a theoretical framework for the book; it gives a selective review of relevant research on the development of children's language and thinking and offers a model for integrating non-fiction into other learning activities. It looks at what is involved in learning from both first hand experience and secondary sources, and considers how the two kinds of learning interact in good practice. Three important principles, well established in sound early years practice, are identified as underpinning informational kinds of literacy. First, children learn actively; they explore their world like young scientists or young researchers. They learn actively before they come to nursery school and this is one of the strategies the nursery team builds on. Second, learning is energised by taking place in social and collaborative contexts. Talk is powerful in all learning, not least when it comes to conversations around texts. Third, the role of the adult is very significant in extending children's learning . I say 'adult' because, in addition to teachers, parents, other relatives, carers and older siblings are important mediators between children and the world.

Chapter 2 enters the world of babies and very young children and considers their response to the environmental print which surrounds them at home and outside. The account then turns to the board, bath and cloth books – many of these are 'informational' in that they help children name, count and label – and the many exciting interactive books which straddle the boundary between toys and books. Short case studies share the encounters of three very young children with early information books. That very important category of early non-fiction, the alphabet book, is the focus of chapter 3. New alphabet books and old favourites are covered and I explore their contribution to children's early attempts to write. Chapter 4 analyses what are often termed 'concept books'; these include books on aspects of learning like, for example, number, colour, opposites and orientation. To end this series of chapters, mainly about pre-school children, chapter 5 is a case study of a young child's experience of books and her drawing and writing in the home setting.

The linking piece, 'Moving forward', introduces the remaining chapters which look at all aspects of non-fiction reading and writing from three to six – the foundation years. Chapter 6 looks at the purposes for which three- to six-year-olds use writing and shows, in some lively case studies, how skilled teachers embed writing in exciting contexts in and out of the classroom. Role play, practical work and outings are shown to be strong settings for making progress in literacy. Attention is given to how we help children think and write in ways important in our society and formalised in National Literacy Strategy requirements. Some important early years issues are discussed – how to encourage both boys and girls to write, how to support young bilingual writers and how to develop children's visual literacy. There is a section on the assessment and recording of young learners' progress.

Chapter 7 examines some different kinds of information text, making a broad division between informational narratives, organised round a time sequence, and the non-narrative kinds, organised round the requirements of a subject or topic. But it is also made clear that many early non-fiction texts are 'transitional genre' which, while clearly serving an informational purpose, do not have all the features of the mature texts of which they are early forms. Criteria for selecting books for the classroom are offered as a starting point for discussion. Case studies sharing the work of children and teachers around texts show how non-fiction can enrich children's learning and how teachers can help children understand each genre and use library and study skills. Finally in chapter 7, there are sections on issues to do with bias in information texts and on those that surround 'genre-based' approaches to children's literacy progress.

Reference texts – dictionaries, thesauruses, encyclopaedias and atlases – are discussed in chapter 8 and annotated lists of some of the best are set out. Chapter 9 looks at children's learning from television and video-film. While media texts are referred to throughout the book, reflecting the fact that they are increasingly becoming important in all learning areas, their use and the issues this raises are brought together systematically in chapter 10.

Early years practitioners have always used texts flexibly and imaginatively to support children's learning. Chapter 11 identifies fiction texts – picturebooks and stories – which seem to provide particularly sympathetic ways into a lesson.

I include a substantial glossary of terms relevant to children's non-fiction reading and writing and I hope this will prove a useful quick reference resource. Appendix 1 provides the information from the official frameworks that is most pertinent to non-fiction reading and writing. The lists of 'star texts' in appendices 2, 3 and 4 offer suggestions to help parents choosing books for the pre-school years and teachers building core non-fiction collections. I have given prices and ISBNs to help here. Children's information books and resources, even very successful ones, can go out of print quickly. This is bound to be the fate of some of the many texts I recommend. I hope that my readers will be able to track down any out-of-print texts they seek through libraries and search engines on the Internet.

My students always tell me to include as much classroom material as possible in my books; I hope that the case studies here of children learning at home and at school make a strong and interesting contribution. Some provide just glimpses of children at work while others follow a learning project in more detail over a number of weeks. This allows us to appreciate the practitioner's skill in placing texts alongside other experiences, at just the right point as the work develops, to help children acquire insights and concepts. So I have set out to share the work and ideas of thoughtful practitioners who want to make children's early forays into non-fiction exciting and purposeful. This has helped me reinforce the belief of so many early years specialists that informational texts are best placed in rich contexts – within broad-based themes which offer opportunities for outings and practical activities. The liveliest work I have seen has been collaborative – young learners working together with skilful input by the teacher in the home corner or in the school garden, as well as in the classroom. It is the teacher who helps children make important links between learning from books and learning from other experiences and who can make their talk, writing and displays deeply satisfying.

Margaret Mallett
Goldsmiths College Education Department
December 2002

Acknowledgements

My students at Goldsmiths College, the teachers and the children I have worked with over the years have been a great inspiration. My colleagues, too, have shared stimulating ideas and often challenged me to take my thinking further. I would particularly like to acknowledge the contribution my friend and former colleague, Marian Whitehead, has made to my understanding of young children's language development.

My thanks are also given to my family – to Anna who is always so interested and supportive of all I try to do, to Katherine who helped with research for the case studies in chapter 2 and especially to David, who reads my drafts with care and rightly pounces on any expression that is vague, inelegant or which descends into jargon!

I appreciate the generosity of a number of parents, teachers and children who provided material for the case studies.

The parents and families I wish to thank are: Pouneh and Morten Bligaard and my friend Parvin Taheri (Yasmine, case study 2.2), Rebecca and Barry Williams (Alexandra, case study 2.3), Siobhan Carolin (Orla, chapter 5), Claire and Paul Kulaway (Beth, figures 1.2 Dulwich Art Gallery and 4.3 Dinosaur maths, and Faith, figures 10.2 Dinosaur account and 6.13 My sister).

My thanks go also to the following schools, teachers and children who shared their work and thoughts with me. These are: Kathleen Doyle and Kingswood School, Norwood for the Whale work (case study 6.6); Elaine Shiel and her five- to six-year-olds for the 'Caring for a pet' case studies and writing, Corstorphine Primary School, Edinburgh (figures 6.10, 6.11, 7.5, 7.6 and 7.7); Claire Pester, both for the work done by her nursery class during her final teaching practice at Clyde Nursery, Deptford (case studies 6.2 and 6.3) and for figure 3.1, the page from five-year-old Nina's alphabet book, Crockham Hill C of E Primary School; John Paine and Terry Gould for putting me in touch with St. Gilbert's RC School in Winton Salford – my thanks go to children and staff for figure 6.3 (Angela's ladybird), figure 6.14 (Samuel's cakes) and the writing display pictures in figure 6.12 ; Heather Ballinger for case studies 4.2 and 7.2 and Norma Fiddler for case studies 9.2 and 10.1 and figures 6.4, 6.5 (which shows Olivia's writing) and figure 10.3 (Abbie's poster), Castlecombe Primary School, Mottingham, Kent; Jenny Lovell, Pauline Donovan and the nursery team for the material on the supermarket theme and figures 6.1 (Yasmin), 6.2 (Tom) and 6.7 (cover of the Waitrose visit book), Dulwich Wood Nursery School; Emma Richardson and her year 1/2 class at Dalmain Primary School, London for the 'Who am I?' writing and pictures in the case study in chapter 5 and figures 6.8 and 6.9; Pat Blackwell, head teacher of Frinton on Sea Primary School and the children, for the recount in figure 1.2 and the Jubilee letter in figure 6.6; Jane Boyd and the staff and children of Perry Hall Primary School, Kent for the material in the case studies in chapter 11;

Elizabeth Bracken, Loughborough Infants School and Clare Kelly, Goldsmiths College for Jamie's map, figure 8.3.

A number of authors and publishers generously allowed me to include book covers and illustrations and, in some cases, accompanying text. They are acknowledged beside the pictures but I would like them to know how much I appreciate their help.

Chapter 1

Language and learning in the early years

Some guiding principles to inform non-fiction reading and writing

Early-years educators now accept that, through actively engaging with the world around them and generating and testing their hypotheses about their experiences and observations, young children bring a great deal of knowledge and a number of established and productive learning strategies to school.

(Ann Browne, 2001: 32)

A coherent and imaginative approach to helping children use and learn from non-fiction texts needs to be underpinned by an understanding of some relevant theories and thinking. There are strong reasons for student teachers to build this understanding because it will help them to play their part in developing early years practice rather than being simply reactive to the prescriptions of others. Journals like *Early Years: TACTYC; Reading, Literacy and Language (UKRA)* and the *International Journal of Early Years Education* all provide a forum for sharing discussions about research, training, advancement and co-operation in teaching young children.[1] Their international perspective helps put our own beliefs and the guidelines we follow in a broader perspective. They remind us that our own practice has developed in the context of our cultural assumptions and is subject to the societal beliefs which influence what is taught in the early years and the ways in which we teach it.

In the United Kingdom there is some tension between the perception that some current official requirements stem from a utilitarian view of literacy and therefore are in conflict with the rich experience of language and learning which early years practitioners want for children. Creative teachers believe that they can work within the guidelines while using their professional skills and judgement to provide the right contexts for exciting work – a belief reflected in the case studies to be found throughout this book.

This chapter looks first at three guiding principles, informed by relevant thinking, which I believe inform good practice in the classroom. These guiding principles and some of the research and thinking behind them will be familiar to early years practitioners and can be observed 'in action' in the good practice of early years teams. These principles are: children learn actively, learning is social and collaborative, and the role of the adult is crucial. I start this book here because I believe they offer a foundation for developing the non-fiction or informational aspects of children's learning. I then move into a discussion of what has been written about the different ways in which we talk and write about what we know and have done, in other words, about ways of representing experience. This is important because these ideas describe the roots from which informational kinds of thinking develop. And this takes us to the central question of this book: how do we help children integrate learning from first hand experience and learning from secondary sources? If we can find powerful and imaginative ways of doing this, then we will help children see writing and reading as a positive and worthwhile part of all their activities and interests.

I end with a model of how this might be achieved in practice.

Some guiding principles

Children learn actively

Children actively engage with their world from very early on in their lives. As Ann Browne reminds us in the quotation that opens this chapter, they are not passive but constantly interact with others and soon try to make sense of everything that surrounds them. For me, Piaget's adaptive model, first described in the 1950s, best captures the notion of the child as an active learner. He uses the metaphor of the digestive system to indicate how we take on new knowledge and information: a new episode of learning is 'assimilated' or adapted so that it can be absorbed just as food is changed within the digestive system so that it can be used by the body. At the same time, the learning structures that the child already has in place change to 'accommodate' the new knowledge just as the digestive organs adapt to the incoming food. This model makes learning seem as natural as eating. If we do not adjust the material we use in the classroom – whether it is on frogs, rivers or supermarkets – to make it appropriate for the intellectual stage children have reached, learning will be as difficult for them as eating raw potatoes would be a challenge to a digestive system. Piaget did not research and write directly for the classroom although some of his ideas have relevance there. You can read about his work in many books and articles. Margaret Donaldson's account in *Children's Minds* is helpful because it puts his work in the perspective of other developmentalists – Bruner, Vygotsky and Macnamara (Donaldson, 1978). If you want a lively new evaluation of Piaget's work I recommend *How babies think* by three American experts on the science of infant minds (Gopnik, Meltzoff and Kuhl, 1999). This book reminds us how Piaget, with the help of his wife Valentine who was herself a psychologist, recorded developments in the unfolding lives of their three children, Jacqueline, Lucienne and Laurent, in some remarkably detailed baby diaries. Piaget's work reminds us that children have powerful learning mechanisms that help them build an internal picture of the world. This internal representation of the world guides action and thought from the earliest stage. Young children behave very much like immensely active research scientists when the urge to learn and 'make sense' comes upon them.

Other cognitive psychologists – Bruner and Macnamara, for example – have agreed with Piaget that the young child has cognitive abilities which are language-free or relatively language-free. But while Piaget tends to underestimate the role of language, they believe that once language is acquired children's intellectual capacities become much stronger and more flexible. Language is a crucial tool in active learning because it helps extend and organise children's actions and thinking.

The child's urge to mean and actively 'make sense' of the world around them is also built into psycho-linguistic approaches to language acquisition. This 'meaning-making' capacity has been illuminated in a fascinating case study of the author's own child in M.A.K. Halliday's book *Learning how to Mean* (Halliday, 1975). Written some decades ago, this book still shows us powerfully that the urge to make sense and communicate is evident long before a child becomes verbal.

All those working with young children find that they are likely to learn best when they are deeply engaged in their activities and understand the purposes of their learning. An active learner, like a scientist, develops theories and expectations about the world and tries them out. We should encourage risk-taking and regard 'mistakes' as part of the learning process. This is why early years practitioners resist an emphasis on getting things right first time. When supporting children's early attempts at spelling, for example, we praise their intelligent and creative attempts to use all their existing knowledge to make meaning while nudging them gently towards the accepted conventions.

The picture that emerges from this selective review of some of the research evidence is of a young child active in the environment from the earliest stages – at stages when the child knows the world through action and perception. Later there comes the pedagogic challenge of combining learning from first hand experience and learning from secondary sources. Any book on the early use and enjoyment of non-fiction needs to show how these can be effectively combined and I make a start on this with the model of non-fiction learning described towards the end of this chapter.

Learning is social and collaborative

Good early years settings take account of a child's need to work alongside others. This helps develop the ability to co-operate on a joint task and to learn from others – from what they do and what they say. There are strong implications here for informational kinds of learning. Perhaps we have too often expected children to research and study alone when the company of others helps animate the 'finding out' and helps them clarify their thinking. In small group work, one child's comment or question can cause the others to reflect and modify their opinions. I remember five-year-olds discussing a video-film that showed a whale eating a seal. Some of them judged this 'cruel' but one child pointed out that if seals were what they ate 'it was not cruel for the whale to kill the seal'. The other children were helped to consider another viewpoint even if they found it hard to accept. And of course, one of the most joyous aspects of finding out is sharing your discoveries with the teacher and the group or class.

An approach which recognises the essentially social nature of learning gives a high priority to speaking and listening. These language processes enable children to organise their thinking and to communicate information, thoughts and feelings to others. Children need to control the spoken language for different purposes and in different situations inside and outside the classroom.

The average five-year-old knows at least 2,000 words and may understand many more (Crystal, 1987). By school age children also control most of the phonemes or sound units of the speech used in their home and community. They command a range of sentence types and are aware of grammatical correctness (Browne, 2001). It is Vygotsky who demonstrates most powerfully the social impetus to learning to talk and the continuing importance of talking through ideas and information to clinch understanding of concepts (Vygotsky, 1986). There is more about Vygotsky's ideas under 'spontaneous and scientific concepts' in the glossary.

Socio-linguistic theories of language acquisition demonstrate that young children begin to 'mean' even before they have words. Halliday, for example, proposes seven functions of 'language' (Halliday, 1975). An attractive feature of socio-linguistic models of language acquisition is that they explain how a child learns the functions and purposes of language, including the social functions, while at the same time increasing vocabulary and control over language structures. You can read about Halliday's model and other theories of language acquisition in Marian Whitehead's book *Language and Literacy in the Early Years* (Whitehead, 1997). The strength of her analysis lies in its presentation of a range of theoretical positions from the point of view of an early years educator.

It is the use of language as a learning tool by children, Halliday's *heuristic* function – 'let's find out', which is of particular relevance to a study of non-fiction learning. This function emphasises the social aspects of 'finding out' not least because children constantly ask questions of adults and other children. It is also through talking with others that children acquire some meta-linguistic terms to talk about their own language and learning. They might, for example, hear a parent or caregiver remark 'I am trying to answer all your questions'. The heuristic function has the potential to engage the child in all sorts of learning situations in and out of the classroom. Although the world is first explored by action and spoken language, a child's questions are later taken to secondary sources.

Halliday's seventh language function, the *representational* function – 'I have something to tell you' – is also of great importance to understanding the social impetus to learning. It develops after the other functions and involves sharing ideas and propositions (Halliday, 1975). Here is the root of some of the more challenging ways of using information and knowledge – perhaps to set out a theory, argue a case or persuade. Children do this first through talk, often modelling what they say on an adult's speech, and later in writing.

The role of the adult is crucial

In the pre-school years it is the parents, older siblings and other caregivers who introduce the young child to the world. They speak and listen – interpreting, repeating, extending and supporting – and they interact with babies, as if they can hear and understand, from the earliest stages. The social impetus to becoming verbal is a lynch-pin of Vygotsky's theory of development (Vygotsky, 1978). When playing with very young children, adults model important elements of interaction like eye contact and turn-taking. We seem naturally to tune into the needs of the very young as conversational partners. Colwyn Trevarthen has shown that children sometimes take the initiative and adults are the ones who follow their gestures and facial expressions.[2] Some adults seem to have the ability to talk to children in particularly supportive and effective ways, linking new learning with what children know already. Gordon Wells finds that this ability is not limited to one gender or one social group. In the Bristol study 'Language at Home and School', which he directed during the 1970s and 1980s, Gordon Wells followed a representative sample of children from their first utterances to the end of their primary school years. After a careful analysis of the data Wells and his team pinpointed four things which were critical for an adult to keep in mind when promoting children's learning through conversation. I list them here as I think they apply helpfully to the sort of conversation we might have with children in school in a 'finding out' context.

- treat what the child has to say as worthy of careful attention
- do one's best to understand what he or she means
- take the child's meaning as the basis of what one says next
- in selecting and encoding one's message, take account of the child's ability to understand; that is, to construct an appropriate interpretation

(Wells, 1986: 218)

Wells' work has had enormous influence in the United Kingdom and beyond on how we think about talk and learning. My student groups found the many examples of children talking at home and in school in Wells' books extremely helpful in reflecting on the right way to intervene to develop children's talking and thinking. Interestingly, the Bristol team found that talk in home contexts seemed more tuned into children's preoccupations and interests than in some classrooms. Many of us were affected by the evidence provided by Wells which showed the dangers of a teacher becoming too concerned with managing the development of a topic and not supportive enough of the young child's efforts to make sense of something. Chapters 4 and 5 of *The Meaning Makers* are packed with examples of children's talk in different settings accompanied by useful analysis.

Many of us adjusted our practice in the light of these observations (Wells, 1986). But early years practitioners are concerned that there may be a move away from more child-centred approaches, which put a high value on oracy, now that there are prescribed programmes and imposed timetables for even the youngest children. No new initiative should be allowed to cut into the amount of time spent listening and responding to what children want to say. In a recent study, Jacqueline Harrett of the Cardiff School of Education, analysed the personal stories and anecdotes of 32 children in an inner city multicultural primary school. She detected 'a lack of vivacity' in many of the children's tellings and wonders if lack of time to practice personal story telling may be a factor. This is a cause for concern since the ability to recount personal history contributes considerably to oracy development and to early writing (Harrett, 2002). It is most important to spend time listening and responding to what children have to say as they ease into a new topic or theme. Their personal experiences, and their feelings and attitudes towards them, help build a bridge to new learning whether through practical activity or through secondary sources like information books.

Conversations around stories read aloud at home and school are judged by Wells and others to be a particularly valuable way of supporting children's intellectual and linguistic development. I believe talk around what I term 'information stories' – narratives which incorporate much factual information – can also lead to interesting and mind-stretching conversations between adults and children. Let me give an example here: Nicola Davies' *One Tiny Turtle*, Walker Books, tells the story of a loggerhead turtle's life from being in a turtle nursery and 'no bigger than a bottle top' to when she is 'as big as a barrow' and about to lay her eggs on the beach where she was born. An American study shows how boys and girls showed an increasing liking for this kind of text as they progressed through school, particularly if the teacher discussed the scientific and social concepts involved (Brabham, Boyd and Edgington, 2000).

The teacher's own effective use of language is central to children's learning: he or she explains, questions, describes and supports developing ideas. Teachers do all they can to extend the child's vocabulary, syntax and understanding of the different functions of oral language to support or, as Bruner would term it, provide 'scaffolding' for their learning (Bruner, 1975a). This has important implications for the level and quality of the education and language abilities of classroom teachers and must therefore set high expectations for the educational levels achieved by classroom assistants if they are expected to extend their area of responsibility. They will need a sophisticated grasp of meaning and vocabulary – marshalling children through government-prepared teaching programmes, check lists and tick lists will not create enquiring and inquisitive minds in young children.

Spoken language is a vital tool for teachers in assessing children's progress. In the case of the youngest children most assessment is carried out by observation and by eliciting the answers to questions. Work around informational themes presents all sorts of opportunities for evaluating progress in speaking and listening: discussion at the start of a new topic to pool existing knowledge; talk about practical activities; discussion of book-based information; and presenting and sharing findings.

Ways of representing experience

This book is concerned with the first steps that children take with non-fiction reading and writing. To do this they need to develop ways of representing thinking and experience first orally and then on the page. Young human beings develop an inner representation of the world or 'world picture'. Before this happens babies know the world through action and perception, but once children can think symbolically – through images and then through language – they can build a much more sophisticated inner representation. James Britton suggests that we can use our 'world picture' either as 'participants' to achieve something practical or as 'spectators' to reflect on and reorganise our experience. So I might use my 'world picture' of a recent train journey as a participant to remind myself or to explain to someone else how to get from Chislehurst to New Cross. Or I might, as a spectator, reflect on a conversation I had on the train and ruminate on its philosophical significance.

You might think that when we are in participant role the language we use, whether spoken or written, is more likely to be informational in function than if we are in spectator role (which is to do with using language to create stories, poems and anecdotes). You would be right – but when it comes to young children's use of language what we find is a quite flexible movement from one role to the other. A six-year-old, asked to tell the class about the elephant he had seen at the zoo, gave some information about size, colour and feeding and then said 'When it was time to go home I leapt up onto the elephant's back and rode all the way home!' This flexibility between fact and fiction is to be found in many texts for young children. Indeed many of the best early texts are 'transitional' in that they may have an informational function but also include some features associated with fairy tale and fantasy elements.

Britton brought his theory of participant and spectator roles to a more practical level with a model in the form of a continuum on which he placed three kinds of language. Britton placed 'transactional language' (all kinds of factual language) on the extreme left of the continuum and 'poetic' language (stories, poems, plays) on the extreme right. But what is particularly interesting is what Britton places at the mid-point of the continuum. Here he places what he terms 'expressive language'. This is talk or writing whose main function is to aid learning – rather like Halliday's heuristic function. Young children, as we would expect, see the world very much from their viewpoint. When they tell us about their visit to the park, their swim or about when their pet went missing, their own interests and preoccupations are paramount. Children's early written 'recounts' are like this and Britton drew our attention to the fact that these early recounts are likely to serve an 'expressive' function.

As children's control over language increases, their talk and writing develops, moving in two directions away from the 'expressive' heart. Early stories will still have an 'expressive' flavour and their early attempts at factual writing will contain all those little 'expressive' touches that remind us that a young child is trying to organise their experience and response. (Britton, 1970). Britton's seminal book *Language and Learning* has remained in print since his death in 1994 but now other ways of categorising children's language hold sway. The six non-fiction text types in the National Literacy Strategy are: recount, report, instruction, explanation, discussion and persuasion. These are compatible with Britton's taxonomy, but

A day out in Colchester

Yesterday we went on the train to Colchester group one went to the
Minories first. We did a picture of the seaside. I got very messy. Getting
messy was the best thing. After lunch we went to the museum but they were
closed. So we went to Castle Park which was fun, when we got an ice cream
it was yummy. Then we went for a walk. We saw some ducks some of the
children ran after a duck. I thought that was cruel so I told the teacher and
she told them not to. Then we saw a water thing and it made us think that
the light would be back on we went to look and they were so we could get
a toy. In the end I got a pencil and some gunge,, My mummy and daddy
plus Darrell don't like the gunge.

Stephanie Jane Cannon

Figure 1.1   A day out in Colchester. Six-year-old Stephanie has word processed her recount of a class
outing and includes 'expressive' touches like 'Getting messy was the best thing' and 'My
Mummy and Daddy plus Darrell don't like the gunge'.

what now seems to be missing is the official recognition that young children's language is
grounded in the 'expressive' function. I believe that we should welcome the 'expressive'
touches children include in their early factual accounts because they signal that the child is
actively 'making sense'.

As children make their way through the education system written material becomes
increasingly important. Writing competence builds on a child's speaking and listening abilities.
There are differences between talk and writing but both are important in conveying meaning.
Through oral work children learn to question, reason, formulate and exchange ideas and so
develop the thinking skills which are so necessary for success in our school system as well as
in the world of work beyond. These thinking skills are carried over from oral work to reading
and writing (Donaldson, 1978; Browne 2001). By talking through information and issues,
children are preparing for the informational writing they will be required to do.

It is important that children see clear purposes for their first attempts at writing. This
notion follows from the work and thinking of the developmentalists, educationists and teachers
mentioned like Halliday, Vygotsky and Britton. One important way of linking purpose and
writing is through children's practical activities. So in later chapters we find children naming
their work, labelling and annotating pictures. We see them making lists linked to cooking
and to simple science experiments where writing down ingredients or setting out a sequence
of procedures goes alongside their activities.

Linking first and second hand experience

To help children to integrate their learning from first and second hand experience we need to
ensure their reading and writing takes place in the context of lively practical activities. Bruner,
above all, argued powerfully that an intuitive understanding of an idea or concept precedes
'its more formal comprehension as part of a structured set of conceptual relationships' (Bruner,

1975a: 25). Indeed his notion of a 'spiral curriculum' reinforces the idea that learning does not always happen in a simple linear sequence but that we constantly revisit topics and concepts in order to achieve a more refined understanding. Knowledge from first hand experience of objects and environments is extended and modified by what people say to us and by what we read or see. What, then, are some of the practical settings which provide energising first hand experiences? They include role play, practical tasks and activities, forays into the outside environment and museum visits.

Role play as a context for talking and writing

Role play in the classroom or in an outdoor area creates strong contexts for talking and for reading and writing. The home corner may become a café, a fire station, a post office or a shop. Each of these gives rise to the need for writing and using texts – notices, labels, posters and rotas to mention just a few. In a nursery school I visited recently the children had been helped to make a café in the home corner. They took turns to put up large notices saying 'open' and 'closed' and menus were prepared, neatly stored and presented to those who went in. Outdoor play is an equally strong context for encouraging all kinds of print. Boys in the nursery years seem particularly motivated to write when their role play is out of doors and centres on familiar locations like garages, plant nurseries and builders' yards (see Chapter 6).

Practical tasks and activities

Following recipes or carrying out simple science experiments using work cards or science information texts with illustrated instructions is a strong context for introducing children to procedural or instructional kinds of writing. Children and teacher can work out a format for recording results of experiments to give experience of writing and making diagrams. There is more about contexts for instructional reading and writing in Chapters 6 and 7.

Forays into the outside environment

Outings to farms, woods, ponds and the seaside are a traditional and worthwhile way of providing children with the first hand experience that can lead to them wanting to consult secondary sources, and also lead to lively talk, writing and drawing. My students often ask how books and other secondary resources can be best introduced to extend the first hand kinds of learning. Sometimes teachers like to start with the experience: children might visit a pond and bring back examples of pond plants and small creatures to the classroom where they can use the secondary sources to identify what they have found. This kind of approach leads to drawings based on children's careful observation of the actual objects they have brought back, but labelled and annotated with information they have found in texts.

At other times, looking at texts, diagrams and pictures before an outing can prepare children for the things they will be observing and recording. I remember a good example of this way of working based on an autumn walk in the nursery grounds. One of my students was working on a 'mini-beast' theme with four- to five-year-olds. The creature of the week was 'spiders' and they were all hoping for the misty sort of day when the sun makes the dewy spiders' webs sparkle. When such a day dawned, the student showed the children pictures of garden spiders and their webs and read out about the places where you are most likely to find webs – under window sills and on plants and bushes. Armed with paper, pencils and clip boards to make little sketches, and tuned into the sort of things to look for – shape, colour and size of the webs – the children brought considerable concentration and enthusiasm to their tasks. Questions followed about how spiders make their webs and kill their prey. This led back to using the secondary sources again once they returned to the classroom and to making their own class book on 'Spiders and their webs'. More recently I noticed a piece about nature walks and spiders in *Nursery Education* which draws our attention to the importance of children having passionate reasons for wanting to read or listen to information from books (September, 2002).[3]

Museum, stately home and art gallery visits

Another context where first hand experience and print can come together is a museum visit. Most museums and many art galleries in the United Kingdom and elsewhere, and many National Trust and National Heritage properties, now provide for very young learners. My late colleague at Goldsmiths College, Vicki Hurst, was one of the first early years specialists to encourage museum provision for pre-schoolers. She worked with the Education Department at the National Maritime Museum in Greenwich to provide programmes centred on handling objects and talking about pictures.

Now I am in a position to do a lot more travelling I often see young children enjoying outings to museums with parents and teachers. During a recent visit to the Aquarium in Vancouver I came across a class of five-year-olds looking at the Beluga whales and asking the teacher to read to them what the explanatory notice said about the creatures. The teacher told me that the museum visit came after the children had begun their programme on living things and looked at book illustrations and video-film. The visit was a chance to extend their learning about whales by looking at their physical characteristics and their behaviour first hand. There was an interesting interplay between what they learnt in school and what the books said, and actually seeing the creatures and looking at the annotations. This link between experience of objects and print is built into the educational programmes of many museums in the United Kingdom; in the London area the Horniman Museum and of course the National History Museum are amongst the favourites. The Horniman has an exciting set of programmes for the nursery years including some centring on animal classification, and on toys, games and music around the world.[4]

The National Trust's 'The National Trust Education' has well-established programmes, ideas and resources for all age groups. To give just one example of provision for three- to six-year olds, at Calke Abbey in Derby they can take 'The Very Hungry Caterpillar Trail' which offers a garden walk 'in the company of a favourite friend' to discover how we use the five senses.[5]

Many art museums are now making provision for the youngest children and adopt an interactive and learner-centred approach. At the Tate Britain in London, for example, one of the main aims where the youngest children are concerned is to help them develop looking and thinking skills. One programme provided a series of workshops for children under three and their parents exploring the theme of 'big and small'. The aspects offered included 'people and faces', 'shapes in space' and 'animals'. The parents were often surprised at what their very young children were drawn to. One child, not yet three years, was drawn to the clouds in Constable's *Flatford Mill* (Hancock and Cox, 2002).

Museum, stately home and art gallery visits expose children to a great deal of print – posters, notices and labels and annotations of the exhibits and so on – and give a strong impetus to find out more in books and from information sources like the internet.

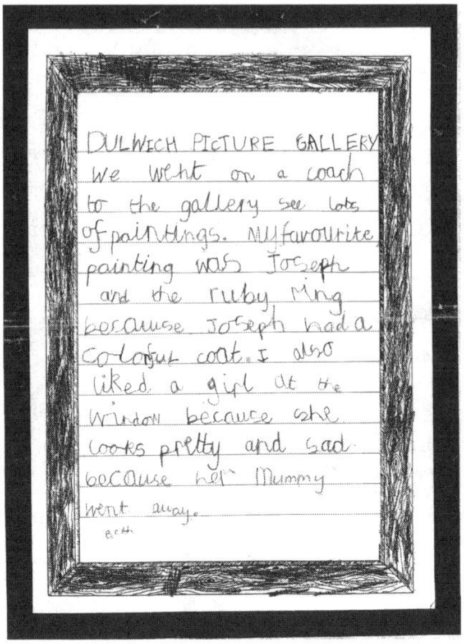

Figure 1.2   Dulwich Picture Gallery. Five-year-old Beth has combined what she saw and what she was told during the class visit to the art gallery.

Reading and writing non-fiction: a 'language and learning' model

This model is built on the three guiding principles, each with its own theoretical underpinning, which are central to this chapter: children are active in their learning; children learn best collaboratively; the role of the adult is crucial. It is also built on the recognition that learning and teaching processes are a dynamic cycle and some basic interacting elements are applicable to short activities and to longer series of lessons and tasks. These interacting elements are planning and resource provision, the teaching and learning activities themselves, assessing the learning achieved and evaluating our teaching, and then feeding all of this into the next cycle of learning. This is a model for rich thematic work on topics like 'food', 'night and day', 'colour', 'pets', 'movement', 'shapes', 'people who help us', 'minibeasts', 'under the sea', 'around the world', 'in the country' and so on, which help organise children's learning over a number of weeks and makes a greater range of non-fiction reading and writing possible. As the many case studies in Chapter 6 and Chapter 7 show, it is often within these projects that even very young children find themselves developing strong views and feelings about issues and ideas. The urge to construct an argument starts early as we see from the zoo case study 11.2.

My model (Figure 1.3) is compatible with the EXIT model of Wray and Lewis which is more detailed in the later stages about how children interact with particular kinds of text (Wray and Lewis, 1997). However, as Riley and Reedy point out, the EXIT model lacks an important stage, the 'offering new experience' stage, stage 2 in the Mallett model (Mallett, 1992). They remark that 'if we are to motivate children to go through the research process, then we must ensure that their curiosity is stimulated, by exposing them to new information or ideas that cause them to want to know more' (Riley and Reedy, 2000: 145). Absolutely – we have to offer children some inspiration!

1. Organising prior experience

Before making a start on something new the teacher and the children talk about, and reflect on, what the children already know. This helps organise their prior experience and prepares the mind to take on new ideas and information. It helps children gain a personal foothold. Sometimes teacher and children make a concept web on a flip-chart or white board to structure and record their ideas.

2. Offering new experience

This might take the form of a class outing to farm or museum, watching a video-film, hearing a text (a story or a factual account) read out loud, considering an artefact or a talk by an adult. Children's interest and commitment often rise a gear if the input is exciting.

3. Formulating questions

The new experience, when combined with organised 'prior experience', gives rise to a number of questions. The teacher can help children organise their questions into categories. So, if a creature is being studied, the questions might be placed under headings like 'habitat', 'body structure', 'food' and 'life cycle'. This helps develop an understanding that an 'exposition', a 'report' or what we term 'non-narrative' text, needs a global or overall structure. The questions put a child in the driving seat when using the books and other secondary sources to inform their own written account. This might be in the form of a book made individually or by a group structured simply around their questions. (Some children will need a lot of support when they use the texts and pictures.)

4. Discussion and planning

Children bring what they have found in books to class or group discussion and are helped to clarify meaning and purpose. A flexible plan for future activity and ways of representing their findings can be agreed. Children often inspire each other with their questions and comments. Writing might include their own books, labelled and annotated diagrams, charts and posters. For the visually aware children of today communicating information by chart and illustration is satisfying. (Teachers read and paraphrase from texts and 'scribe' for the younger children.)

5. Study skills and retrieval devices

This involves finding appropriate books and resources and then using retrieval devices – contents pages, indexes, page numbers – to find the relevant parts of the text. Teachers can model skimming and scanning strategies to show how children can locate just the information they need. Modelling at the point where a child needs to locate specific information is much more likely to be appreciated and understood by a child, as compared with relatively 'out of context' situations.

6. Summarizing, reformulating and reflecting

This stage includes oral summary, note taking and reflecting on what has been found out. Children evaluate what they have achieved and the quality of the resources used. Why were some more helpful than others? The teacher and the other children collaborating on the project are a main and usually appreciative audience. On occasion a presentation may be made, in spoken or written language and with visual aids and children's illustrations and photographs, to a wider audience – perhaps to another class or to parents, governors and other friends of the school.

7. Assessment and record keeping

This is two sided. We evaluate our teaching provision and strategies and the children's learning and we feed the fruits of our findings into the next cycle of planning. Notes on our observations of individual children (taking into account their own comments on their progress) and some examples of their writing and drawing, annotated with date, context and a brief qualitative comment, have a place in their portfolios. It is important that we consult with children about which examples of their work they would like included. This evidence of progress in informational literacy can be summarised at some point on a record-keeping format, for example the Primary Language Record.

Of course actual programmes of work in the classroom never work out as neatly as models suggest. This model is not intended to be linear and stages will often combine, overlap or happen in different sequences so that, for example, a child's most urgent question may occur some way through the project, after hearing or reading about a thought-provoking piece of new information.

Figure 1.3 A 'language and learning' model of non-fiction reading and writing.
Adapted from *Making Facts Matter*, Mallett, 1992.

Summary

A 'language and learning' approach to informational kinds of literacy is best grounded in some guiding principles. These are well known to early years educators and are: children are active in their learning; learning is best supported in collaborative settings where talk is valued; and the role of the adult is crucial in promoting children's learning.

Human beings represent their experience in different ways and for different purposes. Early informational literacy, like other kinds, fares best when it is situated in lively practical contexts like role play, practical tasks and forays into the wider environment. In these contexts texts can take their place alongside all the other activities children are absorbed in.

Notes

1   You will find some interesting articles about the different cultural assumptions held in different countries about young children and their literacy learning and how these shape and influence the nature of the learning experiences provided in *Reading, Literacy and Language*. Vol. 35, No. 2 July 2001. See, for example, 'Cultural constructions of childhood and early literacy' by Tricia David, Kathy Goouch and Marrine Jago, pages 47–54.

2   This insight was expressed by Colwyn Trevathen at an unpublished lecture on 6 November 2002, 'The Vicki Hurst Memorial lecture', organised by Goldsmiths Association for Early Childhood Educators. The talk was accompanied by some remarkable video-film showing babies and care-givers in 'conversations' in which the infants are often the initiators.

3   The 'Spiders' webs' nature walk suggestions (in *Nursery Education*, September 2002. Issue 53) link with 'Knowledge and Understanding of The World' (Early Learning Goal). Barbara Taylor's *Fact File on Spiders* (Southwater) is recommended as a source of pictures and information.

4   For further details of Horniman programmes for the nursery years contact Louise Palmer at: schools@ horniman.ac.uk

5   The internet support site is www.nationaltrust.org.uk/education. The website for families is www.trust.org

References

Brabham, Edna, Boyd, Pamela and Edgington, William D. (2000) 'Sorting it out: elementary students' responses to fact and fiction in informational storybooks as read-alouds for science and social studies', *Reading Research and Instruction*. Vol. 39, no. 4.

Britton, J.N. (1970) *Language and Learning*. Allen Lane: The Penguin Press.

Browne, Ann (2001, second edition) *Developing Language and Literacy 3–8*. London: Paul Chapman.

Bruner, J. (1975a) *Entry into Early Language: A Spiral Curriculum*. Swansea: University College of Swansea.

Crystal, David (1987, second edition) *Child Language, Learning and Linguistics*. London: Arnold.

Donaldson, Margaret (1978) *Children's Minds*. Glasgow: Collins.

Gopnik, Alison, Meltzoff, Andrew and Kuhl, Patricia (1999) *How Babies Think*. London: Weidenfeld & Nicolson.

Halliday, M.A.K. (1975) *Learning how to Mean: Explorations in the Development of Language*. London: Edward Arnold.

Hancock, R. and Cox, Alison (2002) '"I would have worried about her being a nuisance": workshops for children under three and their parents at Tate Britain', *Early Years, TACTYC*. Vol. 22, no. 2.

Harrett, Jacqueline (2002)'Young children talking: an investigation into the personal stories of Key Stage One infants', *Early Years: International Journal of Research and Development*. Vol. 22, no. 1, March.

Mallett, Margaret (1992) *Making Facts Matter: Reading Non-fiction 5–11*. London: Paul Chapman.

Riley, Jeni and Reedy, David (2000) *Developing Writing for Different Purposes: Teaching About Genre in the Early Years*. London: Paul Chapman.

Vygotsky, L.S. (1978) *Mind and Society: The Development of Higher Psychological Processes.* Cambridge, MA: Harvard University Press.

Vygotsky, L.S. (1986) *Thought and Language* (ed.) A. Kozulin, Cambridge, MA: MIT Press.

Wells, Gordon (1986) *The Meaning Makers: Children Learning Language and Using Language to Learn.* London, Sydney, Auckland, Toronto: Hodder & Stoughton.

Whitehead, Marian (1997, second edition) *Language and Literacy in the Early Years.* London: Paul Chapman Publishing.

Wray, David and Lewis, Maureen (1997) *Extending Literacy: Children Reading and Writing Non-fiction.* London: Routledge.

Chapter 2

Early experience of pictures and print

Environmental print; board, bath and cloth books; word books and books functioning as toys

The more encounters with print children have, with experienced readers on hand to answer questions or point things out, the more likely is their understanding about print to develop.

(Weinberger, 1996: 4)

So the learning that occurs when babies are exposed to books … is not just about learning to be literate … but also about how to learn about their expanding world and the emotional and intellectual resources that will make it available to them.

(Griffiths, 2001: 5)

Children's attitudes to print and their understanding of its purposes begin to form early.[1] Pictures of objects in books are recognised by some children as early as about ten months. The task of the adult is to make these early encounters with pictures and print as interesting and meaningful as possible. A most significant development here was the establishment of the Bookstart project in 1991 by Wendy Cooling at The Book Trust, an initiative to provide books for babies.[2] This chapter begins with the role of environmental print in children's early literacy development. It continues with an analysis of the earliest non-fiction books and resources that children encounter, first looking at board, bath and cloth books, then at word books and finally, with some overlap of course, at books as toys. It considers the qualities parents can best look for, bearing in mind that these texts are the very first examples of information texts children see. Some of the books have a narrative form and are 'information stories' about children and families doing everyday things like visiting the park or shops (Butler, 1995). Others are alphabet, counting and concept books. Young children are full of energy and constantly running, hopping, skipping and climbing. So it is not surprising that they like playful books that have levers to pull and flaps to lift.

Young children's thinking moves easily from fact to fiction and back again and this is a feature of many early books. Word books, for example, have an informational purpose – to help reinforce a child's naming of objects – but often fairy tale and nursery rhyme characters appear in the illustrations. Because children love to encounter the same characters in different books and television programmes we find early alphabet, counting and concept books often feature favourites like Peter Rabbit, Miffy and Maisie.

Annotated lists of well thought-of books in each category run through the chapter and there are case studies of young children, Hal, Yasmine and Alexandra, enjoying non-fiction texts at home. These are the sort of texts that help children to name and classify their world and therefore have a very important role in developing children's thinking and language. I end with some thoughts about how we can support these very early forays into the world of information.

Environmental print: living and learning

In our culture print is part of a child's experience of the world from babyhood. Indoors they will see writing on food packages, on the wrappings of household items, on toy packaging and on the free magazines and advertising material that seem constantly to arrive through our letterboxes. Then there are the notes, shopping lists, letters, e-mails and text messages they see their parents and older siblings writing and the print which sometimes accompanies images on television programmes. Out of doors they will come across street names, lettering on bill boards, shops and restaurants and notices in parks and playgrounds.

Much of this print is short lived and disposable. A number of developmentalists and researchers have asked what meaning all this print has for very young children. In an interesting study children's understanding of environmental print was compared with their understanding of the print in their books. On the whole they got to the meaning in environmental print more swiftly: they were able to look at packages of cereal, toothpaste and so on, and to say what they were used for. They understood the message of the print even if they could not say the exact form the words took (Harste, Woodward and Burke, 1984). This suggests that the youngest children may need to see print in context to respond to it.

There is also evidence that children absorb the meaning, if not the exact content, of the many advertisements they come across on posters, in magazines and on television. In Chapter 5 there is a wonderful picture of a bus by four-year-old Orla with a drawing of an advertisement for coffee on its side. Orla has built her environmental knowledge and observations into her own representation. While children want to read because of an interest in stories, they are also stimulated by their interaction with environmental print. As Weinberger points out, environmental print is widely accessible and 'children do notice it and try to make sense of it' (Weinberger, 1996: 5).

Board, bath and cloth books

Publishers work on the principle that very early books need to be sturdy. The laminated pages of board books, the tough plastic of bath books and the robust material of cloth books are all likely to survive the enthusiastic treatment they will receive from a young child. But we also want the books to be of good quality, likely to appeal to young children and to encourage talk and laughter. My forays into the children's sections of a large number of bookshops have convinced me that the choice is wider and the quality of early books better than ever before. This is partly because acclaimed authors are choosing to write and illustrate work for the youngest age groups.

Simple, clear pictures appeal most to young children although small details, perhaps on the borders of a page, can sometimes attract their interest. Practical things are important: the pages should be easy to turn and cloth books in particular should be cleanable. Parents usually enjoy choosing a selection of books but it is the children who decide on their favourites as the case studies in this chapter show. One family known to me remarked that the favourite books are in the kitchen, garden and bathroom while the others stay mainly on the bookshelf!

The annotated list offers some suggestions. Of course it is only a small selection of the large number of books available.

Board

These books have the virtue of being strong but also more like traditional books than a floppy cloth book or a pleasantly cumbersome bath book. Because of this they are more likely to be found in nursery and reception classes as well as at home.

Whose Baby Am I?
By John Butler
Viking Books. 10 months +
This interactive book is made of strong card. Children gain practice in matching as each baby creature seeks its mother. There is emotional satisfaction in reinforcing each small animal's need for its parent. The illustrations are excellent and this is a reassuring book to read at bedtime.

Polar Animals
By Paul Hess
Zero to Ten. 18 months +
Beautiful pictures of polar animals, penguins and bears, are shown in their icy environment and would be an inspiration to children's questions and talk. Others in the series include *Safari, Farm yard* and *Rain forest.*

Jemina Puddleduck's numbers
Beatrix Potter's Mini Board Books.
Penguin Books. 18 months +
A delightful board book just over three inches square and which is just the right size for a young child to hold. There is a figure, a number expressed as a word, a picture from a Beatrix Potter story and a pertinent sentence on each page. They are far from banal – giving people's names, telling us lettuces are 'juicy' and rabbits 'naughty'. Number six shows a mouse with the words 'Anna Maria has **six** bags and parcels'. This opens up the possibility of talking about which pictures show parcels and which bags.

Bath

The idea of a waterproof book is excellent as babies and young children love to play in the bath or paddling pool. They have the advantage of being easily cleaned – just as well, as children often put bath books in their mouths. Children soon learn to hold the book up the right way, to turn the pages and to recognise the pictures.

Baby's Mealtime 'Baby's World'
By Fiona Watt, illustrated by Rachel Wells
Usborne bath books. Usborne Publishing. 6 months +
(with supervision under 36 months. www.usborne.com).
This colourful book presents everyday activities round food and mealtimes. Young children will enjoy pointing at familiar objects like shopping bags, pushchairs laden with carrots, tomatoes and cabbage, high chairs, plastic dishes, forks and spoons, bibs and delightfully messy spaghetti. The family dog and a rabbit toy perched on the pram and sometimes the fridge also provide good talking points. Fun and playfulness are built in – the dog gets a taste of spaghetti and the toy rabbit has a bib.

My First Babies Book; ABC; Number; Truck
Dorling Kindersley Bath Books
www.dk.com. 6 months +
These robust little books all show named familiar objects in a baby's world. Babies are likely
to enjoy playing with them from about six months. By about ten months they will respond to
the bright colours.

Cloth

Technological advances have brought us washable cloth books whose pictures will not easily
fade. Cloth books are often the first that a young child encounters and they are better than
ever. They can be too floppy for young fingers to manipulate. But many now have their pages
strengthened, sometimes with a spongy material, to make them easier to turn.

My Farm
By Rod Campbell
Campbell Books. 2+
The front cover of this spongeable cloth book is in the form of a garden gate and you can see
the sheep on the next page in their field peering over it. And so we have the sense of entering
a farm yard and meeting the farm dog, chickens, sheep and cows.

Bouncy Lamb Cloth Book
By Caroline Jayne Church
Ladybird Books Ltd. 6 months +
This robust little cloth book in the Touch and Feel Play Book series introduces children from
about six months to two years to the world of books. The book won the award from *Mother
and Baby* for the best soft new toy 0–2 years. It is colourful and children will love touching
the coats of the animals which are appropriately textured. It is practical for the age group and
can be hand washed.

Around the Garden
By Lucy Cousins
Walker Books cloth book. 10 months +
One of a series of wordless books which include settings around the house, on a farm and in
the park, *Around the Garden* brings alive in vibrant pictures the things we see in the garden.
So we can talk about a pink butterfly, a red watering can and a bright simple flower.

Word books

These are colourful books full of everyday objects and people, clearly named and usually in
familiar settings. Children enjoy pointing to the items and listening to parents and other
caring adults talking about them. The books offer an opportunity for children to recognise
familiar things and to hear their names so helping the consolidation and development of a
child's increasing vocabulary. Some books in this category are the forerunners of dictionaries
and others of encyclopaedias. Angela Wilkes' *My First Word Book*, for example, is presented
rather like a thematic encyclopaedia, covering 'All About Me', 'At the Seaside' and 'Colours,
Shapes and Numbers'. Word books take different forms including bath, board or cloth books.

There is nothing wrong with parents and older siblings saying the words out loud, but any kind of anxiety-making 'testing' of word knowledge is best avoided. Talking about the objects develops language and social abilities.

Topsy and Tim Word Book
By Jean and Gareth Adamson
Ladybird. 3+
This book, along with the many other Topsy and Tim books, is reassuring and jolly rather than inspirational. But people and objects found in a lot of everyday contexts – supermarket, hospital and station – are included.

The Baby's First Catalogue
By Allan and Janet Ahlberg
Puffin Books. 3+
The concept of difference in family life is explored in this book about babies. On the first page we meet the five different families with their babies. Although a work of fiction, we see the practicalities of caring for a baby and note that there are common experiences that transcend any particular family situation. For example, all families have routines and babies are likely to have some sort of pram and high chair. Children respond to the activities of the babies who are seen doing all the things babies do – smiling, sleeping and crying. It is an exceptionally fine and very human book which encourages children to talk about what is the same and what may vary in different in family settings.

Ian Beck's Blue Book: First Words and Pictures
By Ian Beck.
Scholastic Press. 2+
This robust board book has considerable appeal to the imagination, showing, for example, on the page naming a cow the creature jumping over the moon and thus linking with the world of nursery rhyme. The pages are uncluttered and the illustrations take young children beyond the obvious; for example, showing under 'bed' a cot in a tree that has to be reached by a series of ladders.

The Usborne Book of Everyday Words
By Jo Litchfield
Usborne Books. 15 months +
Words and pictures are arranged round themes like 'The Family', 'The House' and 'The Party'.

Early Words
By Richard Scarry
Random House. Junior Jelly bean book. 3+
If a child likes small, detailed pictures in the distinctive Scarry style this book will be enjoyed. We follow a rabbit character through a day's activities. On the page to do with washing, we have the rabbit vigorously drying his face with a towel and there are small pictures of toothbrush, tumbler and so on all carefully labelled.

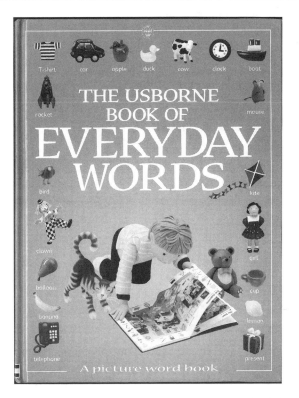

Figure 2.1   Reproduced from *Everyday Words* by permission of Usborne Publishing Ltd. Copyright ©
1999 Usborne Publishing Ltd.

My First Word Book
By Angela Wilkes
Dorling Kindersley. 18 months +
As well as naming huge numbers of everyday objects in familiar settings this word book also
includes action words – sitting and lying down – and some position words – between, above
and below. There are also named fairy tale characters including kings and queens and giants.
At 18 months Yasmine liked the clear, bright photographs and pictures. The book has enough
depth to extend older children of about four or five as the vocabulary ranges from simple
words to 'secateurs' and 'hose-pipe' on the 'In the Garden' page.

Books as toys

Playful books include the bath and cloth books discussed above as well as some new, even
more adventurous, forms which blur the boundaries between book and toy. Some toy books
tell stories but those included here reach out into the real world of objects, sounds and activities.
The 'touch and feel' books allow young children to feel the wool of a sheep, run their fingers
over a fish scale or experience the cool, smoothness of a plastic boot. Some books come in a
package which includes a soft toy of one of the characters or some puppets to help retell the
story or experience. There are also books with pop-up pictures that bring a smile every time

they are shown to a young child and others where you pull cardboard levers to reveal a hidden object. Then there are interactive books which invite participation – for example by making the appropriate noises in Walker Books' *Let's Make a Noise*. But of course these playful books are different from other toys if they have words and pictures. When does a baby start to link objects shown in books with the real world? In case study 2.1, at one year old, Hal does not yet seem to be making such links and his father is right to consider progress will be made here when Hal starts to talk and is helped to label and organise his world using a verbal symbol system. If toy books are associated with enjoyment and being close to parents and caregivers, they play a part in making early encounters with books positive.

Let's Go Driving
By Gus Clarke
Walker Books. 3+
Most children are used to travelling by car and will enjoy being put in the 'driving seat' on a trip to the seaside. This book, with moving parts operated by pulling levers and tabs, gives them the chance to start the car, check the indicators and change a wheel. There is good linkage between the writing and the pictures and there is plenty to talk about and comment on.

Maisy's First Flap Book
By Lucy Cousins
Walker Books. 12 months+
Maisy and her friends enjoy dressing up, gardening, playing in the park and learning about numbers, colours, shapes and opposites. In the garden you can count flowers and find bees, grasshoppers and ladybirds under flaps. A child as young as 12-month-old Hal (see case study 2.1) enjoys manipulating the flaps and seeing the bright colours. Older children will appreciate the more demanding pages with their imaginative use of flaps and levers. For example, on the 'Colour' pages Maisy is painting and the text asks what colour she should paint various objects like carrots and bananas. Lift the flaps and you can check your answers. Good use is also made of the flaps on the 'Opposites' page where for a door is shown with 'closed' written on it. Lift the flap and you see the word 'open' in the doorway.

Digger Power; Tractor Power
By Laura Dollin. Tough Stuff series
Egmont Books Ltd. 3+
These tough little books are circular like a tractor wheel and the cover is formed partly with textured pieces of tyre. This is appropriate since the books are about strong, rough working vehicles. Children will probably use the books as toys at first and enjoy sharing them as an adult reads. The team of characters in the series, including Barley the dog, are pictured on the back cover and each book concentrates on one character and their vehicle. *Digger Power* shows Doug hard at work with his digger on the building site while *Tractor Power* introduces Farmer Finn and his heavy tractor. I like the way we see the tractor in a human context – its huge wheels driving through the mud to pull out someone's car. 'Tough tractor pulls a vehicle out of a ditch. Well done Farmer Finn!'.

Colourful, energetic pictures show the vehicles pulling, pushing and lifting and the text suggests the sounds – the digger 'Blip-blip bzzzz! and the tractor 'Brrrr! Bumpity-bump'. More advanced text – 'tough digger's high force laser beams clear the way for new building' and some technical facts 'rough tractor has a winch capacity of 20 tonnes' – introduce features of information text. Some of the pictures also pave the way for future demands of non-fiction reading by introducing the notion of a diagram, indicating simple things like 'wheel' and 'drill'.

Clothes: Touch and Feel
Dorling Kindersley Board Books. 10 months+
This little board book, one of a series including *Home, Puppy* and *Shapes*, allows children to feel the different textures of the materials clothes are made from.

Tiny Teethers: Zoo
By Cathy Gale
Campbell Board Books. 8 months +
This is an appealing board book combining a teething ring with pictures of zoo animals doing similar things to the babies who are also pictured. Book and teething ring are connected by a plastic strap.

Baby Faces
By Sandra Lousada
Campbell Books. 10 months +
This board book includes seven circular pages joined by thick string, each showing a photograph of a baby smiling, crying or sleeping, with a rattle attached to it. The photographs are in black and white – thought to provide the clearest image for very young children – and below each is a word indicating the baby's feeling – 'noisy', 'happy' and 'sad'.

Let's make a noise
By Amy MacDonald, illustrated by Maureen Roffey
Walker Board Books. 8 months +
Pictures of a truck, a train, a cat, a sheep and so on are accompanied by the sound they make – 'Toot Toot', 'Brmm Brmm' – so that adult and baby can shout out the sounds together. Children love playful, interactive books like this – particularly if the adult can make the sounds convincingly!

Peek-a-Boo!
By Jan Ormerod
Bodley Head Board Book. 8 months +
This is an interactive game book. Each page shows a baby playing the ever-popular peek-a-boo game by holding up an object. The baby can be seen in full when a flap is lifted.

Buggy Buddies: A Bear with a Pear
By Nick Sharratt
Campbell Board Books. 8 months +
Babies can begin to control turning the thick pages of this brightly coloured board book which can be strapped to a pram, cot or high chair with a plastic bracelet. It is a counting book with some amusing rhymes and phrases like 'a cheetah with pizzas' with a picture and the figure 2. Like Yasmine's favourite in the same series, this book features clear uncluttered pictures.

I'm a Little Caterpilllar
By Tim Wear
Buster Books (Michael O'Mara Books). 12 months +
(under supervision because of small puppet)
A latex finger puppet of a caterpillar pokes through a hole in the book so it pops up on every page. On each page the writing says 'I'm a little caterpillar, one day I'll be …'

There are pages showing a lion, a dinosaur and a bat, and then finally the picture of a beautiful butterfly provides the right answer. This is the kind of interactive game children love.

My Little Shimmery Glimmery Playtime Book
By Salina Yoon
Orchard Books. 2+
Pictures of rocking horses, necklaces and sailing boats are made exciting by adding some playful, shiny highlights. The items are not arranged alphabetically but they are labelled clearly. This is one of those books that will appeal a great deal to some children but perhaps less so to others.

Very early encounters with books: case studies

I visited nurseries, schools and children at home while researching for this book. Of course young children depend on adults to provide interesting and appropriate books, but within this limitation I found even the smallest children felt passionately about their favourite books and indeed their favourite part of a particular book. The children I spent time with often liked information type books as much as their storybooks. Interestingly, quite a lot of parents said at first 'I think my child's books are nearly all stories'. But often when we actually looked on the bookshelf we found quite a few examples of the 'experience' books and the ABCs, number and word books which are the foundation of an early non-fiction collection. Children like books about the world and about the objects and experiences they have encountered in their short lives. When I visited Beth and Faith, who are non-identical twins, just before their fifth birthday, they told me they loved reading poems and stories with their mother Claire. Their bookcase, in their bedroom, contained a large number of books some belonging to each twin and others owned jointly. A good proportion were poetry anthologies and stories but there was also a children's atlas, an encyclopaedia and some number and alphabet books. They were both enjoying a dinosaur project at school and some dinosaur books were creeping into their collection. A favourite 'experience' book was Emma Damon's *All Kinds of People* (Tango Books) which is a lively 'lift the flap' book showing people of different shapes and sizes and from different groups in our society. It is often supposed that twins are at a disadvantage in their opportunity for language development because they have to share their parents' attention. But Claire and the twins enjoy being a group of three, sharing and talking about the books.

The three case studies that follow concentrate on children's response to the kinds of very early information books discussed in this chapter. As we might expect, even the youngest children like to communicate and share their response with an adult – to point and smile together. It is this human warmth of shared experience around a text that makes it enjoyable and is likely to ensure a child's positive approach to the world of books. In the three case studies that follow we see what particular children like at ages one year, 18 months and 20 months.

Case study 2.1: Hal

This case study draws on a very interesting diary, in the form of occasional articles about books enjoyed by a young child, written by his father, Roger Mills, for the journal Books for Keeps *(Mills 2002). We join Hal when he is just 12 months old, noting his developing approach to books up to 15 months. He has his own bookshelf – a Hal-high shelf in the kitchen/dining room so that he can easily pull the books down and play with them.*

Twelve months.

Hal gets the books down from his shelf every day but at this early stage he treats them as physical objects. 'He loves turning the pages backwards and forwards in exactly the same way that he loves opening and shutting the doors of our washing machine.' At present he likes books with drawings made partly of textured materials. A 'touch and feel' book called *That's Not My Tractor* is a favourite but he seems mainly interested in touching the textured part of the page. For instance under a picture of a tractor with a trailer decorated with sandpaper, the text says 'That's not my tractor, its trailer is too rough'. Hal likes feeling the sandpaper but is not yet interested in the little mouse pictured on each page. The same enjoyment of physical sensation is evident in his approach to books with pop-ups and flaps. Hal seizes on the flap as soon as he turns a new page. Mills feels that Hal is mainly responding to the colours and interactive format of the books. At this stage, while his father likes to get to the end of the book, *Hal* sometimes wants to turn the pages the other way. A lot of his best loved books are Maisy books but he may not realise that Maisy is a mouse as he has never seen one. Hal's tendency to hold the books upside down suggests he has not yet linked the objects in the books with their counterpoints in the world around him.

Fifteen months

A change comes about at about 15 months when Hal has started pointing at the mouse in *That's Not My Tractor*. 'Before the mouse was just part of the overall pattern, not noteworthy in its own right, whereas now he could see it as an object standing out from the overall pattern'. Pointing at things in books is accompanied by more general pointing at things of interest in the environment. Seeing things as objects separate from oneself is quite a breakthrough. The child psychologist Winnicott referred to this as understanding the difference between 'me and not me' in a book called Playing and Reality (Winnicott, 1965). Once the world of objects begins to have meaning, a child is then able to start to categorise the objects in his or her world. Objects with a seat and a back that you sit on do not all look the same but they are all called 'chairs'. Once you begin to make these classifications you are ready to start to talk. Then when you acquire a verbal symbol system you have a more efficient way of organising your thinking. Hal is now on the brink of naming the objects in his non-storybooks and points to the objects the pictures stand for. Rather than seeking mainly sensation in books – their feel or colour – he now seeks meaning.

Hal's favourite Books

Maisy's First Flap Book
By Lucy Cousins
Walker Books. 12 months +

That's Not My Tractor
By Fiona Watt, illustrated by Rachel Wells
Usborne. Usborne touchy-feely books

Case study 2.2: Yasmine

At 18 months Yasmine can understand a few words in English, her mother's first language, and in Danish, her father's first language. She also responds to a few words in Farsi as her Iranian grandmother is with her a great deal. Yasmine has a particularly rich cultural and linguistic background and she enjoys sharing books with all the adults around her. Her ability to point at illustrations and at objects, noted in Hal's behaviour at 15 months, is well established. When members of the family are mentioned in conversation she runs to a table where photographs are displayed and points appropriately. She can distinguish between numbers and letters.

Yasmine is very attached to her books: when her father selected her favourites from her bookshelf to show me she stopped what she was doing and ran over to pick them up. Many early books are very like toys in their format and design so it is not surprising that one of Yasmine's favourite books is a 'touch and feel' book, *Pets* by Jo Lodge, which can be fixed to a baby's wrist with a springy plastic bracelet. This small board book has a lively picture of a creature – a fish, dog, rabbit and so on – on each page with a sentence containing the name of the animal. So we have a picture of a pet rabbit with a tail of soft material and the sentence 'Bunny rabbit is dozing in the garden'. Three senses are involved in enjoying this early book – sight of course, hearing the text read out and touch, as the bright pictures are textured.

Yasmine has been pointing at objects in book illustrations for several months and now responds to quite small images, for example to the tiny, bright, labelled pictures in Angela Wilkes' large format *My First Word Book*. At present she particularly likes the picture of a small bunch of keys – something she sees her family using. Jo Litchfield's *The Usborne Book of Everyday Words* has the same sort of aim as Angela Wilkes' book – to help children enjoy naming the people and things around them. Yasmine loves the rows and rows of labelled 'things to eat' and points to the things she likes. The 500 simple words and pictures, so well contextualised in familiar scenes, encourage talking and sharing and help with vocabulary building. This is likely to be a favourite book for some time. Later Yasmine can be helped to use the alphabetical list at the end of the book and to enjoy looking for the hidden objects on each page. At the moment she is very taken with the small named objects – 'lemon', 'cup', 'girl' – in the margin round the front and back covers.

Children do not always like what adults predict! Although there are beautiful photographs of babies in Roger Priddy's *Baby's Book of the Body*, Yasmine's attention is caught by the objects arranged on a chess board pattern on the inside pages of the covers of the book. She smiles and points at the pictures of shoes, a fork, a flower, a dog and a ball. The large photographs are organised into sections like 'Look at me', 'Making faces' and 'How many?' – the latter encouraging playful activities like counting fingers, toes, arms and legs. When she was looking at the 'How many' page, Yasmine's family noticed that she already distinguished between words and numbers. So they bought her Kingfisher's *First Number Book*. This is a large format book with large bright illustrations with a playful approach to counting and number. For example we see ten children at a party and some pictures of sweets. We are asked: are there enough for all the children to have a sweet? Yasmine is already pointing to numbers and to words appropriately when sharing parts of the book with adults.

Stella Blackstone's *Bear About Town* and Channel 5's *Bear in the Big Blue House* both use the device of a playful character to introduce information and concepts. *Bear About Town* is full of busy scenes with wonderfully colourful and amusing illustrations. This picturebook shows a lot of environmental print. For example, we have GRANDMA'S BAKERY written over the shop bursting with cakes, bread and biscuits, and on the 'Swimming pool' page, the pool is named SPLASH POOL ALLEY. Yasmine is interested in the pictures at present and points to them, but she will take an interest in the words soon.

Young children today enjoy the opportunities different media offer and sometimes what is in print and what is on screen can interact in interesting and fruitful ways. *Bear's Big Blue House*, a huge colourful book, was bought for Yasmine because she enjoyed the Channel 5 programme *Bear in the Big Blue House*. Like the programme, the book has life, humour and energy. The book consists of double spreads that take us into all areas of Bear's life – living room, bedroom and so on. The objects are named in each context. The bathroom has a towel with a big letter 'B' on it and the bedroom in particular is filled with all the things important to Bear – his models of dinosaurs, his box of feathers and his piggy bank.

There are lots of lively questions to talk about at the end: 'Did you see Bear's globe? Which room was it in?' 'Which is *your* favourite room? 'How many lamps has Bear?' 'Do you have some of the same toys as Bear? Which ones?' Soon Yasmine will be asking her own questions.

Yasmine's top six

Pets
By Jo Lodge
Buggy Buddies. Campbell Books. 8 months +

The Usborne Book of Everyday Words
By Jo Litchfield (designer and model maker)
Usborne. 12 months+

My First Word Book
By Angela Wilkes
Dorling Kindersley. 8 months +

First Number Book
Kingfisher. 2+

Bear About Town
By Stella Blackstone, illustrated by Debbie Hartley
Barefoot Books. 2+

Bear's Big Blue House: A Book of First Words
By Alison Weir and Janelle Cherrington, illustrated by Cary Rillo
Based on the Channel 5 children's programme *Bear in the Big Blue House*. 2+

Case study 2.3: Alexandra

Alexandra is 20 months old, and while her parents say that her favourite books are stories, she also enjoys word books and concept books and is interested in images in her parents' magazines. Alex is looked after with a little boy of the same age while her parents work. Her sibling is due soon and she has recently been looking at some books with a 'new baby' theme and saying the word 'baby' whenever a pram comes into view.

Alex has easy access to her books which are on a low shelf in the sitting room. She gets down her favourites daily and indicates she wants her parents to read to her. Not only has she a favourite book, *Maisy's Colours*, but she also has a favourite author, Lucy Cousins, and particularly likes *My First 123* and *Katy Cat and Becky Boo*. The last of these pictures a colour and then an animal of that colour pops up if you lift the flap. So, as we would expect, Alex at 20 months still likes playful pop-up books. She also likes her bath book *Baby's Mealtime* and has been able for some time to point to her own eyes, ears, mouth and so on in relation to the pictures in the book. Her bookshelf is constantly growing and old favourites keep their place amongst the newer books.

Alexandra is making more and more connections between the objects, animals and people she sees every day and images of these things in books and on television. Hal and Yasmine have begun to do this, but by 20 months, Alex has become able to *name* some of the things and people. Now that she can name bees in a book (*My First 100 Words*) and in the garden, her parents are alarmed at Alex's urge to go beyond pointing to trying to clutch the bees outside!

Being able to name is of course an enormous breakthrough as it is the acquisition of language that accelerates children's developing ability to classify. The signs of becoming able to order things more powerfully were evident recently when Alex and her mother were watching a television wildlife programme together. Alex pointed to a lion and said 'cat'. Children start to make their own classifications of things they see and hear. It seems that the generalisation of a lion to 'cat' happened after Alex had seen real cats, heard the name and seen pictures of cats in books. Because parent and child were sharing the experience of watching the programme, Alex's attempts at naming and classifying were reinforced.

Alex is showing more and more fascination with the words her parents point to in books. It is only when a child is ready that there is any point in directing their attention to the words in books. But once this interest is shown a child's development accelerates as the delights of the world of print open up with new possibilities for sharing and enjoying books together.

Alexandra's favourite non-story books

Animal Names and Noises
By Rod Campbell
Campbell Books. 12 months+

Katy Cat and Becky Boo
By Lucy Cousins
Walker Books. 14 months+

Maisy's Colours
By Lucy Cousins
Walker Books. 14 months+

My First 123
By Lucy Cousins
Walker Books. 18 months+

Spot's Favourite Colours
By Eric Hill
Frederick Warne hbk. 16 months+

Duck Wants to Swim
By Debbie Rivers-Moore
Parragon Pop-up Book. 14 months+

My First 100 words
By Heather Amery, illustrated by Stephen Cartwright
Usborne. 18 months+

Baby's Mealtime
By Fiona Watts
Usborne Bath Books. 6 months+ (adult supervision needed under 36 months)

Patterns of development in early response to books

The children in these case studies come over very much as individuals making their own choices from what has been offered to them. Nevertheless some helpful general patterns in the progress very young children make with books seem to be confirmed.

From about six to 15 months babies treat books pretty much as they do other toys – handling them, pushing them, tasting them and generally playing with them. This fits with the well-known theories of general development, linking with Bruner's 'enactive' phase and Piaget's 'sensory-motor' phase when the child knows the world through sensation and movement. Then, from about 15 to 18 months or thereabouts, children seem to respond to images in books and television, especially when in bright colours. They may not distinguish the finer details at this stage but they are beginning to recognise that the pictures represent things in the real world. Bruner calls this the 'iconic' stage and parents will recognise this point in development has been reached when a child points to an image in a book and then at the actual object. Children at this stage are making a very important distinction, the difference between themselves and other people, between what the child psychologist Donald Winnicott calls 'me and not me'. Children realise that they are separate from their mother and separate from all the objects that can be felt, seen and listened to.

Then we come to that phase, termed by Bruner the 'symbolic' stage, when a child becomes able to understand that words as well as pictures in books, on posters and on television and the computer represent things in the real world. Pointing behaviour becomes more specific and more sophisticated and the child points at words, as Alex is becoming able to do. We see from the case study on Orla (Chapter 5), who at age three is older than the children in these case studies, that becoming aware of letters and their power opens the door to reading and writing and is uniquely empowering.

Important and engaging as first storybooks are, non-fiction also has its part to play in children's development. Sharing a non-fiction book helps children connect objects pictured in books with their counterpoints in the real world. Children's ability to name, order and classify things is reinforced and the fascinating and meaningful patterns numbers and letters make are brought alive in the best books.

Strategies to support early experience with print

A number of studies indicate that children's early experiences of literacy in the home and then in the nursery school have a considerable effect on later progress in reading and writing. One of the most comprehensive accounts of this is found in *Literacy Goes to School* by Jo Weinberger who carried out the Elmswood study with 60 children from different family settings. In their longitudinal study of the effect of books on the learning of very young children Wade and Moore also showed that early activities around books were extremely significant in forming positive attitudes to literacy (Wade and Moore, 1996). But what kinds of intervention are most helpful? Perhaps it is when we take up an early non-fiction book – a number or word book – that we are most likely to adopt an instructional sort of role. However, a less didactic approach is likely to be better when children are very young. Below I summarise some of the pointers from research and my own observations to the kind of things that will support very young children in their early encounters with, in particular, non-story print. So:

- *an interested but relaxed approach seems best* and the avoidance of any sense of 'testing'. So pointing at words and expecting a child to say the word is mechanistic and may be anxiety-making, while an emphasis on enjoyment raises confidence. When it comes to early non-fiction this would mean having a natural conversation about the pictures and ideas in the book, encouraging questions and comments from the child and responding to them. I remember one of my own children with great delight pointing to a picture of an apple and then to the apple in our fruit bowl. Making such connections between what is in books and what is in real life deserves reinforcement (Wells, 1987).
- *anything we can do to support the social aspect of learning is helpful* when it comes to literacy experience. So it is promising when parents, carers, teachers and older siblings talk to the child about signs, labels and notices in context and share, savour and smile at what we read in early books (Taylor, 1983).
- *involving children in what adults are doing* – writing shopping lists, reading letters and bills and so on – helps children understand the purposes of literacy particularly if writing materials are easily accessible so that they can try to write too. These 'naturalistic' activities seem to be more helpful than formal teaching (Harste, Woodward and Burke, 1984).
- *gently nudging children just beyond what they could manage alone moves them forward.* Vygotsky termed the distance between what a child could do alone and what he or she could manage with support 'the zone of proximal development' (Vygotsky, 1978). Bruner calls the support an adult or older sibling provides 'scaffolding' (Bruner, 1975b). This might mean extending what the child says and explaining about ideas in the text and in diagrams and pictures.

And later on:

- *sensitivity on the part of the nursery team to the home literacy practices of individual children makes for continuity between learning at home and at school* (Brice Heath, 1983; Minns, 1997; Gregory 1996, 2000).

Summary

In a technological society babies and young children are surrounded by print inside and outside their homes. Parents, caregivers and older siblings can all help the young child understand the purposes of environmental print by pointing to signs and notices and talking about them in a context that makes sense. When it comes to print in the home, as well as storybooks, children enjoy very early informational material in the form of early 'experience' books,

ABCs, number and concept books. These are produced in different sizes and in different textures and include plastic bath books, thick-paged board books and cloth books. The best of these books have a strong visual appeal, are often playfully interactive with pop-ups and flaps, and help children name and order the many people and things in their world.

Notes

1   The fuller understanding of the role books play in children's development from the earliest stages is reflected in library provision, in that 80 per cent of all libraries offer book sessions for under fives and 92 per cent are involved in a 'books for babies' project (see Griffiths, 2001).

2   Bookstart's main aim is to introduce babies to books and so exciting book packs are offered to all babies at their health check clinics at six to nine months. The project is also linked to research on early experience of books by Professor Barrie Wade and Dr Maggie Moore at Birmingham University. For more information about Bookstart contact Ann Carty at Young Book Trust, 45 East Hill, London SW18 2QZ.

References

Brice Heath, S. (1983) *Ways with Words.* Cambridge: Cambridge University Press.

Bruner, J. (1975b) 'Language as an instrument of thought', in A. Davies (ed.) *Problems of Language and Learning.* London: Heineman.

Butler, D. (1995 edition) *Babies Need Books.* Harmondsworth: Penguin.

Gregory, E. (1996) *Making Sense of a New World.* London: Paul Chapman.

Gregory, E. (2000) *City Literacies: Reading across Generations and Culture.* London: Routledge

Griffiths, H. (2001) 'Babies and Books', *Books For Keeps.* No.129, July, pages 4–5.

Harste, J., Woodward, V. and Burke, C. (1984) *Language Stories and Literacy Lessons.* Portsmouth: Heinemann.

Mills, Roger (2002) 'Hal's Reading Diary', *Books For Keeps.* No.133, March, page 9; 'Hal's Reading Diary', *Books for Keeps.* No.135, July, page 7.

Minns, H. (1997, second edition) *Read it to Me Now! Learning at Home and at School.* Buckingham: Open University Press.

Taylor, D. (1983) *Family Literacy: Young Children's Learning to Read and Write.* London: Heinemann Educational.

Vygotsky, L.S. (1978) *Mind in Society.* Cambridge, MA: Harvard University Press.

Wade, B. and Moore, M. (1996) 'Home activities: the advent of literacy', *European Early Childhood Educational Research Journal.* Vol. 4, No. 2, pages 63–76.

Weinberger, Jo (1996) *Literacy Goes to School: The Parents' Role in Young Children's Literacy Learning.* London: Paul Chapman.

Wells, Gordon (1987) *The Meaning Makers: Children Learning About Language and Using Language to Learn.* London: Hodder & Stoughton.

Winnicott, Donald (1965) *Playing and Reality.* Harmondsworth: Penguin Books.

Chapter 3

Alphabet books

Enjoying letters, words and illustrations

> Alphabet books can be popular because illustrators, freed from the disciplines of needing to tell a story, can concentrate instead on achieving some of their biggest and brightest effects. Learning the typical sounds that letters of the alphabet make can also be helpful.
>
> (Tucker, 2002: 70)

> [Children] will have no chance of appreciating the best if they don't see it.
>
> (Townsend, 1995: 332)

Children and their families enjoy looking at alphabet books together. There is an abundance of these books of all sizes, shapes and designs freely available in bookshops and libraries and early years classrooms. Sometimes storybook characters introduce each letter and illustrators can show great inventiveness, sometimes creating visual jokes, sometimes including puzzles and most recently by creating interactive 'pop-up' books. As Nicholas Tucker reminds us, the best author-illustrators want to make encountering the letters of the alphabet an exuberant, fun-filled experience. Don't be misled by bright covers that hide a dreary content and approach – or be seduced by the 'workbook' brigade that covers the shelves of so many children's sections in bookshops! The latter are never to be found with books of real quality.

From about 18 months to three years sheer delight in a shared experience is the most important thing. Direct teaching can cause anxiety and be counter productive if our aim is to awaken an interest in letters and words. But of course there is no denying that alphabetic knowledge is an important precursor of literacy and, once in school, children need help to understand the names, sounds and shapes of letters and their purposes. A good bridge between the pre-school and school stage is the interest children usually have in the spoken and written down forms of their own names. Seeing their name written down helps children begin to understand the relationship between what is said and what is written. Teachers can build on this and demonstrate sound – letter correspondence in shared reading and writing activities. Young children enjoy multi-sensory approaches which include drawing shapes in the air, in the sand tray and in dough, and singing and dancing to alphabet songs. Early years teachers also encourage children to organise some of their non-fiction writing alphabetically. These approaches go alongside continuing enjoyment of alphabet books, and some of the best for particular age groups are listed and discussed in this chapter. First, however, I want to put today's alphabet books in their historical context, touching at the same time on the development of illustration in children's books – a development relevant to alphabet, number and concept books and other non-fiction picturebooks.

ABCs to picturebooks

The earliest forerunners of the modern alphabet book were printed ABC sheets. Children in medieval times, and for centuries after, learnt to read by saying the names of the letters of the alphabet and spelling out combinations of them. These early ABCs often took the form of a hornbook – you might find examples of these in some museums or stately homes. A hornbook was made of wood with a handle so that it could be held like a racquet. It consisted of a sheet of paper mounted on the wood and protected by a sheet of transparent horn which was held in place by a piece of metal. The book was usually about four inches by three plus the handle. The printed sheet remained much the same over the centuries. It showed the alphabet in upper and lower case, the ampersand, the five vowels and the Lord's Prayer.

In her account of 'Beginnings of Children's Reading' Gillian Avery refers to the experiences of John Martindale who was born in 1623. His godmother gave him an ABC, which was probably a hornbook, when he was just coming up to six years old. With the help of his older brothers and sisters and 'a young man that came to court my sister' he quickly learnt to read it 'and the primmer also after it' (Avery, 1995: 3). This shows us the informal approach to helping children become literate at that time. The role of siblings is interesting in view of recent research into how brothers and sisters support each other's reading (Weinberger, 1996).

The next development was the appearance of the battledore, a form of alphabet book which was used at least until the mid-nineteenth century. These ABCs were printed sheets mounted on a folded piece of cardboard and were more appealing than the hornbooks because they were illustrated.

Another strand in the story is the chapbook. Chapbooks were printed for the mass market and sold by itinerant pedlars from the sixteenth to nineteenth centuries. Some included pages for children with an alphabet and labelled pictures of animals. Then publishers diversified by producing small books for children with prayers, stories and alphabets illustrated with woodblock pictures.

How do we get from these quite roughly produced books to the colourful and sophisticated picturebooks of today? Of course this is part of the interesting but quite complicated story of the development of children's literature – a story we can only touch on here but which you can read about in Townsend, 1995. One figure mentioned in any account of the history of children's books is John Newbery, an eighteenth-century publisher who pioneered work especially written for children, producing fairy and folk tales, and nursery rhymes. His *A Little Pretty Pocket Book* used the alphabet to show children's games and established the link in alphabet books between letter, theme and picture – a link which is still respected by alphabet book creators today.

An important development in the history of the alphabet book was the improvement in the quality of illustrations in children's books generally. One notable event was the inclusion of woodblock illustrations of animals and birds by Thomas Bewick in *The Only Method to Make Reading Easy* – a book written by a school master and printed by Angus, a Newcastle printer. Another landmark publication was *The Alphabet of Goody Two Shoes* printed in 1802 by John Newbery's successor. Here hand coloured engravings of scenes illustrate each letter of the alphabet.

A highly significant figure, the engraver and printer Edmund Evans, 1826–1905, brought colour printing to a high standard for the time. He printed the work of the first three picturebook artists – Walter Crane, Randolph Caldecott and Kate Greenaway. Their alphabet books can be seen in the Opies' collection in the Bodleian Library in Oxford. Walter Crane created a number of alphabet books for Edmund Evans: *The Railway Alphabet*, *The Farmyard Alphabet* and *Noah's Ark Alphabet*. Victor Watson points out that the range of Crane's themes showed an appreciation of the things children are interested in – animals, flowers, names, trains and so on (Watson, 2001).

In 1898 *Alphabet* by William Nicholson, a poster designer, combined a brief text with colourful pictures. John Rowe Townsend, marks this out as 'the first picturebook to look forward to the twentieth century in its graphic style' (Townsend, 1995: 158).

The modern picturebook transcends crude divisions between 'fact' and 'fiction'. It both teaches and entertains from early childhood onwards. Everyone has their favourite picturebook creator from the twentieth and twenty-first century. Amongst the best known are: Hale, Ardizzone, Peake, Keeping, Wildsmith, Burningham, Blake, Briggs, Hughes, Hutchins, Inkpen, Carle, Kerr, McKee, Mahy, Sendak, the Ahlbergs, Hill, Foreman, Browne, Oxenbury and Waddell.

This brief foray into an aspect of the history of children's books shows how books have changed over the years. The technology of a particular time affects what can be achieved aesthetically and pictorally. And of course what people can afford to pay is always a factor – books are more affordable than they were two hundred years ago! But above all, books have changed because our perceptions of childhood have changed. Gradually the book became viewed as something that not only instructed the young – in letters or morals – but also entertained and delighted. The best alphabet books today achieve a welcome balance between instruction and entertainment.

Alphabet books: what to look for

It is unwise to be dogmatic when trying to pin down the qualities which make a successful alphabet book and, of course, there are individual tastes – even the youngest children have preferences. After looking at a lot of books in libraries and bookstores over the years I offer the following features as a basis for discussion. I think appealing books have:

- **an organising idea or theme** to give coherence; for example, by taking a topic like animals, railways or by using a storybook character
- **an imaginative choice of headwords** so that some unusual ones like 'iguana', 'octopus', 'quill', 'yolk' and 'zip' are included
- **an 'alive' feel** so that there is a sense of life and movement and invitations to interact with the text
- **originality** in format and style to catch the young imagination
- **clear letters in both upper and lower case** to make for easy demonstration and familiarisation
- **a lively written text** which is simple without being banal, whether it rhymes or not
- **distinctive illustrations** to intrigue, challenge or amuse

Perhaps the best advice is for children to have alphabet books of different styles and sizes and to see which turn out to be their favourites. So here are some kinds of alphabet book to consider.

First, as a visit to any good children's section in a bookshop will confirm, there are what we might call 'realistic' alphabet books showing everyday objects with their names in print. Children seem to like clear, bright pictures, whether drawn or photographed. Dorling

Kindersley's alphabet books are of this kind, for example *My First ABC Book*. But when it comes to books which use photographs well it is hard to do better than Fiona Pragoff's excellent work, for example her delightful miniature *Alphabet: from a-apple to z-zip*.

Second, there are alphabet books whose appeal comes from using the device of a familiar character from a well known storybook or television programme. Here the characters introduce the letters of the alphabet, often dancing and romping across the pages. These appeal to children's love of meeting the same characters in different books – an early example of what literary critics call 'intertextuality'. In Michael Inkpen's *Kipper's A to Z* Kipper and Arnold, who appear in a series of books by Inkpen, play their way through the book.

Third, publishers sometimes bring out new editions of an early alphabet book, such as those of Kate Greenaway. These have their own unique style and format and the illustrations of children in period dress, perhaps playing with their toys, provide an early social historical perspective.

Finally, I think we would want to have some alphabet books that combine illustrations and print in an entertaining way and make sharing them an enjoyable, fun-filled experience for children and adults. A favourite here is Satoshi Kitamura's *What's Inside? The Alphabet Book* which would amuse someone of any age who loves the quirky, the unexpected and visual jokes. Talking of humour and entertainment, 'movable' or pop-up alphabet books never fail to amuse young children – Robert Crowther's *The Most Amazing Hide and Seek Alphabet Book* (Kestrel 1977) has sold over 200,000 copies

Alphabet books: some annotated suggestions

Animalia
By Graeme Base
Harry N. Abrams, Inc., Publishers. 3+
This international best seller is wonderfully illustrated, teaching about letters and words as well as about animals and wildlife. It can be read and looked at in different ways and is enjoyed by adults as well as children.

John Burningham's ABC
By John Burningham
Jonathan Cape. Board book. 3+
This ABC is a classic to be enjoyed by younger children, but it is demanding enough to intrigue five- to six-year-olds. It has the usual collection of delightfully eccentric characters – clowns, kings and many animals – that make Burningham's work distinctive. The settings for the items on each page are interesting; for example, we see lots of animals in an exciting jungle environment. Children also enjoy the book's vibrant use of colour.

My Most Amazing Hide and Seek Alphabet; My Most Incredible Animal Alphabet
By Robert Crowther
Walker Books. 2+
Much imagination has gone into these two interactive alphabet books, which have both become favourites.

My First ABC Board Book
Dorling Kindersley. 2+

There is a simple but effective approach here: each letter (clearly shown in upper and lower case) is accompanied by objects and animals beginning with that letter. The 'Z' page often challenges writers of ABCs, but here we have a zip, a zebra and a huge red zero. Like other Dorling Kindersley books, this one includes a lot of material without cluttering the pages. Many items are familiar, but children will also come across some more unusual creatures and words. The characters pictured here are also in *My First Word Book* and this would be a good talking point if the child has seen both books.

My First Letter and Word Pack
Dorling Kindersley. 3+
This large pack contains foam letters, picture cards and puppets and there are notes to guide parents. There is a good variety of words, for example 'pumpkin', 'roller skates' and 'sand castle'. Nursery teams like to offer the alphabet letters in many media – wood, plastic and cardboard – and will welcome these foam letters.
   (There is a similar 'concepts' pack: *My First Numbers and Shapes.*)

Alphie's Alphabet
By Shirley Hughes
Bodley Head. 2+
This most original alphabet book draws on pages taken from Shirley Hughes' other books. So we have 'A is for Alfie and for his little sister, Annie Rose'. Older children will like recognising the characters from books they already know, while younger ones will enjoy being introduced to those other books. The children in the illustrations are energetic and playful and shown in the natural situations Shirley Hughes favours.

Kipper's A to Z
By Michael Inkpen
Hodder. 3+
Many children will like the humour of this most original alphabet book, particularly if they already know Inkpen's other Kipper books. Kipper and his friend Arnold do the things children like doing; for example, keeping insect pets and painting pictures. Although this book is often bought for younger children, it is sophisticated enough for six- and seven-year-olds and includes more abstract words like 'on' and 'off'.

What's Inside? The Alphabet Book
By Satoshi Kitamura
Andersen Press. 4+
This is a most unusual picturebook which is also an alphabet book. The things pictured link from page to page in most intriguing and exciting ways. For example, something black appearing out of a dustbin on one page turns out (when more fully revealed on the next page) to be a cat chased by a ferocious dog – this taking care of 'c' and 'd'. Such an imaginative and visually entertaining book will stand many readings.

Know Your Alphabet
Macdonald Books and Posters.
macdonaldbooks@cs.com. 3+

This large, clear, illustrated chart could be displayed in the early years classroom and used to teach about letters and alphabet order.

Dr Seuss's ABC
By Dr Seuss
Beginner Books: I can read it all by myself. 3+
In book, audio cassette and CD-ROM
Dr Seuss aims to entertain as well as teach. As the case study below shows, children love his amusing use of language and illustrations.

Case study 3.1: Dr Seuss's ABC on CD-ROM

Children can now learn the alphabet and have this learning reinforced in different media. This vignette comes from the reception class of Castlecombe school and finds two five-year-olds at the computer. The children had looked at the Dr Seuss book and heard the cassette, and their familiarity with the text and pictures seemed to add to their enjoyment of the CD-ROM.

Nabila and Georgia were securing their understanding of upper and lower case letters of the alphabet by reading through this CD-ROM version of Dr Seuss's well-known alphabet book. When I joined them they were looking at big F and little f, enjoying the entertaining pictures and reading together out loud 'Four fluffy feathers'.

There can be collaborative work round a book, of course, but the CD-ROM version, with its amusing animation, is particularly suited to shared reading and talk.

Making their own alphabets

Alphabet books, charts and friezes and cardboard letters are abundant in early years classrooms, whether in a nursery school or a reception class. Children learn about letters from these resources and also make their own alphabets, sometimes based on the themes they are working with: colour, pets or transport. A transport alphabet might begin as follows: automatic, bus, car, diesel engine. Verb based alphabets could reflect children's activities: I can add, bend, crawl, draw. Adjective alphabets might describe pets: active, brown, calm, dainty. Children enjoy illustrating their own individual, group and class alphabets. Figure 3.1 shows a lively page from a class alphabet book.

Summary

Alphabet books are among the first and most important non-narrative texts encountered by children. A glimpse of their history shows they have always been important in starting children down the path to literacy. There are many to choose from but the best will engage and hold children's interest with a clear text and inviting illustrations. Above all, children must be enthused and entertained, and encouraged to make their own texts around the letters of the alphabet.

Figure 3.1 Nina's ABC page. This is a page from the ABC book made by the children in Crockham Hill Primary School's reception class. Five-year-old Nina has contributed the 'E' page and names and draws her friend Emma, showing she knows how to use the upper case E appropriately. The teacher, Claire Pester, comments that the children had been inspired by *ABC Dictionary*, Collins.

References

Avery, Gillian (1995) 'Beginnings of Children's Reading', in P. Hunt (ed.) *Children's Literature: An Illustrated History.* Oxford: Oxford University Press.

Townsend, J. Rowe (1995, definitive edition) *Written for Children: An Outline of English-language Children's Literature.* London: The Bodley Head.

Tucker, Nicholas (2002) *The Rough Guide to Children's Books, 0–5 years.* London: Rough Guides Ltd.

Watson, Victor (2001) *The Cambridge Guide to Children's Books in English*. Cambridge: Cambridge University Press ('alphabet books' entry, pages 24–5).

Weinberger, J. (1996) *Literacy Goes to School: The Parents' Role in Young Children's Literacy Learning.* London: Paul Chapman.

Chapter 4

Counting and concept books
Books to enjoy and learn from

The best non-fiction involves imagination, invention, selection, language and form as much as any fiction book.

(Milton Meltzer quoted in Watson, 2001:369)

Reading for information in the early years will not be directed towards the accumulation of knowledge as such, but to widening concepts about the environment, and towards ways of thinking which will include observation, hypothesising, comparison and classification …

(Helen Arnold, 1996: 65)

If we have a light touch, we can help children learn about number, colour and other concepts from their very early non-fiction books. But we may create anxiety if the books are used too much like teaching aids. Up to about three, children's encounters with books should be enjoyable for their own sake. This does not mean, of course, that we cannot have many helpful conversations around the texts so that children move forward in their understanding.

There are number and concept books in board and cloth form for the under-threes, and in paper form they are amongst the earliest kinds of non-narrative text used in nursery school and reception classes. However, some are in narrative form and, as we will see in case study 4.1, a story can be an excellent way of drawing young children into the world of mathematics, helping them make 'human sense' of numbers.

Although number and concept books are increasingly written and illustrated by well-regarded authors, there are still some that are rather dreary. The less successful use a bright cover and colourful illustrations to hide an uninspiring and predictable content while others are of the 'workbook' type with an emphasis on constant testing. But it is to the liveliest books that this chapter turns, first on number and then on important concepts like shape, colour and opposites. The books are discussed with a view to identifying some criteria for choosing these very early information books. As in other chapters, there are some vignettes of children enjoying them.

Counting

The notion of number can be particularly challenging. Children learn to count through hearing nursery rhymes and games like 'One, two buckle my shoe' and in the course of everyday life when they may 'help' with cooking, shopping and so on. And of course there is a long tradition of learning about mathematical concepts through story (Mallett, 2002;

Evans, 2001). As we know from the work of Jean Piaget, young children are often confused by the appearance of things. If counters or building blocks are heaped together a child may well think there are fewer in number than if the same objects are spread out over a larger space. For a critical analysis of Piaget's work with children on mathematical concepts and of the work of other developmentalists see *Children's Minds* by Margaret Donaldson. She demonstrates that tasks need to make 'human sense' if children are to understand them, something which Piaget sometimes overlooked (Donaldson, 1978). What research has shown and what teachers know is that in the early years number and other mathematical concepts are learned gradually through first hand experience and with helpful adult mediation.

We know that controlling the vocabulary of number, using words like 'more', 'larger,' 'fewer' and so on, provides a language to talk about and help clinch number concepts. So it is helpful if number or counting books provide number words in an interesting way. Whatever can be done to make a child's first experience of these books positive is obviously very important, so books with a touch of humour and perhaps puzzles and games can be helpful. Criteria for choosing number books are similar to those for alphabet books suggested in Chapter 3. Appealing books have:

- **an organising idea or theme** to give coherence; for example, there might be a theme like counting bugs or monsters or a situation like getting ready for bed, or the counting activities might be linked to a story or TV character
- **an 'alive' feel** so that learning about counting is presented as dynamic and interesting with plenty of opportunity for interaction
- **originality** in format or style to catch the young imagination
- **clear numbers** which appear both as figures and in words
- **lively written text** which is simple without being banal, whether it rhymes or not, and which introduces the names of concepts like 'more', 'less' and 'few'
- **distinctive illustrations** to intrigue, challenge or amuse

The following selective list identifies some lively counting books for different ages to guide the choices of parents and teachers.

Number books: some annotated suggestions

Five Ugly Monsters
By Ted Arnold
Scholastic. 3+
This lively 'song story' encourages young children to role play and talk and helps them clinch the concept of subtraction. (See case study 4.1.)

Little Rabbits' Tell the Time Book
By Alan Baker
Kingfisher. 2+
This book has a playful approach to learning to tell the time by following the activities of the Little Rabbits as they move through a busy day. There is a novelty clock with movable hands to encourage children's participation.

Ten, Nine, Eight
By Molly Bang
Red Fox. 2+
This counting game begins with number ten and ends with one. The story is about a young child getting ready for bed with the help of her father; her shoes, toys and so on are laid out in the sort of rituals children like. There is a nice touch of humour when one shoe goes missing – the cat is found playing with it on another page!

Fruits: A Caribbean Counting Poem
By Valerie Bloom and David Axtell
Caribbean Publishing. 2+
Full of life and colour, this picturebook achieves a number of things: it sets teaching about counting in an interesting rhyming story; it introduces Caribbean vocabulary, explaining the words in a glossary; and it shows ten kinds of fruit in authentic settings.

Ten Seeds
By Ruth Brown
Andersen Press. 3+
Beautifully illustrated and presented in a robust board format, the book takes us through the life cycle of a plant from seed to flower. Nine of the ten seeds do not make it – they are devoured by birds or dug up by creatures; in one case a mouse with tiny pink hands. When the successful plant blooms and produces its own seeds we see a young child about to start the process again by planting them. So children learn about the concept of the life cycle, about the creatures in a garden and about numbers up to ten. It is also a book that helps children think about colour – the brown earth, the green shoots and the bright yellow flower – see case study 4.1.

Engines, Engines: An Indian Counting Book
By Lisa Bruce
Bloomsbury. 18 months +
This unusual counting book takes young readers on an exhilarating journey in some different engines through an Indian landscape. Full of life and colour, it shows exciting environments as well as teaching about number through rhymes and through the numbers on the carriages which each engine pulls.

How Many Bugs in a Box? A Lift-up Counting Book
By David Carter
Orchard Books. 3+
Under careful supervision, as some of the small parts could come loose with rough handling, children will enjoy this book presented as a packing case containing little creatures urgent to get out! It is fun to pull the cardboard levers and to lift the flaps to show one bug in a red box and then reveal butterflies, beetles and so on.

One Child, One Seed: A South African Counting Book
By Kathryn Cave and illustrated by Gisele Wulfson in association with Oxfam
Frances Lincoln. 5+
This is a counting book which also tells us about life in South Africa and Nothando nurturing her pumpkin plant.

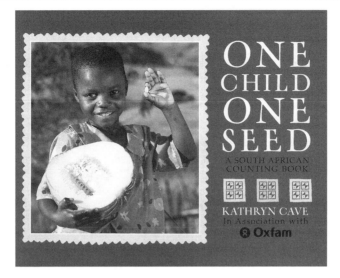

Figure 4.1 From *One Child, One Seed* by Kathryn Cave published by Frances Lincoln Limited, © Frances Lincoln Limited 2002. Text © Kathryn Cave, photographs © Oxfam Activities and Gisele Wulfsohn 2002.

Mimi's Book of Counting
By Emma Chichester Clark
Andersen Press. 2+
Part of the series about Mimi, a small monkey, this picturebook shows Mimi learning about counting with her Grandma.

What's the Time , Maisy?
By Lucy Cousins
Walker Books. 3+
This lovely large 'tell the time' board book takes us through Maisie's day, starting with Maisie's clothes ready for her to put on. There is a large clock with hands you can turn. (Other Maisie books include an ABC, *Maisie at the Farm* and *Maisy's Colours*.)

My First Book of Numbers
By Kim Deegan
Bloomsbury. 18 months +
For a change, this picturebook counts from ten down to one. It shows all the things a young child likes – crayons, bricks and so on. It has very little writing, but the numbers are dramatically large and I think it would appeal to the very youngest children.

My First Numbers and Shapes: Numeracy for the Pre-school Child.
Dorling Kindersley. 4+
In large format, this book includes big foam numbers and shapes which the child can pull out and play with. Numbers are linked with everyday things – two shoes and three teddy bears, for example – and there are mathematical games and puzzles to encourage an interest in number and shape.

Book and Tape 123
First Steps
Ladybird Books. 2+
This package contains a mini hardback book and a 30-minute audio cassette with catchy counting songs and rhymes about counting.

Spot Can Count
By Eric Hill
Puffin Books. 18 months +
Another number book based on a favourite character, this one has a lot of features likely to appeal to young children. It is colourful, is about farm animals and has wittily designed lift-up flaps. The very first flap is a sack which, when lifted, shows one little mouse. Like other Spot books it has text inside speech bubbles driving the story along. While it should please from about 18 months it is also a favourite in nursery school collections.

What's the Time, Titch?
By Pat Hutchins
Red Fox. 2+
Linked to the TV programme, this board book takes us through Titch's day and has clocks telling the appropriate time on each page with a caption like, for example, 'Time for lunch, Titch's favourite sandwiches'. This is a helpful start for young children beginning to understand how we tell the time.

Count and Squeak
Little Ladybird. 12 months +
Big friendly insects help children to count. We begin with one red ladybird with one black spot and end with ten pink snails with purple trails. Children will enjoy pressing the pink squeaker to mark the appropriate numbers.

Billy Bean's Dream
By Simone Lia
David & Charles. 3+
This most imaginative book tells the story of how Billy Bean and his friends (and his friends' pets!) try to build a rocket. There are so many things to count: the jellybeans, the work tools, the sandwiches and the stars as the rocket finally zooms into the sky.

First Time Book
By Claire Llewellyn
Dorling Kindersley. 5+
This book has been widely praised for its clear format and comprehensive coverage. It explains the digital system and looks at the history of number and at calendars. It shows the time in figures, in digital form and in words. It is quite a demanding book which will take children up to about eight years. Younger children would need a lot of support from the sharing adult but could begin to appreciate the pages on 'Day and Night' and 'Days of the Week'. There is a glossary and a clock face which can be used to help children practise telling the time.

(There are also an atlas, a dictionary and an encyclopaedia in this helpful large format.)

How Many Monsters? A Monster Counting Book
By Mara van de Meer
Frances Lincoln. 18 months +
The humour in this book is quite robust at times and includes counting 'smelly feet' and 'picked noses'. But this is the sort of thing children like and the monsters are likely to amuse rather than frighten.

My Oxford Numbers
By Peter Patilla and David Melby
Oxford University Press Board Book. 3+
This useful book gives figures, computer-type digital figures and words. It gives a helpful introduction to order – it has animal characters coming first, second and third in a race. There are also interesting pages on shape, colour and pattern. The latter includes wavy lines, spirals, square teeth and a repeating pattern.

Jemima Puddleduck's numbers
Beatrix Potter Mini Board Books.
Frederick Warne & Co. Penguin Books. 18 months +
This is an attractive mini board book which invites young children to 'learn to count with Jemina Puddle-duck and her friends'. It is just the right size for a small hand to clutch and turn the robust pages. The number on each page is also written out as a word and is illustrated by a picture from a Beatrix Potter book. I particularly like the annotations on each page – they are just the sort of thing that would appeal to young children: 'the two naughty rabbits are called Peter and Benjamin' and 'the three little kittens' names are Tom, Mittens and Moppet'. The ten onions, playfully arranged on the last page are from Mr McGregor's garden.

Ten Clean Pigs/Ten Dirty Pigs
By Carol Roth and Pamela Paparon
North South Paperbacks. 3+
An 'upside down, turn around' book, this book presents two number-themed stories about the same characters. The appealing pictures show familiar bath time scenes and provide plenty of opportunity for talking and laughing together.

Wake Up/Sleep Tight
By Ken Wilson-Max
Bloomsbury Board Book. 4+
A clock with moveable hands makes this an attractive introduction to the concept of time for young children. The hands can be adjusted to show the times of key events in a child's day – waking up at 7 o'clock, breakfast at 8 o'clock and so on.

Case studies

I have recommended quite a lot of number books, but it is only a small selection of quality works taken from the huge array which set out to help children learn about number in an enjoyable way. I have made a point of including several books that take up a narrative approach as stories seem effective in drawing children towards ideas about number. Case study 4.1 offers a glimpse into how a story led to much talk and role play. Learning about numbers can also happen incidentally when children are listening to an adult read picturebooks on other topics. Case study 4.2 shows the response of some four- to five-year-olds to a vibrant picturebook which, while described as a counting book, also helps children to learn about plant life cycles, predators and colour.

Case study 4.1: Five little dollies

This glimpse into some exciting work comes from Janet Evans study (Evans 2001) in which she reads Ted Arnold's Five Ugly Monsters *(Scholastic) to four- and five-year-old children.*

This 'story song' about 'ugly monsters', with its rhyme and repetition, gives a lot of scope for role play. Earlier the children had been carrying out a task which involved sorting some dolls according to their attributes and so when they acted out the song they sang about 'little dollies' instead of about 'ugly monsters'. The children were helped to write down the new, slightly different story song. It began with the line: 'Five little dollies jumping on the bed' and then one by one a dolly fell and bumped her head. Each time a dolly fell off the bed the children stopped and counted the dollies still on the bed and those on the floor. Evans comments 'they had found a pattern and were doing subtraction in an extremely practical and enjoyable way' (Evans, 2001: 73).

Here a story and acting out a song about counting and subtraction made mathematics seem both human and practical. Evans pinpointed lively talk as making a very important contribution to the success of the work, and particularly to the children's growing understanding of the concept of subtraction.

Case study 4.2: Reading *Ten Seeds* with four- to five-year-olds

This book, read to a reception class at Castlecombe school, reinforced the children's counting ability, expanded their understanding of life cycles and predators and also linked with their work that term on 'colour'.

I introduced the children to the book by showing the cover and the little boy counting out ten seeds and then asked them how many of the ten seeds they thought would grow into plants. Some said all ten would but Tommy thought 'an animal might eat some of them'. We had to read the book to find out how many seeds survived. The children joined in the reading, helped by the pictures. They were particularly entertained by the mouse putting its tiny pink hand into the soil to scoop up a seed. They also laughed at the mole emerging from the ground with a seedling on his head! The picture of the cat inspired a lot of talk – Elizabeth told us that 'the cat next door comes under the fence and digs up our plants'. Other children who had cats said they ate small birds and mice as well as plants.

Children are more tuned into visual aspects of literacy in this technological age of mixed media. They quickly saw that the ladybird had eaten the green-fly on the surviving plant before the text was read. And they understood that when the small boy planted the seeds in the final picture, the whole cycle would start again.

The children's theme for this part of the summer term was 'colour' and the colour of the week happened to be orange. So when we came to the vibrant colour spread of the surviving bloom there was a cry of 'Orange and yellow sunflower!' Georgia commented that 'sunflowers look happy flowers'.

This kind of book, sometimes referred to as an 'information story', has the same time sequence organisation that fictional narratives have. The story encouraged the children to bring their existing knowledge to the reading and listening and reinforced their counting skills. Inviting early science and mathematics books such as this one prepare the way for more systematic learning later. The 'how many will survive?' question at the beginning seemed to give a helpful 'let's find out' set towards the account and inspired children's confidence so that they offered relevant anecdotes and observations from their experience. Perhaps the most profound message of the book, which the children commented on, is that nature needs to be extravagant with the number of seeds produced as so many perish before their life cycle is complete. The children's appreciation of the visual humour and Georgia's joyful comment suggest that young children's response to factual kinds of book can, like that to more conventional fiction, include their feelings and emotions. A next step might be the children growing their own seeds and making booklets about the stages of a plant's life cycle.

Figure 4.2 Reproduced from *Ten Seeds* by permission of Andersen Press Ltd. Copyright © 2001 Andersen Press Ltd.

Figure 4.3 Beth's dinosaur maths activity: using a picture to clinch concepts. Five-year-old Beth and her class had been enjoying a project on dinosaurs. The teacher had introduced a labelling game to help the children use the language of dimension. The children were asked to look at the image of the dinosaur and talk about it with their partner. They stuck on labels describing different parts of the dinosaur's body. The intellectual benefits of the activity were expanded when the teacher asked them to discuss their decisions with their partner, thus making their developing concepts explicit.

Concept books: colour, shape and opposites

Visit any children's section in a bookshop and you will find it brimming with early information books on everyday concepts. Like alphabet and number books, concept books may be presented as a story, but may be some of the first kinds of non-narrative text children encounter. Some of the best are quality picturebooks in which text and illustration interact in powerful and sophisticated ways. As we would expect, the criteria that can help us choose are similar to those for alphabet and number books. The best books have:

- **an organising idea** to give the theme coherence; for example, a well-known storybook character might introduce the ideas, or a colour book might be organised round the hues of fruit or creatures
- **an 'alive' feel** so there is a dynamic sense of movement and encouragement to participate, perhaps by including games and puzzles
- **originality** in format and style to catch the young imagination, for example 'lift the flap' and 'pop-ups'
- **clear print** which helps beginning readers
- **lively written text** which is simple without being banal
- **distinctive illustrations** to intrigue, challenge or amuse and encourage talk and reflection

A selective list of concept books

Lorraine Kelly Fun-to-Learn: Colours
By Lynne Breeze
Andrew Deutsch Board Books. 10 months +
Each page of this wordless picturebook is an explosion of a particular colour together with

objects to match – bananas on the yellow page and a cat on the brown page, for instance. As is the case with all wordless books, the adult can enthuse the child with what they say.

Spot's Touch and Feel Book
By Eric Hill
Penguin. 3+
The child listener or reader is invited to join Spot on a walk on a sunny day and to learn about textures. Participation is invited – who could resist feeling the knobbly steps Spot runs down, the rough grass he rolls on and the 'beautifully red and gleaming' smooth ball he bounces?

Colours
By Gallimard Jeunesse and Pascale de Bourgoing, illustrated by P.M. Valat and Sylvaine Perols
Moonlight Publishing. 4+
The transparent sheets allow children to change colours and to hide and reveal things. When the transparent cover is lifted from the giant red pencil, a collection of red toys is revealed. There is a chance to learn about colour mixing: the blue frog is turned green by covering it with a yellow transparency and a squirrel's tail is changed from green to brown with the help of a red transparency. Something of the way colour, or lack of it, can affect atmosphere and mood is indicated by covering a picture of a street with a black and grey transparency transforming it into a dark and shadow-filled scene.

Mimi's Book of Opposites
By Emma Chichester Clark
Andersen Press. 2+
Mimi enjoys learning about opposites with her baby brother. The family context of the learning will appeal to young children.

My First Book of Opposites
By Kim Deegan
Bloomsbury. 10 months +
The pattern of this book is that a word appears on one page, with its opposite shown by turning to the next page. So we have the same baby introducing concepts like 'light and dark', 'asleep and awake', 'up and down' and 'quiet and loud'. Adults can add their own special effects – like speaking loudly and quietly and miming 'up' and 'down'. This input from the sharing adult will bring alive this beautifully illustrated book for a young child.

My Jumbo Book of Colours
Illustrated by James Diaz and Melanie Garth
Gullane Children's Books. 2+
This 'touch and feel' book encourages children's participation by providing textures to feel, colours to delight the eye, flaps to lift and levers to move and slide. When I first looked at it I wondered if there was too much stimulation, but all the novelties are in aid of learning colours in an entertaining way. On the 'yellow' page, an exuberant bee can be moved up and down to alight on a golden flower and you can feel the downy coat of the yellow chick. The colours on each page are named on pictures of giant crayons and there is a poster with questions like: 'Can you see something purple?' Lots to talk about here.

Bedtime; Mealtime
Dorling Kindersley Touch and Feel books. 2+
These books have some satisfying surfaces to feel. *Bedtime* has a splendid padded quilt and rubbery grips on the bear slippers. The jam on the bread in *Mealtime* feels sticky. The adjectives in each contextualising sentence are in bold print.

Who's bigger?
By Dorothy Eiron, illustrated by Sue Cory
Marshall Publishing. 3+
Size and comparison are the concepts explored in this unusual book. The pages get bigger to show the sequence from small to big and there is a pull-out poster showing the child and small animals to encourage comparison.

Kipper's Book of Opposites
By Mick Inkpen
Hodder Children's Books. 3+
This robust board book has eight spreads looking at different 'opposites'. Kipper is a favourite character and children will enjoy talking about the situation in each picture. 'Happy' is illustrated by Kipper rushing along with a lovely big balloon, while 'sad' shows him holding the string after the balloon has burst. Superb!
   (The other three books in the series are *Kipper's Book of Colour, Number* and *Weather.*)

Dog Days
By Krisztina Nagy
David & Charles. 3+
This book helps the understanding of 'opposites' by picturing dogs of different kinds in the park. We have Harriet who is 'hairy' and Sylvester who is 'smooth'. Sometimes just a furry ear rises on the page! The dogs have delightful long alliterative names which adds to the humour of this interactive 'lift the flap' book.

Dinosaur Roar!
By Paul and Henrietta Strickland
Ragged Bears. 2+
(board book or paperback format)
'Dinosaur roar, dinosaur squeak, dinosaur fierce, dinosaur meek' – this is how the minimal text goes in this most original 'opposite' book. Children love seeing the dinosaurs of all shapes and sizes romping and roaring through the pages. An exuberant final page shows all the dinosaurs which have appeared in the book.

My Nose, Your Nose; My Beak, Your Beak
By Melanie Walsh
Doubleday 2+
In this series, children are encouraged to think about differences and similarities. Knowing the words 'similar' and 'different' and using them appropriately helps clinch the concepts.
   In *My Nose, Your Nose* the pictured children have different eye colours but they all have the similar need to close their eyes when they go to sleep. In *My Beak, Your Beak* we meet animals of the same general species that are different in some respects and the same in

others. So we have a small sausage dog and a large dalmatian but both love chasing sticks. Or creatures might have different habitats – a penguin lives at the snowy South Pole while a robin is found in the garden – but they both have pointy beaks. Children and adults would enjoy sharing these playfully illustrated books with their simple text.

That's not my tractor
By Fiona Watt, illustrated by Rachel Wells
Usborne touchy-feely board book. 18 months +
Bright, clear pictures in primary colours (outlined in black) help young children explore the concepts of 'like' and 'not like'. There are some lovely surface effects – shiny, textured headlights, squashy tyres and scratchy seat material. The rhythmic text repeats 'That's not my tractor' on the left of each double spread. The opposite page gives the reason, for example, 'its funnel is too smooth'. A little mouse appears on most pages.

Creature Feet; Creature Hair; Creature Noses; Creature Tails
By Nicola Whittaker
Creature Feature series. Watts. 3+
The fact that animals' bodies are adapted to particular habitats and lifestyles is the main insight that this book aims to impart. It does so by using pictures of animals placed on the page in interesting ways. So in *Creature Tails* a picture of a huge rattlesnake curves its way round the page, holding its tail ready to rattle. The text sweeps around the pictures, with important words in larger print and witty touches that children will enjoy. A glossary provides more information about the animals and could be handy when answering children's questions.

Using concept books

Children under three will enjoy sharing books like those suggested above with an adult or older sibling, pointing to favourite pictures and beginning to question and comment. In nursery and reception classes teachers often use these books to support work on a theme. Here the book and the conversation it generates will extend children's understanding of the concept. Colour books may complement work on colour mixing in art while shape and size books help clinch mathematical learning. Children gain great satisfaction from making their own individual, group or class books to celebrate and record their work alongside reading the books introduced to them by the teacher. In case study 4.3 we join four children from a reception class who have been working on 'colour' and find them bringing their prior experiences to the reading.

Case study 4.3: Colour mixing

Reception class children at Castlecombe were working on the theme 'colour'. In the following vignette a group of four listened to 'colour' by G. Jeunesse and P. de Bourgoing.

It was the coloured transparent sheets interspersed between each page that appealed most to the children. Putting the sheets over the pictures could both hide and reveal things. Four-year-old Elizabeth looked at the giant red pencil on the red page and remarked that red made her think of toys. So she was delighted on lifting the flap to find a toy engine, car and building brick.

The transparent sheets also helped demonstrate the principles of colour mixing. A pink ice cream in a cone was changed to orange by placing over it a yellow transparency. 'These pictures are like summer' remarked five-year-old Courtney who also reminded us that orange was their colour of the week. The blue frog was turned green by a yellow transparency and the squirrel's tail was transformed from green to brown by a red transparency.

The children were also shown how colour could affect atmosphere and mood. A picture of a sunny street became dark and full of shadows when a grey and black overlay was placed over it. This was the transformation that generated most talk. Tommy said he preferred blue skies and that black stopped you seeing colours. There was some talk about animals that come out at night time. Hannah mentioned that her young cousin brought a doll when she came to stay overnight – to comfort her in the dark. Another child said they took Pooh to bed for the same reason and that they tried to 'think of something happy'. Elizabeth said 'The only thing I like about the dark is the moon'.

The book encouraged children to share their thoughts about the physical effects of colour mixing and to bring their own personal anecdotes to explain the emotional impact of colour and to help make human sense of these concepts.

Summary

Early information books about number and about concepts like colour, shape and opposites need to achieve a balance between teaching and entertainment. Some are early examples of non-narrative text, but stories and story songs can also be exciting ways into learning about numbers and other concepts. Alongside counting games and first hand experience, the best number books help make a child's first encounters with figures and counting enjoyable rather than threatening.

In both number and concept books talking and sharing the ideas, whether with an adult or older sibling, both makes the experience pleasurable and encourages active participation.

References

Arnold, Helen (1996) '"Penguins never meet polar bears": reading for information in the early years', in D. Whitebread (ed.) Teaching and Learning in the Early Years. London: Routledge.
Donaldson, Margaret (1978) Children's Minds. Glasgow: Fontana.
Evans, Janet (2001) 'Four little dollies jumping on the bed – Learning about mathematics through talk', in P. Godwin (ed.) The Articulate Classroom. London: David Fulton.
Mallett, Margaret (2002) 'Mathematics and English', in The Primary English Encyclopaedia. London: David Fulton.
Watson, Victor (2001) The Cambridge Guide to Children's Books in English. Cambridge: Cambridge University Press.

Chapter 5

Reading and writing non-fiction at home: Orla's books and writing

Beginning to control your world

> We want children to write a lot and through their experiences with writing to see writing as enjoyable, as a powerful way of communicating.
>
> (Godwin and Perkins, 2002: 109)

> If young pre-school children are writing at home, then their family are probably involved in some way, since it is they who provide the context for learning.
>
> (Weinberger, 1996: 12)

In Chapter 2, there are three case studies where children under two years are looking at their first books and having their first experience of non-fiction print. The case study on which this chapter is built covers a longer span of time – from the first year of life up until age four. It looks first at the books that Orla enjoyed and continues with some examples of the early non-fiction writing she did at home.

The analysis here has links both with previous chapters on early years non-fiction, including those on alphabet books and number books, and with the chapter which follows, Chapter 6, which looks at non-fiction writing in the nursery school and in the reception class. Orla always writes to serve a very real purpose, whether to stop children entering her parents' room or to puzzle out how people get to Heaven when they die. This need to write for a purpose, a need so very evident in looking at this case study, is something we need to bear in mind when encouraging children to write in a school setting.

Orla's experience with books and her attempts at writing overlap, but I have looked at each in turn for clarity.

Case study 5.1: Orla – a very young reader and writer

Orla enjoyed books of all kinds from a very young age. She had an exceptional opportunity to do so as her mother, Siobhan, is an early years teacher with special expertise in children's literature. When I was preparing to write this book I explained to Siobhan that I was interested in the very early interactions of children with non-fiction; Orla's mother remembered that while she had many storybooks Orla had also enjoyed quite a few early non-fiction books at different stages. The following analysis draws selectively (the emphasis is on non-fiction) on Siobhan's diary of Orla's progress.

Orla: listening to and reading non-fiction

Birth to one year: miniature board books and novelty books

From about six months Orla enjoyed sharing Jan Pienkowski's concept books and responded particularly positively to *Zoo* and *Faces*. But the book her mother remembers as being the favourite when Orla was still under a year was *My Big Book of Beautiful Babies* by David Ellwand. This is a book that goes along the lines of 'baby happy, baby sad, baby good, baby bad' and so on. Orla liked the last page which had a mirror and the words 'And last of all a place for you!'

Twelve to 20 months: more board books – with photographs

During these months Orla showed a preference for board books with photographs. Her mother remarked 'Photographs were definitely preferred to other forms of visual representation at this stage, continuing up to about two years'. She particularly liked the 'naming' board books like *My Home, Who's That?* from Campbell Books. Orla and her mother found them in their local Early Learning Centre. Fiona Pragoff's colourful photographs and simple text were appreciated. I often see these in public and nursery libraries – they have a simple but very effective design. One attraction seems to be that you can find a Pragoff book which shows a child the same age as your own child and doing the same sort of things. It is satisfying for both child and adult to have their lives reflected back to them.

Once, when in America, Orla's mother bought some number and shape board books – *123*, *Triangle*, *Square* and *Circle* – that she rightly predicted that her daughter would appreciate. These were by the American artist, William Wegman, who often uses photographs of his dogs, dressed up, to illustrate his books.

Age two to three years: reading to learn the ABC

Siobhan found that ABC books were popular with her daughter at this stage, particularly Brian Wildsmith's *ABC* which has delighted generations of children since its first printing in 1962. Although she describes Margaret Tempest's *An ABC for You and Me* as 'rather twee' she points out it did help Orla to learn the names of the letters at about two years and eight months. 'The calligraphic text is as striking as the illustrations. I adapted it by using the names of people she knew instead of those in the text. So, for example, "Oliver had an orange" became "Orla had an orange"'.

Age three to four years: enjoying Anno and others

Two textless books by Anno – *Anno's Britain* and *Anno's Journey* – were great favourites as Orla moved through the pre-school years. I was interested that a child still so young should like these very sophisticated books. As her mother comments: 'Both books have an enormous amount of illustrative detail, most of which is historical and intertextual'. *Anno's Counting Book* is not published here but was ordered in small format paperback for Orla from Amazon. The big book version is apparently very well liked for teaching numbers in America.

Siobhan and Orla also loved reading Dorling Kindersley's *Children Just Like Me* and *Millennium Children of Britain Just Like Me*.

Reflections

Of course young children can only show their early preferences if they have a good supply of books to choose from, and in this respect Orla was fortunate. Not only were many books provided, but also her mother enjoyed sharing them with her.

Two things which particularly interested me were Orla's partiality for photographs as illustrations in the second year of her life, and the fact that, in her mother's words, 'she adores Anno books'. Children soon become visually aware in these days of television, DVDs, video-film and e-books. Orla also had many fine fiction picturebooks read to her and so probably became able to make subtle connections between visual images and the written text at a young age. It is also true that her mother talked to her about the pictures and texts. It is well honed talk that helps children tune into all the subtle meanings the author of a sophisticated book like Anno's offers. We know from many studies – that of Gordon Wells, for instance (Wells, 1986) – that fiction can be a bridge to abstract thinking. We know less about the intellectual pay off from early exposure to non-fiction texts. My guess is that quality non-fiction helps young children make connections, form categories of phenomena and ideas, and note similarities and differences both visually and verbally. In other words, it develops their concept-forming ability.

Orla's first writing

Important as stories are to young children, their first attempts at writing are more likely to have an informational or communicative function – a card to wish someone a happy birthday, a notice to control people's behaviour or a label to denote something significant: 'my book, teddy, toy'.

Orla's mother notes that her daughter's interest in writing began when she started to understand the significance of letters. So the ABC books encouraged her and she 'has quite a lot of stamina for it, and loves writing in cards'.

Orla became convinced of the power of writing as a way of communicating at an early age. When Hallowe'en came around in October 2001 and she was three years and four months old, she became worried that witches might come into her room while she was asleep. After talking about this the result was that she asked her mother to help her write out 'Orla knows no witches come into my room'. Siobhan writes 'This features Orla's idiosyncratic early handwriting – I was rather fond of her R s with "running legs"! Writing this down and pinning it to her door seemed to help her cope with her fears by being in control.' (See Figure 5.1.)

This use of writing and image-making to control things happening in her world is evident in the work shown in Figure 5.5. Orla made this notice just as her fourth birthday celebrations were drawing near. It was pinned to the door of her parents' bedroom as she did not want any child who visited to go into the room and peep at the birthday cake that was stored there. Nor did she want anyone bouncing on the bed – a privilege which she felt should be hers alone! The notice has a girl with a cross drawn over her – using the principle of some prohibitory traffic signs. Orla sought help to write 'No Children' underneath. This example shows her ability to use environmental print and images creatively for her own intentions.

Siobhan told me that Orla likes to label and explain her work. On one occasion she wrote around a picture (an illustration clearly intended for older children) which her friend had left behind (Figure 5.3). The writing said: 'Elizabeth was at Orla's house'. Children are quickly exposed to the norms of their culture – in this case through a picture showing the clothes and

Figure 5.1 'Orla knows no witches come in my room'. Three years, four months.

Figure 5.2 'A bus – Orla's picture of a bus with advertisement for coffee on the side showing the impact of environmental print on a very young writer. Three years, ten months.

body language of a romantic teenage couple. The intention of this example was to record, as older people might do in a diary, a significant event – the visit of her friend.

Siobhan's favourite picture from all those that Orla has done so far seeks to record what she has seen in the world outside her home and to comment on her experience in the environment (see Figure 5.2). 'This is a drawing of a London bus, complete with passengers looking out of the windows, and an advert for coffee (with appropriate slogan and illustration) on the side!' It shows the impact of a consumer society – an impact which has been strong enough to become a natural element in her pictures at an early age. (This sensitivity to environmental print and the ability to adapt it for her own purpose is also evident in the bedroom notice shown in Figure 5.5.)

Young children often puzzle over aspects of the world and try to make sense of it. Orla talks to her mother about these puzzles and uses drawing and writing to hypothesise – to suggest some possible answers. On one occasion she was drawing a map of how to get up to the sky (see Figure 5.4). Her mother comments that it was a busy post-lunch occasion when she was entertaining three other four-year-olds and their mothers and she was trying to have a conversation with the adults. Orla was insistent that her mother help her write out 'This is a map to get to the sky'. She did not feel inclined to wait until the adult conversation had stopped and Siobhan remembers it as a rather uncomfortable situation during which she gave Orla advice across the room in a rather disjointed manner while she continued to talk to the adults. The origin of this map-making was that an aunt had told her that when people die they go to Heaven and that Heaven is in the sky. Orla, who thinks deeply about things, wondered how they got from the earth to high up into the sky. One theory she expressed to her mother was that giants, like the giant in *Jack and the Beanstalk*, lifted people up in their

Figure 5.3 'Elizabeth was at Orla's house'. Three years, 11 months.

Figure 5.4 'This is a map to get to the sky'. Three years, 11 months.

Figure 5.5 'No children' – a notice written by Orla just before her fourth birthday to discourage children at her party from entering her mother's bedroom.

long arms. Another theory was that people climbed up to Heaven on long ladders, and the map was Orla's way of working through how this journey was accomplished.

Orla has pre-occupations which she needs to puzzle out in her own way. Piaget called this passionate feeling and need to sort out puzzles a state of 'disequilibrium'. Only a satisfactory answer will make the mental state comfortable or in 'equilibrium' once more.[1] Navarra describes his own young son's intense search for answers to his wonderings. On one occasion he noted that snow melted first on the sunny side of the house and struggled to make sense of this and to solve the puzzle of why this happened (Navarro, 1955).

Reflections

There is a lot here in Orla's development that fascinates anyone interested in children's development and particularly their language development. I'm still puzzling over some questions the work raises. Was there, for example, a strong link between Orla's early experience of books and her own writing? There are interesting studies showing links between children's writing and their experience of fiction in both print and video-film (Fox, 1993; Browne, 1999). (Stories about giants seem to have influenced one of Orla's theories of how people get to Heaven – but this was a spoken rather than a written hypothesis.) Stories about witches have had a strong effect and have affected her choice of writing in the form of her notice made for Hallowe'en. It is as if Orla felt that expressing her hope in language made her safer. In this book, of course, the emphasis has been on early non-fiction literacy even though the boundaries between fact and fiction often blur in early years work. Here it is difficult to be sure about effects, but the labelling and annotation of images evident in Orla's work is found in children's information picturebooks – so there may be some linkage here. But the most striking influences seems to come from the environment at home and from the world outside – Orla's writing accompanies images of advertising on buses and images from road signs. These are adapted creatively to meet her purpose.

One interesting thing about the examples of Orla's writing that I have included is that she has clearly wanted to get things right first time. She has asked her mother how to spell words so that not many of the developmental spellings often found in the work of children this age are apparent. This may be connected with the fact that her mother presents a strong model of a writer. She writes a great deal using longhand and sometimes the word processor and spell check in connection with her job and the part time Masters degree course she is following. So Orla has had a particularly strong example of writing as a part of everyday life. She has been able to learn early on that writing has purposes and that adults have intentions when they write and she wants to share in that. Orla's purposes for writing are clear: for labelling, for recording events, for controlling other people's behaviour, for making observations about her world and for problem solving and theorising. Children are individuals with their own interests, preoccupations, worries and priorities and we would expect this to be reflected in their choices as writers. The important thing to appreciate is that this sense of purpose is essential to mustering the sheer energy and effort to write – always a challenging activity. In doing so children draw on all the resources of the society in which they are growing up.

Orla's non-fiction

Anno's Britain; Anno's Journey
Anno Mitsumasa
Bodley Head (textless books)

Anno's Counting Book
Anno Mitsumasa
Bodley Head
(Published in America only)

My Big Book of Beautiful Babies
By David Ellwand
Ragged Bears

My Home, Who's That?
By Rod Campbell
Campbell Books

Children Just Like Me; Millennium Children Just Like Me
By Barnabus and Anabel Kindersley
Dorling Kindersley

Zoo; Faces
By Jan Pienkowski
Heinemann (miniature board book format)

Fun to be One; It's Great to be Two
Fiona Pragoff
Gollancz

An ABC for You and Me
By Margaret Tempest
Medici Press (also published in poster and wrapping paper format)

ABC
By Brian Wildsmith
Oxford University Press

123; Triangle; Square; Circle
By William Wegman
Hyperion Books for Children, New York

Note

1   For a more detailed explanation of Piaget's concept of equilibrium and disequilibrium in learning, see David
    Wood (1988) *How Children Think and Learn*. London: Blackwell, pages 39–41.

References

Brown, Naima (1999) *Young Children's Literacy Development and the Role of Televisual Texts*. London:
    Falmer Press.
Fox, Carol (1993) *At the very Edge of the Forest: The Influence of Literature on Story Telling by
    Children*. London: Cassell.
Godwin, Diane and Perkins, Margaret (2002, second edition) *Teaching Language and Literacy in the
    Early Years*. London: David Fulton.
Navarra, J.G. (1955) *The Growth of Scientific Concepts in the Young Child*. New York: Teachers College,
    Columbia University.
Weinberger, Jo (1996) *Literacy Goes to School*. London: Paul Chapman Publishing.
Wells, Gordon (1986) *Learning Through Interaction: Learning to Use Language and Using Language
    to Learn*. London: Hodder & Stoughton.

Moving forward

The early chapters described some of the books pre-school children enjoy. These included the playful books in plastic, cloth and board that children first encounter. Case studies were included to bring a personal and human dimension and showed that it is never too early for children to have preferences. The early alphabet, number and concept books that start to be enjoyed after about age two were discussed in some detail with suggested criteria to help choose them. These books can provide a link between home and school because children will often find them in nursery school and reception class collections.

In the chapters that follow the analysis is concerned with what happens in school to support children's developing control over informational reading and writing and, to some extent, what happens at home as well.

Chapter 6 explores the kinds of non-fiction writing which children attempt first and how we can support them. At this age, control over language is growing and teachers try to meet the challenge of giving this support – extending study and research skills and so on – while not pressing mature forms on young children too soon. The links between reading and writing are quite subtle and complex when it comes to non-fiction. Indeed, finding a 'voice' in writing may precede children's informational reading. In dealing with this complexity I have found it helpful to place the writing chapter before the reading chapter.

Chapter 7 attempts a classification of the non-fiction texts for the three- to six-year-olds that we find in school and which I hope will inform our choice for thematic work and lessons across the curriculum. In both this chapter and in Chapter 6 there are case studies of teachers and children at work which explore the issues at a practical level.

In both Chapter 6 and Chapter 7 I have identified the early learning goals most specific to children's experience of non-fiction and there is more on the official frameworks in Appendix 1.

The final chapters look at the contribution of references books, of television, of the computer and of fiction as ways of developing informational literacy. Each has its own chapter so that the issues that arise can be given greater weight and developed in more detail than perhaps is usual in more general books about early years literacy.

Chapter 6

Early informational writing three to six years

Making a start with informational genre

Children's writing should always be set in meaningful contexts that are familiar to the experience of young children.

(Riley and Reedy, 2000: 135)

[Primary teachers encourage narrative] as a means through which children can learn to express their feelings about their world.

(Czerniewska 1992: 134)

Children's non-narrative texts are different from mature non-narrative ... because they express a certain stage of thinking.

(Barrs, 1987: 14)

The first attempts that children make at writing go alongside, or may even precede, their first attempts at reading. Reading and writing are processes that nourish each other, but when it comes to early non-fiction kinds of writing the links between what children read (or listen to) and what they write are complicated. This seems particularly true of non-narrative kinds of writing which, as Barrs argues above, seem to be connected with the stage reached in a child's intellectual development.

If you want to read about children's very earliest mark-making and writing of all kinds there are a number of interesting studies to consult, for example, the early chapters in Riley and Reedy, 2000; Bissex, 1980; Whitehead 2002; Clay 1975; Temple *et al.* 1988. All these writers show that children reach out creatively to the principles of written language and that our teaching should support this. It is an insight informing the analysis in this chapter where the emphasis is on early informational or non-fiction writing and how it can be supported in the years from three to six. I begin with a discussion of role play both in the home corner and in play areas outside and its potential for developing early writing. Then I move to a consideration of 'Writing to help children organise their world' and children's early attempts at naming, labelling, annotating, listing and summarising. Children enjoy writing when it is linked to all the other things they are doing including physical activity. The emphasis then turns to 'Writing to communicate with others' and a look at making posters and notices and at writing letters and e-mails. Next in 'Moving on: kinds of thinking, forms of writing' I discuss how teachers help children control the kinds of writing valued in our society while keeping purpose and enjoyment to the fore. This section takes a critical look at genre theory and suggests strong contexts for encouraging writing – role play, exploring the local area and practical work. The writing that emerges from the rich contexts of the early years classroom, with its emphasis on talk as a major force in language and learning, gradually begins to differentiate into writing to recount, instruct, report, explain, discuss and persuade – the six non-fiction genres identified in the National Literacy Strategy.

'The writing corner', an essential resource for all kinds of writing, has its own section, and under 'Further issues' I comment on drafting, writing and gender, young bilingual writers and the role of teachers and parents, visual literacy and on how teachers create a community of young writers in the early years classroom.

Finally a consideration of 'Assessing and recording children's non-fiction writing' recognises evaluation of children's and the teacher's work as a crucial part of the learning cycle.

The two early learning goals most pertinent to this chapter are:

- children need to write their own names, labels, captions and simple sentences
- children need to attempt writing for different purposes (QCA, 1999)

These goals and the requirements of the National Literacy Strategy and National Curriculum, English, provide a check list to hold up against the learning programme (see Appendix 1 for further details). However, it is teachers who put the life and creativity into the learning programme as the case studies in this book show.

Play and literacy

Children growing up in a literate society are surrounded by print and see adults and older children writing for all sorts of reasons. So it is not surprising that they try to write themselves and we have all seen the waving lines of their first 'pretend' writing. Playing at being a reader and a writer and 'getting closer and closer to the real thing' is very much part of becoming literate in the earliest years (Whitehead, 2002: 60). Both the home corner and the outside play areas, so important for children in nursery school and in reception classes, are strong settings for the many informational kinds of writing which are the subject of this chapter. The home corner is a changing environment, sensitive to the theme-led nature of much good early years work. It may become a café, baby clinic, post office, fire station, museum, vet's surgery, space station, travel agency or shop associated with a wealth of interesting print and writing opportunities. Some of the children involved in the Food Theme work (case study 6.1) enjoyed role play in the Red Café which the teacher had helped them set up. When I visited they were eagerly putting up the 'Open' and 'Closed' notices and making menus, posters and bills.

Outdoor play settings can also provide rich opportunities for language and literacy development. Talk and writing can be kept together and we can link literacy with the sort of exciting, noisy and adventurous activities so many young children enjoy (Bromley, 2002). There is some evidence that boys in particular feel comfortable learning in an outdoor setting (Millard, 1997). Later in this chapter resources for a writing or literacy area are considered. But there is no reason why a literacy area with books and writing materials should not be created outside during fine weather. For writing outside, huge flip charts are particularly practical or paper can be attached to large clip boards. Some nursery staff help by fixing chalk boards to a wall. To the usual implements for writing we might add jumbo chalks, large crayons and extra big brushes. Books displayed might support the role play activity in process: there could, for example, be some books on plants to support play in a garden shop context or books on cars to link with a garage setting. We can also use ICT resources imaginatively, providing remote control toys, play video cameras and so on. In a very interesting article, Terry Gould suggests that role play outside is particularly suited to robust contexts like a market garden, a garage or road works. These create a strong purpose for writing signs – 'Go', 'Stop', 'Danger', 'Sand', 'Cement', 'Entrance' and 'Exit'. Children also like writing bills for building materials and writing down a telephone order (Gould, 2002). They can also be helped to make labels and captions for digital images of themselves engaged in outdoor role play. Gould notes that talk and writing work together in extending children's vocabulary and use of language. Overheard in a 'builders' yard' were the following comments: 'Can't you read? It says CLOSED, so come back later', and 'O.K. just sign there and we'll send the bill to you in the post' (Gould, 2002: 10).

Writing to help children organise their world: naming, labelling, annotating, listing and summarising

In the early years classroom, children begin to use their knowledge of letters and sounds in their own writing in a creative way. The intelligent developmental spellings children use are familiar to teachers of this age group and we see some of these in the case studies and figures in this chapter. In this section we are concerned with one of the first functions that writing serves for the young child – helping them to organise their world.

Names are important

Writing their own name is one of the first instances of conventional writing by children. Some children come to school able to write their names. Parents who help their children to do this are providing them with a good start. Research into which school entry abilities auger most strongly for success in literacy consistently show this. Jeni Riley, for example, who studied 191 children from school entry to the end of the first year at school, comments that 'the ability to identify letters of the alphabet and to write one's name at school entry are the most important predictors of successful readers at the end of the first year' (Riley, 1996: xv). The same claim is made by Weinberger in assessing the results of the Elmswood study of literacy experiences at home (Weinberger, 1996: 150).

Why is the ability to write one's name early on so significant? First, when children write their name it shows they are coming to realise that their name symbolises 'them' and who they are in all their complexity. This is an enormous step forward and most important to the emergence of a strong self-image. Second, it marks the emergence of literacy and is the beginning of the journey towards conceptual understanding of the alphabet system. This sounds a big claim – but if you think about it, writing your name means you have some knowledge of directionality as you write from left to right, you may know that you use upper case for the first letter, and, if you can write both your names, you will soon learn to place a space between the words. Early years teachers encourage using names on belongings, pegs and work to reinforce the symbolic nature of writing.

In case study 6.1 children name put their names on their pictures and also name the objects in their illustrations, see Figures 6.1 and 6.2.

Case study 6.1: Food theme – children name their work and the objects in their illustrations

Teachers and four-year-olds at Dulwich Wood Nursery School enjoyed a range of activities – a visit to a supermarket, cooking, role play in The 'Red Café', drawing, writing, sharing books – during a project on 'food'.

The children drew food they had seen during the supermarket visit and wrote the name of the food and their own names on the work. They had books and picture cards to help them as well as their memories of the visit. The black and white illustrations in the figures here give an idea of the vitality of the work but cannot do justice to the vibrant colour with which the children brought their pictures of pizza, pineapples, mangoes and oranges to life. Some children, like four-and-a-half-year-old Yasmin, drew and painted their favourite food and named them below. Others, like Tom, integrated their drawing with the names of the foods.

Everyday good nursery practice like this provides opportunities for meaningful naming and labelling.

Labelling

The nursery and reception years provide many opportunities for children to move on from writing their names to helping the teacher to name and label the objects in the classroom. Writing labels such as 'reading/writing corner', 'weather chart', 'helpers chart', 'timetable' and so on creates environmental print for the classroom. Role play in the outside play area or in the home corner also gives a reason for labelling – 'plant nursery', 'café', 'post office' and 'waiting room'. Being able to write labels helps children feel in control of their world. In case study 6.2 we join young children whose teacher made learning to write labels part of a bigger topic which included a number of interesting activities.

Case study 6.2: Naming body parts

Four-year-olds at Clyde Nursery School in Deptford were helped to become familiar with the names and positions of parts of the body as one topic within a broader one entitled 'features of living things'. Both a picturebook and a factual poster were used to help children label the main parts of the body on their own drawings.

Listening to the teacher read Eric Carle's picturebook *From Head to Toe* (Puffin) gave a dynamic start to the lesson. Then, with the help of a 'My Body' poster (this one was from *Child Education*, December 1995, but any large, clear poster would serve the purpose), teacher and children talked about the name and position of the main parts of the human body.

Next, in pairs, each child took turns to lie down on a huge piece of card while their partner was helped to draw around them. Then the teacher helped the class to write the names of the parts of the body – arm, leg, neck and so on – on their outlines. These

Figure 6.1 Yasmin's pineapple. Yasmin four and a half, has concentrated on her picture of a pineapple, placing her name at the bottom of her work.

Figure 6.2 Tom's burger. Tom, aged four and a half, has integrated the names of his chosen foods with his drawings.

giant pictures were then cut into simple jigsaws after which the children 'reassembled' them. When this was done the children and teacher talked about the parts of the body and their positions with reference both to the poster and to their jigsaw. The lesson ended with the song 'Head, shoulders, knees and toes'.

Significant here was the variety of activity the children enjoyed and the way in which practical work and use of secondary sources were integrated to promote learning. They talked about two very different resources – an amusing story and a factual, labelled poster. Then there were some exciting practical activities in pairs – drawing round each other and making jigsaws. This 'enactive' mode of learning helps secure knowledge from secondary sources, supported by the teacher's mediation.[1] Returning to the poster and story helped the children clinch the names and positions of the parts of their body. The work extended into role play round a hospital theme in the home corner where there were more opportunities for making labels and posters.

Annotating poems, pictures and diagrams

Annotations are an extension of labelling. Children enjoy adding notes and pictures to drawings and writing, as they did to the poem in case study 6.3. The 'news' that children write in school often consists of a drawing and some written annotation of the illustration: 'This is me swimming with my sister' or 'I had a lot of cake at my party'. In case study 6.3 the teacher created an interesting context for children to write and draw annotations to place round a large piece of card on which an action poem had been written out.

Case study 6.3: Annotations of 'I can' poem

Four-year-olds at Clyde Nursery School, Deptford annotated a poem they had enjoyed, 'I can' by Rozalia Makinson (Collins 'Pathways to Literacy' series).

The poem was read to the whole class and they talked about the things children of their age can do – tying shoe laces, banging drums, climbing trees and so on. In response to the poem and the discussion, the children were invited to write, draw or take photographs of something they thought they could do well. One child asked the teacher to help her write 'I can catch a ball'. Another drew a picture of himself cleaning his teeth while another child asked for a photograph to be taken of her riding a little bike.[2] The teacher placed the children's written and pictorial annotations round a copy of the poem which had been written out in large writing. The children talked about their drawings, writing and photographs using, with encouragement from the teacher, the language of position – 'I lift my hand to brush my hair'; 'I bend down to put my dog's lead on'.

The student teacher observed that the children took notice of what was said in the discussion of the poem. In her notes she wrote: 'we must take care that children do not become concerned about what they cannot do in comparison with others'. In this work

Figure 6.3   Angela's ladybird. Five-year-old Angela has annotated her drawing.

the teacher took care to put the emphasis on what each individual could do. The lesson shows how a poem can lead to reflections on practical aspects of our own lives and competencies as human beings. It proved the starting point for a particularly rich response – not least a growing understanding of how annotation can extend thinking.

Listing – an important kind of early non-fiction

One of the earliest kinds of non-narrative writing is the list. Even the youngest children can understand that lists are used for different purposes. Teacher and class often list things like what to bring on the school outing, the ingredients for cooking or the food for the classroom snails. Figure 6.4 shows Olivia's word processed list of the items needed for her sandwich.

When planning a piece of writing a list can be the first step. A group of children writing their own book about snails listed their questions, and with some rearrangement, the questions provided the organisation for the whole book (see case study 3.1 in Mallett, 1999). Here a

Our Sandwich

Things we need for our sandwich

jam   butter

bread   knife

plate

Figure 6.4   Olivia, age six years lists items needed for her sandwich.

list was used by some young researchers as a basis for thinking and a preliminary means of organisation. For adults, too, a list can help us plan an essay, letter or other piece of writing.

A list can also clarify the sort of things we want to find out about in the first place. Stephanie Harvey gives us a most interesting glimpse into a classroom in America where children are encouraged to have enquiring minds and to make lists in their 'wonder books' (Harvey, 1998). At eight Jordan is a year or two older than the children in the age range in this book, but his wonder book list makes encouraging reading. He lists 22 topics, with illustrations, that he would like to investigate. These include 'volcanoes, dogs, the human race, black holes and electricity' (Harvey, 1998: 18). This kind of list can lead to genuine interests and the burgeoning of hobbies.

When young children first start to write more than a sentence or two of non-fiction it may seem to be no more than a miscellaneous stringing together of facts or their thoughts about them. But is this the first attempt to turn the list into a piece of continuous text? In a very interesting article, 'Mapping the world', Myra Barrs suggests such writing may actually be a collection or inventory of things to do with a topic. It may sometimes serve as a young child's way of 'mapping out' or ordering an aspect of the world (Barrs, 1987).

Summarising

Can young children write summaries to organise their experience of the world? You might imagine this is a relatively late achievement, but in fact children make oral summaries in all sorts of contexts and this is a step towards becoming able to write them. For example, children are often asked to say what their favourite and least favourite foods are or what they most enjoyed about their holiday. In a school known to me the children are invited at the end of each school year to say what they enjoyed most, what they had found most difficult and what their main aim is for the next school year. Then there is an enjoyable concert including some of their favourite things – so games are played again, poems and writing read out and songs sung. This provides practice in the sort of selection process we go through when we write summaries. Six-year-old Olivia has managed to write a summary of the significant things in her year with brevity and honesty: see Figure 6.5.

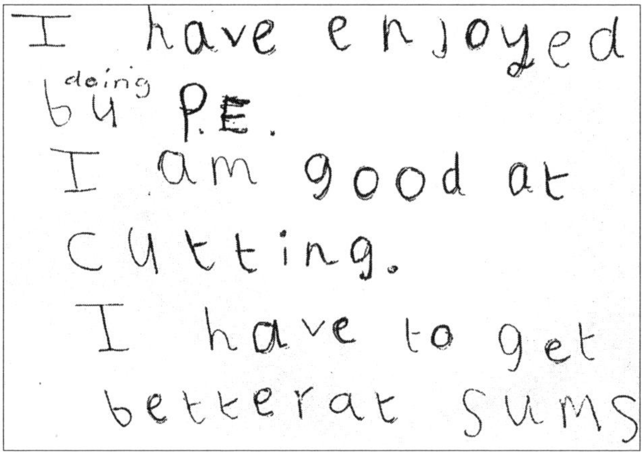

Figure 6.5 Six-year-old Olivia wrote this summary of her skills and of what she enjoys and notes where she needs to improve.

Writing to communicate with others

We have been looking at the writing young children use to help organise their world. Now we turn to another main purpose for developing children's non-fiction writing – to help them make a start with the task of writing to inform and communicate with others. Here the intended audience – the teacher, the other children or visitors to the classroom – affects the form and tone of the writing and illustration. This purpose is a very motivating one – children are enthusiastic about sending cards and messages to friends and family and they are encouraged by positive and swift feedback from the recipients.

Making posters and notices

Designing posters to advertise school fetes and book sales shows the positive side of advertising and introduces children to persuasive kinds of writing. All sorts of useful things can be taught, including how picture and text work together to get the message across, and how size of lettering and use of upper case make an impact. It shows how punctuation can be powerful – when we use an exclamation or question mark, for example. Above all it shows that language needs to be clear to get the message across, whether using slogans or strong phrases.

There is usually particularly high motivation when posters are made in drama or role play. One of my students carried out some drama work with seven-year-olds who had heard *The Giant* by Julia and Charles Snape read aloud by their class teacher. The gist of the story is that a giant mountain covered in beautiful plants and flowers and home to many animals leaves the village because the people have not taken care of the environment. The children, 'in role' as the villagers, decided to try to change people's ways by making posters to put up in the streets and on trees. Considerable thought and effort went into designing the posters. One child drew a little rabbit caught in a large discarded tin with jagged edges. Below she wrote 'Rubbish can kill!' Others focused on 'leave flowers for others to enjoy' and 'putting rubbish in bins'. Children and teacher agreed it was better to stay positive and say what people should do rather than what they should not. The teacher showed some ways of using relevant computer programmes and other techniques like stencilling, newspaper print collage and freehand bubble writing. The teacher, Louise Grayson, wrote in her notes: 'I can honestly say that I have never seen a class of young children so eager and enthusiastic about a writing activity as these children were during this session. They worked with a strong sense of purpose and children who had not finished asked to stay in at lunch time to complete their work'. The children talked about their posters and read and commented on each other's so that the sense of being part of a writing community was fostered. This project, which also provided an inviting context for letter writing, is described in more detail as case study 3.3 in Mallett, 1999.

Letters

Perhaps letters, both business and personal, are less important in our society now that the text message and e-mail have taken hold. But they still have a secure place. Business letters are still needed to communicate complex issues – to record agreements or signal disputes and to provide the confidentiality less guaranteed electronically. Personal letters to share news and thank people for gifts are still much appreciated. My very computer-literate daughter wants letters from home as well as e-mails during her studies abroad. There is a tradition of card- and letter-writing in early years work and children soon get to know that the purpose of and audience for letters affect the degree of formality with which they are written.

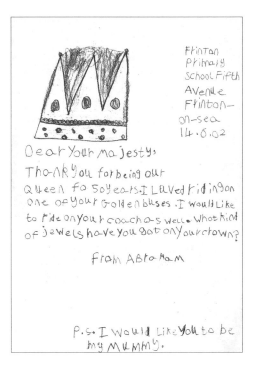

Figure 6.6 Abraham writes to the queen in Jubilee year.

Contexts for letter-writing include writing to thank a museum guide for their help, to invite parents to a school event and to send news and good wishes to a child in the class who is ill. Role play – the clinic, the post office or the builders' yard – provides strong and motivating contexts for letter writing as the case study 3.3 in Mallett, 1999, shows.

E-mail

E-mail is one of the new kinds of communication which is increasingly important in the world young children inhabit, perhaps to keep in touch with a parent travelling abroad or with grandparents. At school children are increasingly using e-mail to send information to each other and to children at other schools in their own country or abroad.

E-mail is also beginning to mark a return to the art of communication formerly seen in letter-writing. Stephanie Harvey gives us a wonderful image of the letter, reborn as e-mail 'rising from the ashes like some cyberflight of the phoenix' (Harvey, 1998: 121). Of course e-mail has been criticised for encouraging a cavalier approach to both punctuation and elegant expression. But we would expect a new medium to have its own form and style and there is no reason why an e-mail should not be powerfully written and share interesting knowledge. Even the youngest children can share interests and information with other children and sometimes develop global relationships.

Moving on: forms of thinking, kinds of writing

So far in this chapter I have looked at the ways in which children first begin to organise their non-fiction writing – to name, label, list and so on and to communicate with others through making posters and notices and writing letters and e-mails. Children then go on to attempt more extended written accounts and teachers help them to enlarge their writing repertoire to include the kinds of writing valued in our society. How we support children's progress raises some important issues for early years practitioners. To understand these issues we have to know something about genre theory and how this has affected classroom literacy practices in some countries – Australia and the United Kingdom, for example. Genre theory evolved from the work of a group of scholars and teachers, including J.R. Martin, F. Christie and J. Rothery, who carried out research in Australian schools to find out how children were taught to write for different purposes. They found that a great deal of children's writing, whether fiction or non-fiction, had a narrative or chronological organisation. In other words, children's writing in the primary school tended to be either stories or recounts of their experiences, sequenced through time. These genre theorists argued that much more of the writing done by young children should be of the non-narrative kind where a measure of competence is needed to make progress in the secondary school and thereafter to function in many jobs and professions. They concluded that these 'high status' kinds of writing should be taught to quite young children to ensure they started on the journey to controlling them as readers and writers as soon as possible. If you would like to read more about the genre theorists and their work, I recommend Pam Czerniewska's *Learning About Writing: The Early Years*, Chapters 7 and 8, which provide a particularly lucid and detailed analysis (Czerniewska, 1992).

Another helpful analysis is Alison Littlefair's in *Reading All Types of Writing* which shows the different genres children need to control as readers and writers as they move through the school years (Littlefair, 1991).

The 'genre' approach came to influence United Kingdom practice through the work of Wray and Lewis, directors of the EXEL project, who (drawing on the work of Martin, Christie and Rothery) identified six non-fiction genres or kinds of writing (Palmer, 2003): recount, report, instruction, explanation, discussion and persuasion (see definitions in glossary). These run through the National Literacy Strategy *Framework for Teaching*. The reasonable assumption is that 'recount' can be viewed as a generic strand leading to the development of narrative genres and 'report' as a generic strand leading to the development of expository genres (Czerniewska, 1992). We have, perhaps, been more successful at supporting children's 'recount' writing than 'report' or the non-narrative kinds that lead to some of the forms of writing most valued in our society. This means we need to reflect on children's language development in terms of the 'big shapes' of genre types. But while everyone wishes children to control all the genres important in their society there is debate about the best ways to do this, particularly where the youngest children are concerned. In its more extreme form, a genre approach with its stress on text models and direct teaching is not compatible with a developmental or constructivist model of learning. I must make it clear here that Wray and Lewis have not recommended this stress. Indeed they share the concern of scholars and teachers who are anxious that mature kinds of writing might be pressed on the young in ways that are unlikely to make them feel confident about their writing or to enjoy it. We must remember that writing progress is very much linked to intellectual development and there is no point in asking children to struggle with forms beyond their reach. We can help by reading aloud non-fiction texts to familiarise children with their distinctive 'tunes' and patterns but we cannot assume that this will lead to them being able to write in such ways themselves. We need to value their spontaneous writing as an attempt to make sense of things of great interest and as offering 'a window on how they are organising their experience and thoughts' (Barrs, 1987: 12). This is why we still need to make room for 'expressive' writing, writing which allows children to get a personal foothold in their learning, before moving towards more mature forms (Britton, 1970).

Can we then sympathetically introduce children to the mature non-fiction genres important in our culture in ways that allow them to keep their writing and thinking together in a creative way? The first results of a research project on creativity in children's writing show that the children in the foundation and key stage 1 years 'were markedly more enthusiastic than the older children about their writing' (Grainger, Goouch and Lambirth, 2002: 136). So what do gifted early years teachers do? Their success seems to be connected with the provision of strong and imaginative contexts which throw up purposes for different kinds of writing (Palmer 2003). One of these is role play which is a powerful setting for children's talking and writing. Two main benefits from embedding writing in play are, first, that children understand the purpose of the different kinds of writing and the audiences they are intended for and, second, that interest and motivation are usually very high and the effort involved in writing seems to them worthwhile. In case study 6.4 children are helped writing menus, lists and charts to extend their role play in the 'red café'.

Another setting likely to generate a lot of language work, including writing, is the school's local area. A school near a pond or park has rich possibilities for studying wildlife and then producing labelled diagrams, writing recounts of visits and writing reports on particular creatures. Even in a relatively built up area there can be a 'round the block' safari looking perhaps at different house styles and building materials, at chimneys and vents and roof shapes, and producing labelled diagrams. Another idea is to focus on the different styles, colours and materials of front doors, perhaps taking photographs and making sketches which could be labelled in a display back at school (Kenyon, 2002). It is self-evident that young children need a lot of teacher support and input to help them with their writing. The following analysis of some of the main non-fiction genres is accompanied by case studies and examples of children's work, which show how this can be achieved.

Recounting experience

Children hear narrative accounts in the stories and some of the factual texts adults read to them. Some of the factual texts are about the life cycles of a particular animal or plant and so have a natural time sequence. Then there are books with titles like 'A Day at the Seaside', 'Flora Goes to School', 'At the Park' and so on. These accounts are also chronologically ordered and tell us what happened through time.

When they begin to write their 'news' sentences children are writing short recounts: 'Last Saturday Mummy took me swimming, then we went to the park and ate our sandwiches'. The quotation from Pam Czerniewska's book at the beginning of this chapter reminds us of the power of narrative as a way of allowing children to express not just what happened, but how they feel about it. So we find children's recounts which include comments like 'I did not like it when my friend sat next to someone else on the bus' and 'we got a shock when Jamie picked the flower'. Shannette, aged just seven years, mentions in her recount of a visit to the Toy Museum her wish that the guide would choose a particular doll to talk about – 'I was saying to myself I hope the lady will show us that Indian doll because it looks so nice'. James Britton would regard these asides in children's recounts of their outings as 'expressive' elements which show the children are actively making sense of their experiences (Britton, 1970).

Of course children aged only six years or under will mostly only manage to write very short recounts. Often teachers 'scribe' for them. When children have been on a special outing or visit teachers often help them to make a book to share their experience with other children. Figure 6.7 shows the front cover of a book made by the teachers at Dulwich Wood Nursery telling of the class's trip to the supermarket. The teachers showed the children the photographs and asked them to relate the story of the visit and what each picture showed. This kind of exchange helps children gain control over the recount genre as speakers and so helps them write their own recounts when they are older. At age three to four years the children need their teachers to weave a written text round the photographs. The book is on display so that children can savour the photographs of their journey, visiting the cake-icing section, the cold room and the offices.

Reporting on a topic

'Report' writing is non-chronologically organised and informs us about a topic or subject. The typical children's non-narrative information book – perhaps on ships, on rivers or on frogs – is a good introduction to this genre. When children learn about a topic the foundation is being laid, through talk and discussion, for getting a grasp on the characteristic report

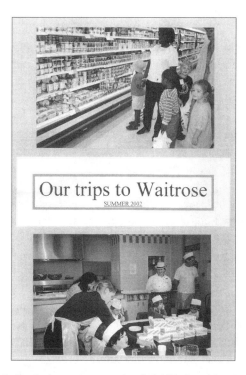

Figure 6.7 Front cover of a book about nursery school children's visit to the supermarket.

structure of classification and description. Becoming able to write a report helps children learn to think in ways which help them control information and leads to their attempting kinds of writing important in our society. In case study 6.4, six- to seven-year-olds were helped to classify a wild animal they had chosen by talking about it in pairs. The next step was to draw the creature showing its distinctive features and then to write a sentence naming it. The interest and enjoyment that accompanied the talk and drawing made this a most sympathetic introduction to classifying. Although the writing task was to name the creature in a short sentence, in fact the children moved a step further, towards thinking in a scientific way. The teacher noted that both boys and girls found this a particularly enjoyable activity combining talking, drawing and bookmaking.

Case study: 6.4: Who Am I? Towards report writing

Children in a vertically grouped early years class at Dalmain Primary School enjoyed Owl *by Moira Butterworth from the 'Who am I?' series as the text chosen for the work in the literacy hour during one week. One aim was to help children distinguish between fact and fiction texts and to become more secure in recognising the features of a non-fiction text. In the book, clues are given about the animal followed by some factual information.*

The book was read out in the 'shared reading' part of the literacy hour over three days and the teacher, Emma Richardson, discussed a different aspect of a non-fiction text each day: how it is designed and structured, what kind of ideas and words we usually find and illustrations.

In the guided reading and writing part of the hour the children worked in pairs each day, studying their chosen animal and compiling lists of its characteristics. Attention was then drawn to the need to order the information with most important features first; for example, giraffe's neck and crocodile's jaw. In the plenary over the three days, some of the pairs read out the characteristics of their animal and the other children guessed what it was.

The teacher told the children that their writing and drawing was so interesting that it would be a good idea to make some books to share it with other children in the school. She took the opportunity to show children the potential of the computer in making books and, using Clarisworks, the children were helped to choose a suitable size and style of text. The teacher writes that 'they were able to learn the advantages of making word processed copies – they could make several copies and they could experiment with different presentation styles'. Two large colourful books were produced.

Just in case you are wondering about the other requirements of the National Literacy Strategy, phonic work, attention to spelling, and work towards SATs were all incorporated into the teacher's long and short term plans. But the important thing to note is that she managed to make the children's activities with non-fiction texts alive and creative while working in the literacy hour framework. The book she read was the starting point, model even, for their work but they managed to burst out into their own forms of expression. They enjoyed their research, writing, word processing and illustrating and also moved a step closer to controlling what is quite a challenging genre for a young writer – report or exposition. The collaborative flavour of the work was especially helpful. Early experiences of non-fiction should be fun, not dreary. Figures 6.8 and 6.9 show samples of work from a truly exciting early years book-making project.

Writing to instruct (procedural writing)

A child's first experience of this genre may be when they describe the stages of a simple science experiment and are then helped to write them down. I once worked with six-year-olds to find out how much faster jelly cubes melted when the water they were put in was hot than when it was tepid. We constructed a diagram together to show our results. Work of this kind helps children understand the procedural language in science books and to follow instructions for experiments. Teachers can also help children write their own simple recipes for making sweets and biscuits.

Creating a human context for writing nearly always results in a strong written response. I used to visit a year 1 classroom where one of my students was carrying out his teaching practice. The classroom bear, called William, needed to have some written instructions about how to use the classroom computer, how to make his favourite biscuits and how to use the telephone. (He was a forgetful bear and just telling him how to do things did not always work!) The children were very happy to labour over writing down instructions with copious pictures.

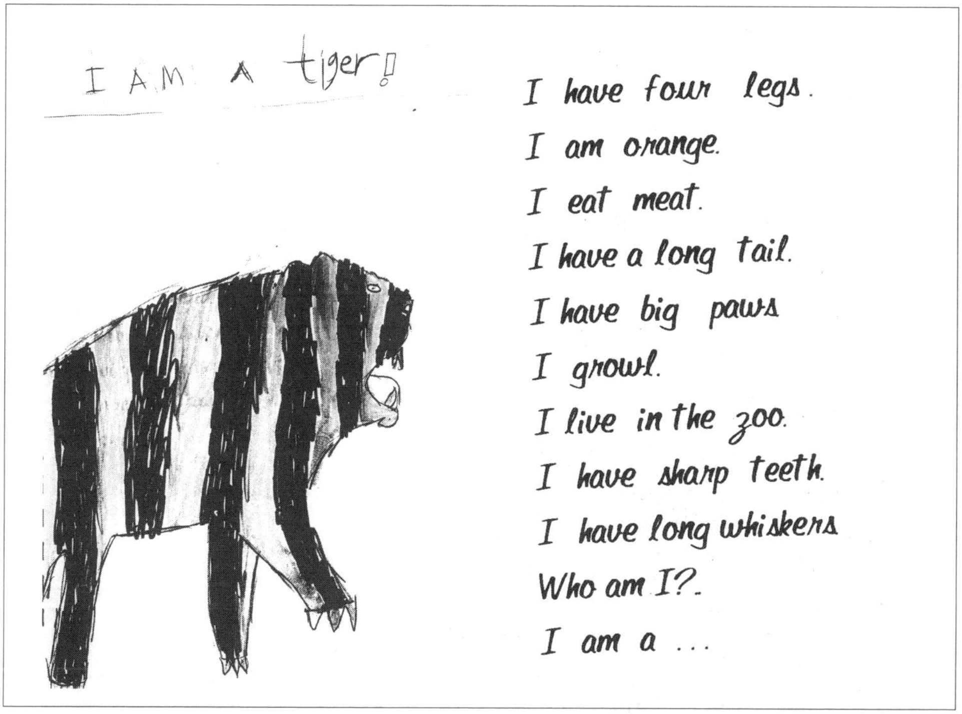

I AM A tiger!

I have four legs.
I am orange.
I eat meat.
I have a long tail.
I have big paws
I growl.
I live in the zoo.
I have sharp teeth.
I have long whiskers
Who am I?.
I am a . . .

Figure 6.8 'I am a tiger' by Daniel and Jason, just under seven years.

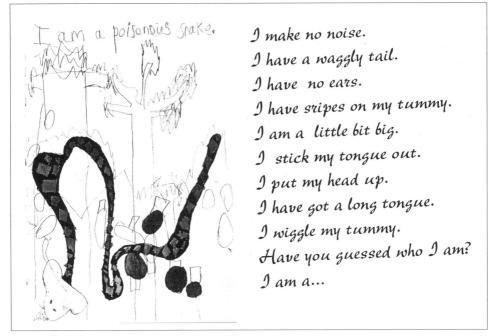

I make no noise.
I have a waggly tail.
I have no ears.
I have sripes on my tummy.
I am a little bit big.
I stick my tongue out.
I put my head up.
I have got a long tongue.
I wiggle my tummy.
Have you guessed who I am?
I am a...

Figure 6.9 'I am a poisonous snake' by Alexander, six years.

One of the most brilliant classroom case studies I know of showing how exciting purposes were created to encourage children's writing is to be found in *Mr Togs the Tailor* (SCC, 1987). The teacher of the six-year-olds in a Scottish school was given a tailor's dummy by a parent who no longer needed it for his clothes shop. Teacher and children created a character by dressing the dummy as a tailor and called him 'Mr Togs'. This led to creating a family for him and a shop with tape measures, sewing materials, old clothes, a counter and everything needed to make it seem authentic. It was a powerful context for all kinds of writing. Steps towards instructional writing were taken when the children wrote out Mr Togs' favourite recipes and the instructions for the burglar alarm which he installed after 'thieves' broke into his shop.

Another motivating context for procedural writing is shown in case study 6.5. Here four- to five-year-olds became very involved in thinking about how to care for a pet cat and were helped to make some instructional booklets.

Case study 6.5: Writing 'Caring for a Cat' booklets

Elaine Shiel and her five-year-olds at Corstorphine Primary School were involved in a science project with the title 'animals and their homes'. This included talking and writing about 'caring for pets', a favourite area for early years children who are so often interested in animals.

We joined the class at the point at which the teacher talked with the children about the responsibilities that come from owning a pet. The children talked enthusiastically about their own pets, and particularly pet cats, and shared many anecdotes. The teacher saw an opportunity to help the children move into an early kind of procedural writing. Using a flip chart, she wrote down the children's ideas about what you needed to include in a booklet to help people care for their cats. They decided on a title page with picture and author's name, food, things needed for sleeping and toileting, and appropriate toys.

The children, some of whom were barely five years old, were at an early stage in controlling this kind of writing. Ross's booklet (see Figure 6.10) is typical; he lists the food you need to buy for the pet and then labels a diagram of some of the other items which need to be provided which include a basket and a litter tray. Sarah managed some sentence-like annotations of her pictures. She drew a special tray in two compartments, perhaps like that provided at home for her own cat, and has written 'Tray wiv the food and the milk' (see Figure 6.11).

It was the lively talk which built the enthusiasm which in turn gave energy to the writing task. Talk also helped the children, with the teacher's help, to think in a particular way about pet care. This led to carving out together an organisation for the booklets which suited their purpose. Producing the booklets was only possible with much effort on the children's part and support from the teacher. The children had been helped, in a quite structured but sympathetic way, to order their thoughts in the booklets in something approaching instructional writing.

Figure 6.10   Ross's cat care booklet.

Figure 6.11   Sarah's cat care booklet.

Writing to persuade

It is sometimes assumed that children are not able to cope with argument and the persuasive genre until they reach about age nine years. Yet ethical issues come up in a great deal of early years work: learning about the environment, for instance, is bound to include such topics as animals and plants in danger of extinction, problems in the disposal of refuse, people in countries where basic things like the right to clean water are not available and how we treat animals. As I argue in Chapter 11, often it is a story or picturebook that inspires children to feel strongly about such things. It is when passions are stirred that children will want to find out more from information texts and feel the need to write their thoughts in the appropriate form. One of the case studies in Chapter 11 draws on David Reedy's powerful series of lessons with six-year-olds who were helped to build arguments for and against zoos after reading Anthony Browne's picturebook *Zoo*. As Reedy notes, Browne's book with its stress on family tensions and bored animals in cages is 'closer to the reality of many a young family's visits than the one depicted in the non-fiction "A Visit to The Zoo" type books for young children' (Riley and Reedy, 2000: 160). So often it is when children's feelings are awakened by a story that they are ready to be taught a form of writing in which to present their arguments. After much focused talk and after putting points for and against zoos on a flip chart, the children were helped to structure their views in written accounts starting with an opening statement, then moving to the supporting evidence and ending with a summary and conclusion.

The case study below also shows how young children can be stirred by a narrative and helped to take up a position on a matter of ethics. I have referred to this example on a number of occasions because it shows so powerfully that young children are capable of profound thoughts given the right support and can summon up the sheer stamina needed to put these thoughts in writing.

Case study 6.6: The plight of whales

Rising-five-year-olds who had just joined the reception class were learning about whales as part of a bigger project on creatures of the sea. Kathleen Doyle, the student teacher, had collected an impressive collection of fiction and non-fiction texts to support the work.

The children were helped to write down their questions about blue whales. The teacher used the device of asking them to address these questions to 'Bluey', – a huge blue whale they had been helped to make out of *papier mâché*. The children arrived in school one morning to find a huge envelope containing a large letter – 'Bluey' had 'answered' their questions by directing the children to particular parts of the books in the classroom. Some of the questions needed to be taken to books intended for much older children, including one published by the BBC in connection with a wildlife programme on whales.

However, it was only when the teacher read from story and picturebooks that the ethical issues were made available to the children in a way they could understand. One of these stories made a particularly strong impact on the way the children thought about the issues. This was Diane Sheldon's *The Whales' Song* which tells the story of Lucy who visits her grandmother near the sea. Within the narrative we learn of contrasting views on whales – Uncle Frederick thinks they are for their oil and blubber. Lucy's grandmother considers them beautiful creatures who should be respected and valued and not allowed to die out through over-hunting.

The children drew pictures of blue whales which were annotated with short but passionate pieces of writing, sometimes to do with whales being killed and cut up for food. Facts are not neutral! They were beginning to learn about how they could express a viewpoint. One of the children feared that 'children in the future might not be able to see a whale because they have all been killed for their blubber'. It is from such heartfelt beginnings that teachers can build children's abilities to structure persuasive pieces of writing.

The writing corner

Writing is encouraged throughout the early years environment but the writing corner, usually part of the reading area, provides a haven for children's reflection and literacy activities. We would expect to find different materials to write on – card, paper, booklets, chalk boards and sand trays – and a variety of writing implements – pens, pencils, felt tips, pastels, chalks, brushes, crayons, charcoal – anything that can make a mark. Marian Whitehead reminds us that while children like thick brushes and chubby crayons, they also 'love to write and draw with biros, fine pencils and thin markers and brushes' (Whitehead 2002: 71). Writing their own name with different tools helps children develop an interest in letters of the alphabet and supports developing ability in handwriting. Rosemary Sassoon believes that children must be taught the correct letter formation as soon as letters begin to appear in their mark-making. Early teaching, she considers, makes it more likely that children will develop a style that is comfortable, legible and fluent (Sassoon, 1990). And of course there will be at least one computer in a well-stocked writing corner.

Like other kinds of writing, non-fiction gives an opportunity to develop spelling ability and we help children to develop strategies to transcribe words correctly. Vocabulary used in current lessons and activities can be displayed in the writing corner. Resources that help children segment words into syllables, onset and rime and phonemes have an important place.

For non-fiction writing in particular we provide materials suitable for different purposes, for example small pieces of sugar paper for tickets and large sheets to make posters, post cards, post-it notes, envelopes, calendars, diaries, till receipts, cheque books and the sort of pads people list things in.

Book-making materials like card, paper, wall paper (for a cover), glue, staplers, rulers, sticky tape and safe scissors encourage writing and illustrating. The writing corner can be made interactive by providing a notice board which teacher and children use. Messages, posters, interesting information in words and pictures, examples of letters and advertisements and examples of children's work can be pinned on it.

The more arresting labels and notices are more than just a name and can be powerful examples of the purposes of writing. The more interesting ones will stimulate discussion (Godwin and Perkins, 2002). So we might have 'Things to help you make a book' and 'Use these scissors carefully'.

Some further issues

Is drafting appropriate for very young writers?

Mature writers usually find it helpful to plan their account, make a first draft, read it through and redraft and finally proof read for secretarial errors. Something like these stages is suggested in the 1999 National Curriculum English orders. When it comes to young children, re-writing is problematic, even on the computer, and teachers usually accept that the first draft will be the only draft. Too much fussing about secretarial errors or organisation of content might be de-motivating. But there is everything to be gained from the teacher modelling something like these stages in shared writing. We can also help children to carry out 'oral drafting' by encouraging them to talk through their writing, perhaps scribing for them (Godwin and Perkins, 2002).

Paintings about me and my family

Maths display linked to number song 'one elephant went out to play upon a spider's web one day ...'

Pictures painted by children in response to dentist-structured play area and their ideas of what we can do if we have teeth.

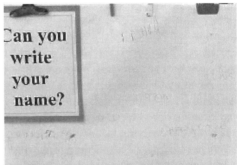

Daily signing/writing board.

Figure 6.12 Writing corner displays.

Gender: do boys and girls need different kinds of writing support?

The language we use reflects and emerges out of values, attitudes and practices in the wider society. In the 1970s and 1980s there was a lot of concern about girls tending to speak out less than boys in the classroom and about teachers unwittingly conniving in this. This seemed to be connected with the secondary roles women tended to have in the work place, a social reality which is changing. Now the emphasis is on the disadvantage some boys seem to face when it comes to literacy. In the United Kingdom, SATs results show girls consistently performing better than boys across the range of writing tasks at key stages 1 and 2. A closer

Figure 6.13 Four-year-old Faith has asked the teacher to scribe her sentence about being kind to Beth, her non-identical twin, before writing it out underneath.

analysis shows some interesting gender differences in writing abilities. While, very generally, girls do best with writing tasks that are open ended and expressive, boys shine when they are asked to write to inform and explain. Many believe that, just as a general reluctance on the part of some girls to speak out in class can be explained in societal terms, so can boys' relative preference for factual and informative writing. Boys seem to model their literacy practices on adult males in their family who in turn are affected by the roles they have played in work and home contexts. For a detailed analysis of recent evidence of gender difference as it affects children's writing see Judith Baxter's excellent booklet *Making Gender Work* (Baxter, 2001: section 5). Baxter believes that teachers should keep in mind how boys and girls differ in the ways in which they come to literacy, as these understandings support good practice. When it comes to non-fiction kinds of writing boys respond well to map-making and technical drawings and diagrams as ways of representing their experience. This reflects their preferences in play and role play. Quoting Kate Pahl's research, Baxter suggests that we should regard boys' diagrams as texts to be 'read' and valued just as written texts are (Pahl, 1999). It is important that children have the strongest possible self-images of themselves as writers from the earliest stages. So we need to support and praise what they do well, and help them to add to their range of writing expression. For instance, some girls would benefit from being shown how diagrams can enhance and extend their writing while boys need support in extending their written responses and enriching them with their reflections and feelings. In case study 6.6 we saw how all the children were helped to think deeply about the future of whales, to care about it and to begin to put their feelings and thoughts into written form.

Supporting young bilingual writers

Definitions of bilingualism vary from meaning equal competence in both languages as speakers, readers and writers, to much greater competence in one language or incomplete competence in either. The term 'emergent bilinguals' can refer to children at the beginning of the journey to becoming competent in two or more languages (Gregory, 1996: 8). There is a lot of evidence that young bilingual children bring additional strengths from their community literacy practices. They have an ability to get 'outside' a language in some way and see it as one of several options for labelling and categorising the world (Whitehead, 2002: 21). But the predetermined nature of U.K. literacy hour objectives means that teachers sometimes find it difficult to build on bilingual children's 'other' literacy experiences. This is a pity, not only for the young bilinguals themselves but also for the other children in the class who would benefit from sharing some of the opportunities cultural diversity brings. Seven-year-old Ikram is able to read and write in Urdu, classical Arabic and English and can talk about his learning in each one of these languages. It would be well worthwhile finding ways for him to share his varied literacy experiences and abilities with his peers. Robertson, in sharing the case study about Ikram's progress, refers to Philip Pullman's 'butterfly' metaphor which suggests all children should be encouraged to read like butterflies and write like bees, for 'only then will they make honey' (Robertson, 2002: 125). The bilingual child is well placed to move with the dexterity of a butterfly from one type of literacy to another. The circumstances of young bilingual children vary considerably. Some come from families who have lived in the United Kingdom for many years. These children may have sophisticated control of more than one language and therefore much to teach their monolingual peers. Their situation is very different from children who are newly arrived here and just beginning to learn English as a second or additional language.

Listening to stories with their helpful rhythms and repetitions helps young emergent bilinguals as well as all the other children in the class but information texts – those children read and those they write – also have a strong potential role in helping bilingual children make progress in their new language. Reading and writing about every day topics like names and food help children learn about their new culture as well as a new language (see Gregory, 1996, Appendix 3). Just as learning a first language involves creativity, so can learning a second language which involves a child in flexible thinking, in language switching and in translating. Marian Whitehead reminds us that early years settings are helpful to emerging young bilinguals because of the tradition of respect for individual children, recognition of the value of play and exploration, emphasis on things that matter, purposes children can understand, and the presence of interested adults.

Homing in to the informational side of things, how can we help young emergent bilinguals?

- By showing our respect for children's language and culture in the texts (print and electronic), photographs, pictures, signs, and play materials we provide, and becoming informed about, for example, scripts, names and counting systems.
- By welcoming help in creating continuity between home and school, not least continuity of literacy experiences (Hurst, 1997). Parents can translate books and recipes into home languages (perhaps by using a computer programme with language and scripts other than English) and by bringing to school texts from home like airmail letters, calendars and newspapers.
- By recognising the crucial role of talk as a way of sharing and explaining meanings and of course exposing children to patterns of intonation in their new language. Gesture and

facial expression make talking contexts particularly valuable. Talk around practical activities like science experiments and cooking gives the opportunity to write labels, notices and messages. And of course talk in role play where children act out roles in cafés, space ships, clinics and so on is extremely helpful as a precursor to writing. Talk around information books helps bring the ideas and facts alive for all the children. Wordless information picturebooks give the opportunity for teacher and child to create a text first orally and then perhaps in writing.

- By recognising that some non-fiction texts are challenging for all children, but perhaps particularly for young emergent bilingual learners who will not bring the same degree of cultural and linguistic knowledge to the texts. We can help by reading aloud life cycle books and 'experience' books with their accessible 'time sequence' organisation as well as ABCs and counting books to help children with the 'tune' and pattern of the different texts.
- By organising visits to community centres, places of worship and specialist food shops which can lead to exciting writing activity back in school.

Words and pictures: how do we support the development of visual literacy?

Children are more visually aware than ever before. They watch television, DVDs and video-film before they come to school and many of them play games on the home computer. They look at advertisements in print and at the moving multi-modal ones on screen. Do teachers respond to children's need to develop these visual aspects of their experience? Some say many of us do not. Millard and Marsh, for example, argue that too often drawing is regarded as 'a dispensable embellishment'. They note that there is sometimes lack of attention to encouraging the visual aspects of children's understanding and its way of communicating alongside writing (Millard and Marsh, 2001). Boys, in particular, seem to want to integrate their drawing with their writing. Some ways of making meaning, for example explaining processes like the digestive system or how a machine or vehicle works, call out for labelled diagrams and, in the case of a CD-ROM, the showing of moving parts in action. The pleasure children take in drawing and the care they take over it is evident in case study 6.4. But even the visually literate children of today need help in both 'reading' diagrams and producing their own. Learning to interpret and understand labelled diagrams is essential in some subjects like science and geography.

While developing children's visual literacy, we must never forget the importance of the verbal. There are many things which can only be made clear in words. Pictures often need to be put in an historical, geographical and scientific context. There are some books which show beautiful pictures, using all the latest computer and colour printing technology but without enough explanatory text to make them fully coherent.

Creating a community of young language users: how do we encourage a supportive writing environment?

The most important single element in a lively writing environment is probably to do with the way teacher and children talk with one another. Talking together about their plans for writing, discussing ideas and showing each other the fruits of their work, add energy to the writing children do. The provision of quality resources in the writing or literacy corner helps give

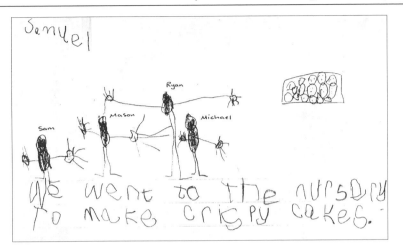

Figure 6.14   Samuel's cakes. Five-year-old Samuel shows a good understanding of how illustration and writing complement each other: the pride in their cooking is shown by the children pictured showing their cakes in outstretched hands and by the cake display on the table.

children's writing activity focus and value. Children like to see their work displayed and read out loud by the teacher. Quick, sensitive feedback from the teacher is also motivating. The essentials for a vibrant writing culture in the classroom in a nutshell?

We need to keep in mind that:

- *Social aspects* of writing are important in two ways. First, we need to link what is done in school with the wider society by bringing in new literacies – not least, visual and computer literacies. Second, writing gains energy if it reinforces social interaction and children are encouraged to collaborate and co-operate.
- *Significant* writing tasks are those that children understand and even feel passionate about and which link well with their current activities and preoccupations.
- *Support* from teacher, parent or older sibling is essential because writing involves such an effort for a young child. The best support, be it modelling, demonstration, scribing, discussing ideas for writing or help with secretarial aspects, arises from an adult's intense and genuine interest in a child's writing progress
- If the first three element*s* are well embedded in the writing programme, children will be likely to have the *stamina* for the challenge of learning to write.

Assessing and recording progress in non-fiction writing

It is helpful to think of assessment as part of the whole learning cycle. Teachers assess children's competence in writing and their understanding of its purposes so that they can help them take the next step. So evaluation of children's successes and identifying what help they need and what they should attempt next feeds into the next cycle of planning. Thoughtful evaluation ensures that parents can be given helpful information on progress. A positive response from the teacher is also helpful and motivating for the child. In the case of young children, teachers usually talk to them about their writing and make notes on their observations and 'next step' ideas.

Early years teachers keep portfolios of each child's work, including samples of writing – some of it in the non-fiction category. It is good practice to consult the child about which pieces of writing they would like included. The non-fiction writing in a child's portfolio at the end of nursery school might include a drawing with their name on, a simple labelled diagram, a list used for gathering the ingredients for cooking, writing for the home corner, a copy of a card sent to someone and an e-mail or letter. At the end of reception we would add examples of recounts of visits – perhaps to a farm, museum or supermarket – notices made for role play, instructions for a recipe or experiment in science and an illustrated book on a topic like 'pets' or 'ourselves'. Some of the writing will probably have been done on the computer.

At points in the year agreed by the whole team, teachers will enter a summary of children's progress in a format like, for example, the Primary Language Record (Barrs *et al.*, 1988). Children's progress in informational kinds of writing can be summarised in the writing section on the record-keeping sheets or booklet (whether in print or on the computer). These notes will be a summary of observations and sampling of children's work over a period of time. Nursery and reception class teachers keep a portfolio of samples of children's work, including non-fiction writing. Good record-keeping formats have a place to record children's comments about the writing they enjoy and what they want to achieve next and for parents' comments. (See Appendix 1 for details about current assessment frameworks for the Foundation Stage.)

Summary

Much of children's first writing is to do with organising their world, by naming, labelling and listing. It is also often to do with communicating with others through cards, notices, letters and e-mail. Practitioners do all they can to embed early writing in the things children are doing and experiencing. This is the key to helping children understand the purposes for what is an extremely demanding activity. Play, role play and drama provide exciting contexts for a range of writing as children create cafés, space stations, baby clinics and offices. The themes which structure so much good early years work – 'ourselves', 'growth', 'changes', 'seasons', 'food' and 'pets' for example – also invite interesting writing which, crucially, is embedded in children's and teachers' wider intentions and purposes. The most passionate writing emerges when we tap into things about which children really care, really feel strongly about – their environment, their family, their pets and their most interesting experiences in and out of the classroom. Writing situated in such contexts is the springboard to give the energy to control the forms of writing necessary to progress in subjects across the curriculum – history, geography, science and so on. So we see children making the first steps towards using writing to recount experiences, report on topics, compile instructions and explain processes – all important functions for written language in our society.

Given the right sort of opportunities, not least the chance to talk about their thinking and their writing, young children can also reach out towards the challenging persuasive kinds of writing.

There are a number of interesting and important issues around helping to support children's non-fiction writing, including the challenge of responding to children's growing visual awareness and the implications for the role of pictures and diagrams in their written output. Our response to the impact of powerful electronic tools on ways of communicating is most important. Then there are issues to do with genre, with gender and with helping young emergent bilingual writers.

Creating a well-stocked, lively and interactive writing corner is a great spur to children's writing efforts and can help support the sort of culture we want. This is one where children feel part of a community of young language users. Careful and imaginative evaluation and recording of children's writing achievements helps teachers monitor progress and to develop the writing programme.

Notes

1   The 'enactive' stage was identified by J. Bruner as the period when the young child knows the world through physical action and perception. This is similar to Piaget's 'sensory motor' stage.
2   Where taking photographs is part of a project the school's policy needs to be checked and adhered to.

References

Barrs, M. (1987) 'Mapping the world', *English in Education.* NATE, Vol. 21, no. 3, pages 9–15.

Barrs, M., Ellis, S., Hester, H. and Thomas, A. (1988) *The Primary Language Record Handbook.* London: Centre for Language in Primary Education.

Baxter, Judith (2001) *Making Gender Work.* University of Reading: Reading and Language Information Centre.

Bissex, G. (1981) *GNYS AT WRK: A Child Learns to Write and Read.* Cambridge, MA: Harvard University Press.

Britton, James (1970) *Language and Learning.* London: Allen Lane, the Penguin Press.

Bromley, H. (2002) 'Can you fix it for Bob the Builder', *The Primary English Magazine.* NATE, Vol. 8, no. 1, October, pages 12–16.

Clay, M. (1975) *What Did I Write?* London: Heinemann.

Czernieska, Pam (1992) *Learning About Writing.* London: Blackwell.

Glen, Pat (1987) *Mr Togs the Tailor: A Context for Writing.* Scottish Consultative Council on the Curriculum.

Godwin, D. and Perkins, M. (2002, second edition) *Teaching Language and Literacy in the Early Years.* London: David Fulton.

Gould, Terry (2002) 'Language and literacy through outdoor play at the Foundation Stage', *English 4–11 (The English Association)*, Summer, no. 15.

Grainger, T., Goouch, Kathy and Lambirth, Andrew (2002) 'Research in progress: the voice of the child, "We're Writers" Project', *Reading, Literacy and Language* UKRA. Vol. 36, no. 3, November.

Gregory, Eve (1996) *Making Sense of a New World: Learning to Read in a Second Language.* London: Paul Chapman.

Harvey, Stephanie (1998) *Nonfiction Matters: Reading, Writing and Research in Grades 3–8.* York, ME: Stenhouse Publishers.

Hurst, V. (1997, second edition) *Planning for Early Learning: Educating Young Children.* London: Paul Chapman.

Kenyon, Pauline (2002) *Nursery Education.* September, Issue 53, page 4.

Littlefair, A. (1991) *Reading All Types of Writing.* Milton Keynes/Philadelphia: Open University Press.

Mallett, M. (1999) *Young Researchers: Informational Reading and Writing in the Early and Primary Years.* London: Routledge.

Millard, Elaine (1997) *Differently Literate: Boys, Girls and the Schooling of Literacy.* London: Falmer Press.

Millard, E. and Marsh, J. (2001) 'Words and pictures: the role of visual literacy in writing and its implication for schooling', *Reading, Literacy and Language* UKRA. Vol. 23. no. 2, pages 54–61.

Pahl, K. (1999) *Transformations: Making Meaning in Nursery Education.* Stoke on Trent: Trentham Books.

Palmer, Sue (2003) *Teaching Writing Across the Curriculum at Key Stage 1*. London: David Fulton.

QCA (1999) *Early Learning Goals*. London: Department for Education and Employment.

Riley, J. (1996) *The Teaching of Reading*. London: Paul Chapman.

Riley, Jeni and Reedy, David (2000) *Developing Writing for Different Purposes*. London: Paul Chapman.

Robertson, L.H. (2002) 'Parallel literacy classes and hidden strengths: learning to read in English, Urdu and classical Arabic', *Reading, Language and literacy* UKRA. Vol. 36, no. 3, November.

Sassoon, Rosemary (1990) *Handwriting: The Way to Teach it*. Cheltenham: Stanley Thornes.

Temple, C., Nathan, R., Burris, N. and Temple, F. (1988, second edition) *The Beginnings of Writing*. London: Allyn & Bacon.

Weinberger, J. (1996) *Literacy Goes to School: The Parents' Role in Young Children's Literacy Learning*. London: Paul Chapman.

Whitehead, M. (2002, second edition) *Developing Language and Literacy with Young Children*. London: Paul Chapman (chapter 4).

Chapter 7

Non-fiction texts and resources three to six years

Choosing and using quality texts

When choosing information texts, we seek books which arouse curiosity and share, in a way young readers can appreciate, some careful observations, ideas and feelings about the phenomena involved.

(Mallett, 2002: 149)

You have only my word for it, but the more I work with beginners on topic search and 'writing up', the more I am struck by their rituals and the similarity between those of my most advanced research students.

(Meek, 1996: 118)

How can we make early forays into information texts a positive experience? In the past 'information books' have had rather a dreary image, perhaps because some have had uninspiring pictures and a less than fully coherent text. But the best non-fiction can, in its own way, appeal to young imaginations just as much as fiction. Children deserve information books which, however simple, 'are still individual, strong and alive' (Fisher, 1972: 25).

This is the first of a series of chapters about non-fiction books and resources which aim to illuminate how they can be used to support children's learning in lessons, activities and projects in nursery and reception classes. The series includes chapters on reference texts, computer resources and televisual texts.

This chapter categorizes information texts into two main groups: narrative non-fiction and non-narrative non-fiction. 'Narrative non-fiction' refers to texts that are chronological in organization – books about life cycles, journeys or everyday experiences. 'Non-narrative non-fiction' is organised according to the logic of a subject or a topic and includes books ordered around questions, information picturebooks and first books about science, history and geography.

The texts for young children in these two main categories have some of the features of the mature forms written for older readers; for example, retrieval devices, diagrams and headings. The secret of success is making the texts exciting and accessible. So some authors try to interest young learners by using devices like humour, questions and story characters; Baker and Freebody (1989) refer to such texts as 'transitional genres'. The division into narrative and non-narrative is best regarded flexibly: some early books combine the two kinds of organization; for example, the books in Walker's 'Read and Wonder' series are written in story form but also have factual information indicated by italic text. The chapter includes a consideration of non-book print which teachers bring to the classroom, because of its importance in our culture. This tends to fall into the non-narrative category; here we include posters, charts, notices, flyers, brochures and charts.

Because the texts for this age group are largely 'transitional' I have not attempted to organise my account around the U.K. National Literacy Strategy's six categories of non-fiction – recount, report, instruction, explanation, discussion and persuasion. However, I have indicated where an early book can help nudge children towards an understanding of these text types.

Teachers keep in mind some criteria when choosing books for the non-fiction element of their class and library collections, and some criteria are suggested together with examples of quality texts. Even the best information books have a relatively short shelf life and so developing criteria is important.

How do teachers use the texts to further children's learning both about a topic and about the form and purpose of the texts themselves? Here we see how talking with the teacher and talking with other children in their class about their reading helps children link 'book information' with existing knowledge and with first hand experience. This dialogue helps keep up momentum, sustain focus and maintain a high level of interest and energy. We also see that children are most ready to acquire study and research skills when they are fully absorbed in their learning. Case studies provide glimpses into classrooms to see how skilled practitioners use information texts to enrich and extend children's learning.

Since the implementation of The National Curriculum in the late 1980s, the curriculum in the United Kingdom has been organised around subjects. This contrasts with the more flexible approach in many schools before this, an approach in which much of the work was arranged around themes and topics. Nevertheless, as I visited primary schools during this project, I found that many Early Years teachers still managed to work flexibly, often linking subjects and including imaginative cross curricular tasks while still meeting the official requirements. And, while I have no facts and figures to support this, my impression is that teachers are more aware that information texts can add interest and focus to children's work. This may be partly because of the recognition of the value of non-fiction in the National Literacy Strategy's 'Framework for Teaching' (DfEE, 1998). The best strategy here lies partly in providing an appropriate book to develop the work at a particular point. And many of the teachers I spoke to showed great skill in using the same text both in the literacy hour and to support work in another lesson. This flexibility is evident in case study 7.2.

Finally, there seemed to be some other things I wanted to comment on which needed separate treatment to do them justice. And so the chapter ends with some discussion of the current emphasis on genre, of bias and of gender and reading under the heading 'Some other issues'.

I have kept in mind three of the Early Learning Goals for reading which are particularly pertinent to non-fiction.

Children need to:

• show an understanding of how information can be found in non-fiction texts to answer questions about where, who, why and how.

The practitioner needs to:

• encourage children to add to their first hand experience of the world through the use of books, other texts and information communication technology (ICT).

- encourage children to use a range of different reading strategies by modelling different strategies and providing varied texts through which that range can be used (QCA, 1999; QCA, 2000).

(See Appendix 1 for further comment on the U.K's official frameworks.)

Narrative non-fiction

There is no doubt that narratives, imagined or real, with their chronological structure offer an appealing and coherent listening or reading experience for the very young. So it is not surprising that many early non-fiction texts have a narrative structure. In her article 'Narrative as a Primary Act of Mind' Barbara Hardy points out that we experience the world in a time sequence and much of our conversation takes this form (Hardy, 1977). Reflecting on the many early narrative non-fiction texts that I have reviewed, used or seen used in the classroom, I have concluded that it would be helpful for the purpose of analysis and discussion here to distinguish between life cycles, journeys, instructions (e.g. for experiments and recipes) and information stories. Any attempt to classify brings some overlap but I feel sure that teachers will recognise something like these categories when they look at their own collections.

Life cycles

Early science books are often based on the life cycle of a creature or plant and therefore have a natural time sequence as we follow the main stages from egg or seed through to maturity. The chronological form of this kind of text can help make it comfortable and accessible reading material for young learners in a number of ways. For instance, a narrative can communicate a strong sense of how living things change and develop through time (Mallett, 1999b). The authorial 'voice', too, is likely to be friendlier than that in some other kinds of information books. And because we are following through one life history there is a coherence about the language not always present in the more 'fragmented' text in some simple information books. So we find a good 'life cycle' book often has a distinctive 'tune'[1] and may include some poetic images; for example, in *The Barn Owl* we read that the creatures play in the dark 'like ghostly acrobats'. They may introduce technical terms, well contextualised, and we may also find imaginative vocabulary to suggest movements and characteristics. In *The Otter* Sandy Ransford contrasts the 'fumbling steps' of otters on land with their 'lithe and graceful, spiralling' antics in water. Like other quality 'life cycle' books, the illustrations in *The Otter*, drawings by Bert Kitchen, complement the text by showing the creatures in their distinctive habitats. The best life cycle books are appreciated by children because of their beautiful illustrations of the natural world and they awaken genuine interest through sharing careful observations giving just the right amount of detail. If we believe that, on the whole, children learn by moving from the particular to the general, we can see why books concentrating on one creature or plant suit children in the younger age groups. Many do children the courtesy of pointing out when knowledge is incomplete. Some of Walker's 'Read and Wonder' books achieve a welcome speculative stance: *Think of an Eel* by Karen Wallace explains that there is a secret at the heart of an eel's life history – no-one has seen the elvers being born. In her book *One Tiny Turtle*, Nicola Davies points out that no-one sees the young turtle leave its nursery for 'cool seaweed jungles and turquoise lagoons and it is a mystery how the mature turtle finds her way back to the beach where she was born to lay her eggs'.

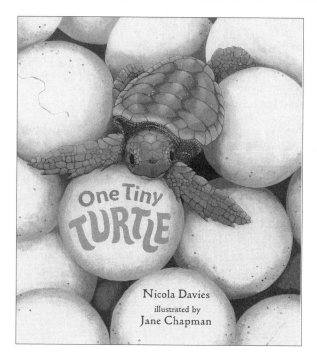

Figure 7.1   Cover illustration © 2001 Jane Chapman. Reproduced from *One Tiny Turtle* by permission of Walker Books Ltd.

This kind of speculation, with different theories offered, can help children think critically about the issues and, like scientists, form hypotheses and develop an enthusiasm for wanting to find things out.

Journeys

Books with a journey theme have an inbuilt momentum which can sustain a young child's interest and enrich work in geography, history and English. *River Story* by Meredith Hooper takes young readers on an exhilarating journey from the river's source to its arrival at the sea using poetic language echoing the movement of the water. Like other good 'journey' books this one uses fine pictures and evocative text to create environments vividly. Often these are changing environments. Those pictured and described in Jannie Howker's *Walk with a Wolf*, for example, show the harshening wild North environment as the back drop to the journey of a wolf pack. So these books can show powerful images, both verbal and visual. The raw side of nature is not hidden from children in Howker's book; we see and hear about an elderly deer being killed and torn to pieces. Other information books can show the robust side of things of course, but perhaps because they are set in the natural environment and have a narrative form, journey books can do this with particular vitality. Children are not inspired by the bland and cosy but sometimes are by what is disturbing, and this can bring thinking into top gear.

Instructions

Young children enjoy practical activities and making things so it is not surprising that quite a lot of early books give instructions for simple science and mathematical experiments or for cooking and growing things. These books provide an introduction to the 'instructional' or 'procedural' genre. They may begin with a list of items to be used in a science experiment or recipe before going on to describe each step. Children's early writing in this sort of genre complements their reading.

Sometimes we find instructions for scientific or mathematical experiments within an information book whose main organisation is non-narrative. Claire Llewellyn's *My First Book of Time* is of this type; it covers the main aspects of the topic 'time' under headings but it is also packed with instructions, for example on how to create a calendar, grow beans and make clock cards.

There are many cookery books for the young to use alongside an adult, for example Jane Asher's book *Round the World Cookbook* and *Making a Chapati* from Collins 'Pathways to Literacy' series.

Information stories and picturebooks

These are narratives which might well be first seen as stories, but which in fact give a lot of help with children forming an understanding of the practical world. One type is the 'experience book' which reaches out to their everyday activities – to meal times, shopping, playing, school and visiting the doctor or dentist. In her excellent account in *Babies Need Books*, Dorothy Butler calls them 'descriptive' books and praises the work of Sarah Garland whose titles include *Having a Picnic* and *Going Shopping* (Butler, 1995). 'Experience' books have a simple text, but they need not be banal. As well as teaching concepts they can also impart some truths about human experience. So as well as introducing the language of size, the universal dilemma of being the youngest child is explored with gentle humour in Pat Hutchin's *You'll soon grow into them, Titch* (see case study 7.1). Children enjoy having their own experiences reflected back in books like these from the pre-school years onwards and they remain a well liked genre in the nursery and Reception class. Those that are built round photographs, for example, by Fiona Pragoff (*Starting School*) and Angela Wilkes (*See How I Grow*) signal that the books have an informational purpose.

As well as seeing familiar experiences in books, children learn by reading about other people and their lives. There is a well-established kind of book often with a title like 'A day in the life of …' which tells us about life in another country by telling the story of one child's day or week. Frances Lincoln's 'Child's Day' series includes carefully researched books on children in many countries including India, Egypt, China, Ghana, Lapland and Peru. Other 'day in the life of' books tell us about the working life of a doctor, nurse or fire officer and these books often help resource 'People that help us' themes in the early years.

Then there are information stories and picturebooks poised between fiction and non-fiction which have the potential to help learning in particular lessons. Early history lessons can be enriched by Janet and Allan Ahlberg's *Peepo!*, a story about a family showing the life style and artefacts (including clothes horses and perambulators) of people during the First World War. Information picturebooks also enliven geography work. *Lion in the Grass* tells an engrossing story about a pride of lions and also creates in the illustrations a vivid impression of the African plains where they live. In science and nature study lessons books which explain science concepts within a story have a valid place. *Growing Frogs* could be regarded as a 'life cycle' book, but it is as much about a mother and daughter's relationship as they develop a shared interest as it is about the stages of growth from frogspawn to frog. Many of Walker's 'Read and Wonder' books show the personal element in learning science because the authors share the reasons for their interest in the topic. One of my personal favourites is *A Ruined House* – a strongly autobiographical story by Mick Manning which includes detailed pictures of all the small plants and creatures that live in an old building. When it comes to religious studies there are books which, like *Apples and Honey: A Rosh Hashanah Story*, follow a family's celebrations of religious festivals including Christian, Jewish and Islamic festivals. These books show the human and personal side of religious observation. Stories from sacred books are found in every nursery and reception class. We look for versions that, like Jane Ray's *Noah's Ark*, stay close to the spirit and meaning of the story while showing its significance for believers.

Criteria for choosing narrative non-fiction

There are several good journals which review children's non-fiction: *Books for Keeps, The School Librarian, English 4–11, The Times Educational Supplement* and *Language Matters*. Teachers can also see reviews by other professionals on a number of websites; for example, *National Grid for Learning*: www.ngfl.gov.uk, or *The Booktrust*: www.booktrust.org.uk.

In the analysis above I have tried to indicate some of the features we look for in the different books within the narrative non-fiction category. Here I summarise some of the general qualities which seem most important, although any such list needs to be used flexibly. We look for:

- a strong 'global' or overall structure
- lively language which explains things well
- linked to this, an authorial voice that latches onto a child's interest but does not patronise
- the well-contextualised introduction of technical vocabulary where appropriate
- helpful and appealing illustrations, whether photographs or drawings, which complement, explain or extend the writing
- a spark of originality and the qualities which fascinate and involve young readers, encouraging them to talk, reflect and want to find out more

Using narrative non-fiction

Narrative information books are a useful resource in lessons across the curriculum and in the literacy hour. They are often read aloud by the teacher to launch a new project or add new insights to a project already underway. One of my students found that *River Story* by Meredith Hooper provided a dynamic start to work on 'water', and case study 7.1 below shows how *You'll soon grow into them, Titch* helped both humanise and focus work on 'sorting'. Perhaps teachers often begin with these books because, as well as the sheer enjoyment that comes from reading them, pictures and text in story form seem to help children recall those personal anecdotes that link their existing experience with the concepts they will be learning about.

In the literacy hour the language and illustrations used in the different kinds of narrative non-fiction provides material for discussion. Teacher and children can see how procedural texts set out the different stages, in the instructions for a recipe for example, perhaps using

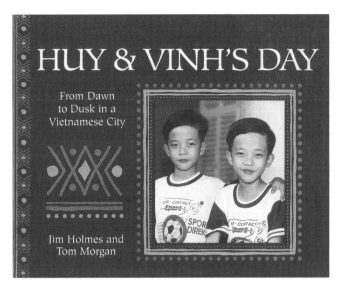

Figure 7.2 From *Huh and Vinh's Day: From Dawn to Dusk in a Vietnamese City* by Tom Morgan, photographs by Jim Holmes, published by Frances Lincoln Limited, © Frances Lincoln Limited 2002. Text © Tom Morgan, Photographs © Jim Holmes 2002.

numbers or bullet points. Links can then be made with the children's own instructional or procedural writing. With a light touch we can also discuss the structure of a book organised as a life cycle or a journey.

Study skills

Wordless books following a plant or animal's life cycle or the progress of a journey provide the opportunity for children to talk through a sequence of events. This is a helpful step towards them becoming able to structure their own time-sequence writing. A number of publishers are producing wordless non-fiction books including Collins' *Butterfly*.

We mainly associate the learning and application of study skills, using retrieval devices for instance, with reference books and non-narrative kinds of information text. On the whole, these books are not designed to be read through in one sitting. However, narrative information books can offer more of a literary experience and may be read all the way through like a fiction text. Some 'life cycle' and 'day in the life of' books combine such narratives with notes and an index so that children can find where particular information is located. An example is Frances Lincoln's 'Child's Day' series which includes detailed fact pages structured by headings.

Case study 7.1: Sorting clothes

A student teacher used an information story at the start of some work on sorting, matching and set-making with four-year-old nursery children. This encouraged the use of mathematical language in a strong context.

The student teacher read out Pat Hutchin's story *You'll soon grow into them, Titch* and talked with the children about the different kinds and sizes of clothes mentioned. Then the children went into self-selected groups of four to tables on which there were clothes similar to those in the story in different sizes, colours and materials. First, the children were asked to place the clothes into sorting rings using whatever criterion they wished. Then they talked about how they had sorted the clothes. One child, influenced by the story, had sorted the things by size and the teacher asked 'shall we all sort by size now?' They then went on to sort by colour, material type, use and so on.

There are two particularly useful things to note here. First, the information story which introduced the work created a human context for the lesson. The children related strongly to the experiences and feelings of the little boy in the story who had to wear hand-me-downs as he was the youngest in the family. So interest and motivation were high at the start of the activity. Second, the text led perfectly into the sorting tasks because the children had been encouraged to use language to do with size, shape and colour as they discussed the story with the teacher. This helped them focus on the sorting tasks and to articulate the thinking behind their choices.

Selective list of narrative non-fiction

Life cycles

Butterfly
By Barry Wade, Hilary Minns and Marie Duonocore
Pathways to Literacy, Collins
Photographs without words tell the story of a butterfly from egg to insect. Adult and child or children can construct the sequence of events in words together.

The Waterhole
By Graeme Base
Abrams
This beautifully illustrated counting book shows us ten waterholes in ten different locations. Children will learn about the different animals – tiger, toucans, tortoises, kangaroos and so on – and their habitats from the illustrations. The written text tells how the animals move – moose 'wallow', catfish 'flounder' and tortoises 'lumber'.

Little Turtle and the Story of the Sea
By Sheridan Cain, illustrated by Norma Burgin
Little Tiger Press
Clear, inviting and sometimes poetic language explains the struggle of a young turtle to reach the sea once it has broken free of its egg. The rhythmic refrain, the song of the sea, 'Come Little Turtle, Come home to me' helps children understand the power of instinctive longings. This is a 'life cycle' book which also describes a dangerous and exciting journey.

A Seed in Need – a first look at the plant cycle; The Drop Goes Plop – a first look at the water cycle
By Sam Godwin
Macdonald Young Books. M.Y. Bees
Many teachers have told me how much children love these books which explain the plant and water cycles with a witty text and energetic illustrations. Does mixing storybook characters with factual information cause confusion? Children do not seem to have a problem with this. In fact they like the snail and ladybird narrators in *A Seed in Need* and the Mama and baby seagull in *The Drop Goes Plop.* In the latter book, the conversation between the creatures is very like a parent–child conversation.

How did I begin?
By Mick Manning and Brita Granstrom
Franklin Watts
An appealingly illustrated story of the early stages of human life.

The Otter
By Sandy Ransford
The Barn Owl
By Sally Tagholm
Illustrated by Bert Kitchen
Animal Lives series, Kingfisher
Illustrations and written text combine to give a good introduction to the main life events of each creature. Glossary and fact file included.

Think of an Eel
By Karen Wallace
Read and Wonder, Walker Books
Illustrations which are wonderfully evocative of environments deep in the ocean accompany a poetic text. This is another 'life cycle' book which also describes an epic journey. Karen Wallace is one of the best writers of children's non-fiction.

Duck; Snail
Both by Barrie Watts
Watch it Grow, Watts
As we would expect from this distinguished writer of children's information books *Duck* and *Snail* are well written and illustrated with exceptionally fine photographs and diagrams. In each book, children are introduced to a glossary and there is an annotated picture summary of the life cycle.

See How I Grow: A Photographic Record of a Baby's First Eighteen Months
By Angela Wilkes
Dorling Kindersley
Excellent photographs and a simple text show a baby's development – the basket holding the babies gets bigger on each page. This book fits perfectly with thematic work on 'ourselves' and 'growth', see for example case study 2.2 in *Young Researchers*, Mallett, 1999.

Figure 7.3 Reproduced from *Snail* by permission of Franklin Watts. Copyright © 2002 The Watts
Publishing Group Ltd.

The Little Penguin
By A.J. Wood, illustrated by Stephanie Boey
Templar
This inviting book about the nurturing of this young great emperor penguin goes beyond
sharing interesting information and tells us about the universal pains and pleasures of growing
up. The confusions and worries of the creature, not least about losing his baby feathers, give
way to the delight of exploring the underwater world with the mature birds.

Journeys

Pi-shu the Little Panda
By John Butler
Orchard Books
Pi-shu's journey with his mother takes him over mountains and snowy landscapes until a
valley is reached and a 'lush grove of bamboo' well away from the humans that threaten to
destroy the pandas' habitat. It is never too early for children to learn what is valuable in our
world and how we should protect it. A good fact page helps adults answer children's questions.

Bat Loves the Night
By Nicola Davies, illustrated by Sarah Fox-Davies
Walker Books
Bat, 'a pipistrelle no bigger than your thumb', wakes at dusk and prepares for her journey
through the night. As is the case in many other Walker books, two kinds of text are featured:
narrative in large print to describe the journey and interesting and relevant information bites

in smaller lighter italic print. There is nothing 'cosy' about the bat's predatory instincts – she 'bites hard and the moth's wings fall away like the wrappers from a toffee'. The pictures are excellent and have great imaginative appeal – we see, for instance, the bat returning at the end of the night to the roof space where the batlings 'like velvet scraps' are clustered together.

Authors of information texts for children are not as well known as story writers – so let me say here that Nicola Davies has helped encourage young children's interest in nature by writing many excellent books on animals.

River Story
By Meredith Hooper, illustrated by Bee Willey
Walker Books
The respect and knowledge, and indeed love, of rivers which this author and illustrator share comes through clearly. The changing environments, including snowy mountain landscapes and the winding meadows of the lowlands revealed in a clear text and in vivid illustrations provide much to think and talk about.

Walk with a Wolf
By Janni Howker, illustrated by Katherine McEwan
Walker Books
This tale of a dangerous journey is full of powerful images to encourage talk and interest. The environments of the far wild North are magnificently captured in the pictures. We see wolves at rest, their heads tucked behind their legs and their noses covered by the fur of their tails. The large main print tells the story powerfully while extra pieces of information wave along the bottom of the pages in italic script.

Emeka's Gift
By Ifeoma Onyefulu
Frances Lincoln
This counting story takes the young reader on a journey through an African market to the next village. Emeka takes a gift to his grandmother and, on the way, he meets people and sees landscapes, food, water vessels and children playing games. Vivid, sunny photographs help give a strong impression of the environment of a Nigerian village and so this book would enliven early geography work.

Instructions

Round the World Cookbook
by Jane Asher
Dorling Kindersley
One of a number of good cookbooks on the market, this one has step-by-step instructions for dishes from the Middle East, the Caribbean, Uganda and China.

My First Book of Time
By Claire Llewellyn
Dorling Kindersley
This is perhaps the finest book on the theme of 'time' written for young children. As well as providing a lot of information about clocks, calendars and seasons which can be mediated by the teacher, the book is full of interesting puzzles and ideas for simple experiments. It is the

interactive nature of the approach which fits so well with the nature and needs of the very young.

Making a Chapati
By Barry Wade, Hilary Minns and Chris Lutrario
Pathways to Literacy, Collins
Through clear written text and photographs this book shows all the stages in the cooking, and the family enjoying the results.

Information stories

The Usborne Children's Bible
Retold by Heather Amery, illustrated by Linda Evans
Usborne
The text of these well known Old Testament and New Testament stories is clear and interesting – just the thing for reading time with older nursery children or to support early readers. Bright and interesting pictures, with colourful borders that enliven the pages, make this a good introduction to the Bible.

Lion in the Long Grass
By Ruth and Kenneth Brown
Andersen Press
This truly involving story is set in the African plains where lions live. A vulnerable young lion cub is protected by an old lion who knows the dangers that predators like the circling jackals pose.

Growing Frogs
By Vivien French, illustrated by Allison Bartlett
Walker Books
This picturebook is beautifully illustrated and written in a lively manner with a lot of dialogue between parent and child. It shares a deep interest in how living things grow and develop.

Going Shopping; Having a Picnic
By Sarah Garland
Puffin
These are just two of Garland's beautifully illustrated books structured round everyday events and activities.

You'll soon grow into them, Titch
By Pat Hutchins
Puffin
Titch is the last one in the family to wear the clothes and often they do not fit. This very human story creates a strong context for discussing the size, colour and material of different clothes.

Boushra's Day
By Khaled Eldash and Dalia Khattab

Child's Day series, Frances Lincoln
(other countries include India, China, Ghana and Peru)
Like the others in this series, this story follows a child's day from dawn to dusk, taking in religious observances, food and schooling. There is a detailed fact file divided into sections on history, people and religion in Egypt and an index.

A Ruined House
By Mick Manning
Read and Wonder, Walker Books
Mick Manning takes young listeners or readers on an imaginary visit to a house which he remembers from his childhood. Once the house was abandoned it became home to many wild plants, insects and birds. The clear text is accompanied by appealing annotated illustrations. For example there are the lichens and foxgloves that are found in wild gardens and the insects that live in ruins – spiders, craneflies, ground beetles and woodlice. The story form gives a coherence to learning about the creatures and plants living in the old house. Helpful explanation is given – fungi break down old wood and 'once it gets damp, beetles tunnel into it'. (Quentin Blake, the first Children's Laureate, includes this book in his 50 favourites in *The Laureate's Party.*)

Starting School
By Fiona Pragoff
Collins
Like other books by Pragoff this one has a simple text structured round appealing photographs.

Noah's Ark
By Jane Ray
Orchard Books
This is a lively re-telling of the Bible story with illustrations showing how Noah built the Ark and chose the creatures to take refuge in it. Children will enjoy re-enacting the story using the pop-up characters at the end,

See How I Grow
By Angela Wilkes
Dorling Kindersley
This is a photographic record of a baby's first 18 months with a simple yet appealing text. It is a favourite book to use to support themes on 'growth' and 'ourselves' – see case study 2.2 in *Young Researchers* (Mallett, 1999).

Apples and Honey: A Rosh Hashanah Story
By Jonny Zucker, illustrated by Jan Barger Cohen
Frances Lincoln
This tells how one family celebrates the Jewish New Year by eating apples with honey and planning for a joyful year ahead. There is a fact file and a short glossary.

The world came to my place today
By Jo Readman, illustrated by Ley Honor Roberts.
Eden project. Transworld Publishers.

Figure 7.4   The World Came to My Place Today by Jo Readman, published by Eden Project Books. Used by permission of Transworld Publishers, a division of the Random House Group Limited.

When George has to stay at home, Grandpa helps him spend an interesting day finding out where all the things he eats and all the things he uses come from. Excellent introduction to a 'products' theme in geography.

Non-narrative non-fiction

A very important category of non-narrative non-fiction is the reference book – dictionaries, thesauruses, atlases and encyclopaedias. Such a very substantial category deserves considerable discussion and you will find this in Chapter 8. So here I turn to the sort of books people mostly think of when they hear the term 'information book'.

The typical children's information book is an illustrated text on a single topic such as spiders, space or supermarkets. Unlike the texts discussed earlier in this chapter, those texts organised in a time sequence, these texts organise information under headings and subheadings to give coherence to the different aspects of the subject in question. The documentation for the United Kingdom National Literacy Strategy describes this kind of writing as 'report'. One of the most helpful studies of the global or overall structure of the typical children's information book was by Christine Pappas in 1986. Her study, which was built on the examination of a large number of books, led her to identify three 'obligatory elements' of the genre – the things that will always be present. The first is 'topic presentation'; for example, 'A spider is ...'. The second, the 'representation of attributes', describes the different parts of the subject – on the lines of 'Spiders have eight legs and most spin webs and produce a poison to paralyse their prey'. The third element describes the 'characteristic events' and in the case of the spider would include breeding, birth, food and hibernation. Pappas argues that children develop expectations about the order and nature of these obligatory elements and these expectations help children to develop competence in this kind of reading (Pappas, 1986).

While Pappas has illuminated the global structure of information books, other writers have concentrated on mechanical guiders – headings and subheadings – and retrieval devices – contents pages and indexes (Neate, 1992) – and illustrations (Mallett, 1996/7). For an inspirational and profound account of how children read to learn and how books help or hinder this learning, see Margaret Meek's book *Information and Book Learning* (Meek, 1996). Helen Arnold also offers a particularly clear analysis of the language of the best information books (Arnold, 1992).

Information books for very young children are, as we would expect, a 'transitional' genre – texts with some of the features of mature 'report', but with some modifications to make them accessible to young readers. So Pappas' three obligatory elements may well be present, but not in the conventional information book format. For the purposes of this book I have found it helpful to organise these early books into three groups: question books, non-fiction picturebooks and fact books.

Question books

Young children constantly ask questions about their world and it is perhaps not surprising that quite a lot of the books for their age are organised by questions. My preference is to start by helping children to think of some of their own questions and then seeing whether the books they are using have similar questions in them.

When it comes to the better books the questions are not miscellaneous, but are grouped under sub-topics and again it is a good idea to help children to organise their questions in this way. The questions in *Are you a Snail?*, one of Kingfisher's appealing 'Up the Garden Path' series, move through the creature's life taking in breeding, feeding and so on, and would reinforce this approach. The books in this series help children to start to classify animals by establishing their habitats, structure and behaviour.

The best 'question' books anticipate the sort of things children are likely to ask and answer them clearly and imaginatively. Oxford's 'Question and Answer' series manages this well. 'Why doesn't that bird fall off the branch? in *Why do Stars Twinkle and other Nighttime questions* is answered in detail in words, helped by a simple but clear diagram of a bird's long tendons locking its claws onto a branch.

I appreciate it when 'question books' make it clear that not all 'answers' are definitive. *I Wonder Why Triceratops Had Horns* explains we are not absolutely sure what colour dinosaurs were. We have fossil evidence of their skin type of course 'but this only shows that it was scaly'.

Sometime whole books are devoted to answering one question in great detail. Mick Manning and Brita Granstrom in *What's Under the Bed?* take the amusing answers in text and pictures to an extreme with great effect. Readers are shown what is immediately under the bed, under the house foundations (taking in a cross-section of an ant colony) and then deeper and deeper into the earth until its boiling centre is reached. This is one of those books that delight adult and child and show that a non-fiction book can be hugely imaginative and original.

Questions seem much more 'alive on the page' than statements and make a young reader feel truly actively involved in ideas and concepts. Children enjoy organising some of their own writing around questions. A group of children structure their own book around questions about snails in the case study in chapter 3 of *Young Researchers* (Mallett, 1999a).

Information picturebooks

The boundary between fact and fiction blurs to a fine line when it comes to the children's picturebook – that important cultural form which emerged in the last decades of the twentieth century. These are not just stories with a lot of illustrations, but are often highly sophisticated works of art. As well as the wonderfully inventive fiction picturebooks, there are some information stories which deserve to be regarded as picturebooks. *Ten Seeds* by Ruth Brown has wonderful pictures of plants and animals supported by a simple, but never banal, text. When it comes to picturebooks with a non-narrative organisation we would include a lot of the best alphabet and concept books discussed in the earlier chapters, by author illustrators like Shirley Hughes, John Burningham and Brian Wildsmith. We think of the Anno books, with their copious small pictures, and Stephen Biesty's cross-sections as being for older children, but some under-sevens love looking at them with an adult. As other information sources become available including software and the internet, the print book has to compete. Aidan Chambers, speaking in January 2002 to the London Association for the Teaching of English, predicted that even if information is carried in future mainly by electronic means, we will still have some books and their value will rely even more on their individuality and on their appeal as beautiful objects appealing to our aesthetic sense. You can read more about this in *Reading Talk* (Chambers 2001).

Of course, as is the case with all books and resources, we need to keep a firm hold on our critical hats when choosing them; and we should avoid paying a lot of money for fairly miscellaneous collections of attractive pictures tenuously linked by an unimaginative written text. In fact there needs to be a strong coherent theme to stimulate the sort of talk and discussion around a book that helps link the content with children's learning. So one good question to ask when choosing is: will this book arouse interest and promote useful talk? Franklin Watts 'Creature Feature' series helps children classify creatures by looking at particular parts of their body – hair, feet, noses and tails. The simple written text has a distinctive 'tune' and weaves round appealing illustrations which include welcome touches of humour.

Some of the books mentioned above are produced in big format to support shared reading in the literacy hour or lessons across the curriculum. In case study 7.2 a teacher reads Alan Whitaker's book *My Skin* to a reception class, making links with children's science work.

Fact books

'Fact books' is my shorthand term for those early information books written to support lessons across the curriculum and these days the literacy hour. A teacher remarked to me that she regarded these as 'bread and butter' books – often less aesthetically appealing than information picturebooks but useful to resource particular lessons. Science, history, geography, mathematics, technology and art books pour out of the publishing houses for different age groups. They are produced in abundance by publishers of reading programmes and resources who link their use in the literacy hour with use in other lessons. Publishers love to produce books in series, each book disciplined by the same general format and with sub-topics shaped into the Procrustean double spread! The trend is towards having the books in small and big format and increasingly on CD-ROM as well as on cassette and video-film. Publishers of children's non-fiction of all kinds include Dorling Kindersley, Kingfisher, Ladybird and Franklin Watts. Reading programmes and resources well known for including a strong non-fiction element include Collins Primary Literacy, Cambridge Reading, Oxford Reading Tree, Literacy Land, Ginn's All Aboard!, and Heinemann Library.

Many of the books for the sixes and under are of the 'time sequence' kind, including recounts and instruction texts discussed in the first part of this chapter. However, there are also books organised as simple reports providing an early taste of non-narrative text, for example *Waste* and *Firefighters* in Collins 'Pathways to Literacy' titles. Oxford Reading Tree 'Fact Finders' series has books to support topics on *Food, Clothes, Schools, Families* and *Houses and Homes*. Fact Finders Topic Starters are intended to encourage talk and can provide early experience of 'discussion texts' with titles on *Different Homes* and *Everyone is Special*. Heinemann Library also supports topic work with some broad collections round themes, including Collection 2 'Ourselves' which has a number of titles – *Food, Tasting, Hearing, Safety First* – which introduce children to non-narrative text in the course of their work on a topic. Oxford's *Web Non-Fiction* provides a range of early 'fact books' for children from nursery to Year 2, gradually building in non-narrative text features like captions, labels, lists and colour coding.

Non-fiction books in series, whether part of a structured reading scheme or not, have come in for some criticism over the years. They can seem rather 'recipe written' to fit with government programmes and the worst are dull and predictable. Sometimes scraps of information are attached to a series of pictures and young readers are not helped to see how a particular 'fact' fits with the 'bigger shapes' of learning. If you would like to read more about this I recommend Margaret Meek's book *Information and Book Learning*. Things have improved. Publishers now often seek the help of well thought of reading consultants in designing and developing their programmes and it is gradually being accepted that not everyone can write a good information text for children! Some people are rather good at it and the signs are that the books of distinguished writers of non-fiction are being used in reading schemes and for other non-fiction series. Meredith Hooper's fine wildlife books are used in the Cambridge Reading Programme, for instance. Other excellent writers and illustrators of early non-fiction to look out for, whether in books from reading programmes or not, include Ruth Brown, Nicola Davies, Vivien French, Sarah Garland, Claire Llewellyn, Mick Manning and Brita Granstrom, Ifeoma Onefulu, Fiona Pragoff, Karen Wallace, Barrie Watts, Angela Wilkes and Bee Willey.

Some teachers choose one main published reading programme and supplement it with strands from other programmes and with other fiction and non-fiction texts and resources. Others feel that they stay in control by developing their own core books for different stages, including some scheme books. The important thing is to ensure that children have the opportunity to enjoy some of the books by the best non-fiction writers and illustrators.

Criteria for choosing non-narrative non-fiction

Whether chronologically or non-chronologically organised, we seek a text which in content, style and approach serves our purpose at a particular time. Our purposes need to match with the author's intentions. We also have to estimate the readability level of the book for the child. Of great help here is Cliff Moon's annual list *Individualised Reading* which divides large numbers of books, including titles from reading schemes, into categories according to reading level. *Core Books: A Structured Approach to Using Books Within the Reading*

Curriculum and the companion *Core Booklists*, including the best non-fiction, from the Centre for Language in Primary Education, help teachers select the most appropriate books for different reading levels and interests.

Many of the qualities listed below are similar to those which we look for in chronological non-fiction. The ones I have added are to do with retrieval devices, diagrams and the greater emphasis in some early non-narrative books on contextualising a technical vocabulary. Any list of criteria needs to be used flexibly and not all will apply to a particular non-narrative book. We look for:

- a coherent 'global' or overall structure
- a format which enthuses and invites
- uncluttered pages that are inviting and coherent
- clear, accurate content with just the right amount of detail and offering something new and interesting for the intended readers
- appropriate retrieval devices
- language with life and vitality which explains things well
- an authorial 'voice' which invites the young reader into the topic, communicates with them and gets them to reflect
- a text which is cohesive so that the sentences have a good rhythm and meaning is crystal clear
- well contextualised technical vocabulary
- accurate, useful and attractive illustrations which, whether photographs, drawings, diagrams or charts, have a clear purpose, work well with the written text and where appropriate are annotated
- a spark of originality and the capacity to fascinate and involve young readers, encouraging them to want to find out more

Using non-narrative non-fiction

I have organised my thoughts on using non-narrative texts under three headings. The first is the role of these texts in learning; the second is their role in developing knowledge and understanding of the text as a genre; and the third is their contribution to building library and study skills. The third is particularly pertinent to non-narrative kinds of non-fiction – to the typical 'information book'.

Role of the texts in learning

I put this first because it concerns the main reason for which we use information texts – to illuminate an area of learning. The teacher uses books and resources to support learning at different stages – at the start of the work to invite interest, or later to answer children's questions or to move their thinking and understanding forward. We might choose to read a text, or part of a text, aloud at the start of new learning. One of the books in the lively 'Creature Feature' series would help children to think about similarities and differences at the beginning of a topic in mathematics or science. One advantage of starting this way is that the text and pictures provide a focus for children's comments about their existing knowledge as a preliminary to taking on new ideas and understanding. Sometimes a book links perfectly with a particular lesson. The teacher of a reception class whose theme was 'colour' read out

Moonlight Publishing's book *Colours* at the point at which the children were learning about colour mixing. This book featured transparent coloured overlays to produce different colour effects. Even the visually aware children of today need help in making their response to illustrations explicit and in having these responses extended or challenged. Looking at this book gave rise to talk about the effects that colour or colours can have on one's perception of a scene or object. Yellows and reds were thought to be mood enhancing by some children, while the darker colours seemed to make buildings and objects smaller and more mysterious.

Sometimes a particular image in a book makes a special impact on individual children or even a whole class. I remember the imaginative appeal a picture of a Victorian horse-drawn fire engine had for a reception class studying firefighters as part of a 'people who help us' project. The book showing the picture is now long out of print but the teacher found the children referred to this old engine in their discussions and many of them made their own pictures of it (Dalton-Vinters and Mallett, 1995).

Teachers set up displays of books, pictures and objects to support lessons and topic themes; children enjoy browsing and should be encouraged to do so. But we also need to be active in bringing books into lessons, making explicit to the children how they contribute to their learning. This helps them become accustomed to the rhythm or 'tune' of information books and ensures that less forward readers benefit from the information they contain. Talking together about new ideas is quite simply the best way of helping their assimilation and of linking book knowledge to other experience. When there is a mismatch between what we read and what we know from experience things can become exciting and demonstrate to young learners that they must be critical readers. A student teacher was reading to six-year-olds who kept snails in a classroom vivarium. The book said snails preferred 'green leaves – lettuce, cabbage and so on'. Their own observation of the classroom snails showed that their snails very much preferred carrot. This led to talk about some quite profound things and, not least, to considering what can best be learnt from books and what from observation and experiment (Mallett, 1999a).

The children learning about snails went on to write their own book, drawing both on what they observed and on what they had found in books. Writing, as well as talk, can be a way of assimilating and evaluating new information. But let us not underestimate how challenging it is for the older children in this age range to be asked to use books as a source for their writing. Knitting together information from first hand experience or our existing knowledge with new discoveries in books is no small intellectual achievement.

A great spur to both talking and writing is a little bit of controversy – as we saw in the snail work. Books giving different theories of why dinosaurs died out, those which speculate on the dangers of over-fishing our seas and those which comment on the behaviour of predatory creatures have all, in my experience, led to passionate debate and writing. You would not expect perhaps to be terrified by a counting book, would you? However, in her book, *One Hungry Spider*, Jeannie Baker mentions that spiders sometimes eat their young. The illustration shows six spiderlings which have fallen into their parent's web and the text tells us they were devoured. A five-year-old remarked 'You wouldn't think it would eat a creature the same as itself, would you?' Illustrations as well as text can move children's responses up a gear and create that feeling of disequilibrium that Piaget believes leads to truly energetic learning. I remember six-year-olds being mesmerised by a photograph – in a long-out-of-print book – of a bedraggled baby sea bird contaminated with oil and slowly dragging itself along the shore line. As one of the children said, you could feel how heavy its wings must have felt, saturated as they were with oil causing them to drag along the ground as it moved. Seeing and talking about this powerful image transformed and made real the children's perception of pollution and they wanted to learn more about it and how it could be prevented. Including fascinating, even disturbing things help an information text serve its purpose – 'to develop the will and the mental equipment to assess facts and ideas' (Fisher, 1972: 474).

Understanding the text as a genre

Teachers have always known about different texts and their purposes and have drawn children's attention to 'book language' of different types, but current United Kingdom requirements make an even more systematic knowledge and understanding necessary. Children are introduced to different text types as soon as they begin literacy hour work in the Reception class. Thus in the 'shared reading' part of the literacy hour teachers draw attention to features at text, sentence and word level.

What, then, are some of the features we note in the typical information book? At text level we would look at how the content is organised, often under sub-headings. In the case study that comes later, the teacher looked at a big book on *Skin* in the literacy hour and linked it with the children's work on science. This approach helps children understand that different books have different purposes and that their layout, language style, illustrations and content relate strongly to this. At word level, young children can be helped to tune into the technical vocabulary of some information books – 'holt', 'prey' and 'forepaws' in a book about otters, for example. I find children like glossaries and often manage to incorporate this feature when they make their own books.

Perhaps it is at sentence level that we have to take care not to press difficult aspects like 'voice', 'tense' and 'syntax' on young children. They can, however be helped to appreciate and identify the distinctive 'rhythms' of non-fiction text and to understand how punctuation affects meaning.

Building library and study skills

Library skills are to do with locating particular books and learning how to sample a book swiftly looking at the cover and skimming through the contents page and index in order to discover if it serves your purpose. Most English co-ordinators agree a plan with their colleagues to ensure coverage of library skills in the teaching programme, including later on how to control the Dewey system. Now library skills include selecting CD-ROMs and software and becoming able to use the internet for information retrieval. Some publishers of reading resources have produced ICT texts which simulate the operation of 'the web' to help children become familiar with the digital environment for information retrieval and study purposes. Collins, for example, has such ICT texts suitable for use on PCs, Macs, projectors and interactive whiteboards.

'Study skills' is a term referring to all the strategies that researchers of any age use when finding out about a topic. In the quotation which began this chapter, Margaret Meek remarks on how similar the approaches of the very young are to those of mature researchers. Adults begin research with clear purposes and young children also often begin with a strong need to find out about something. Early years teachers demonstrate the use of retrieval devices – contents pages and indexes – in the classroom or library, to help children find what they need. The only sensible way to demonstrate this is within the context of learning about a topic or wanting to find out something quite precise like the size of a creature or the diet of a frog. I will never forget the passionate way four-year-olds urged the teacher to find answers to their questions about the blue whale. She had to seek out an encyclopaedia for much older children to answer their detailed questions about size, structure and breeding. The information and reference books for their age group on the topic did not have such detailed information.

If, from an early age, young children are helped to see that finding their way round books can serve important purposes for them, not least providing answers to their questions, they start off with a dynamic and positive approach to research in secondary sources.

In the case study that follows we join a reception class teacher who combines learning about the features of an information book with reinforcing some of the concepts the children have been learning about in science.

Case study 7.2: Using a big science book in the literacy hour

Heather Ballinger, used the big book Skin *by Alan Whitaker in the shared reading portion of a literacy hour with her reception class at Castlecombe Primary School. She made links through discussion with the children's science work on 'colour' and on their work on 'similarities and differences'.*

The teacher began by letting the vibrant colour of the picture on the front cover make its impact. It shows the head and shoulders of a little girl of about five years in a swim suit with water in the background. Elizabeth commented that 'The girl is in a swimsuit so she might be learning to swim' and Craig thought the water behind 'might be a swimming pool or a children's pool – not too deep'. Next the teacher drew attention to the title and author on the front cover and asked the children what they thought the book would be about.

The children's study of colour made them sensitive to the subtle shadings of the animals – so that they were able to say the crab was a brown colour with some black, yellow and pink areas.

The teacher nudged the children towards thinking about similarities and differences when they came to the page featuring the large pink worm with a moist skin. Georgia was able to say that slugs also had slippery skins although they were shorter than worms. Katie said that snakes were like huge worms but their skin was dry and scaly. 'Caterpillars', said Lauren, were 'dry creatures usually but they were much smaller than worms. Christian said 'I don't want to touch a worm' and Georgia was glad to be reassured that worms, unlike snakes, do not bite. Jack was beginning to think about the reasons why animals have different skins, remarking that the turtle needs a hard thick shell 'to protect it from other animals'.

When I first looked at the book I noted it said, above a large picture of a tiger, 'A tiger's skin looks best on a tiger'. I thought ethical issues were being touched on as something like this has been a slogan for the Ban Fur in Fashion movement. But the next page shows a child with the sentence 'And your skin looks best on you'. I was seeing issues where none were intended! Jack was preoccupied with what his father had told him: 'never touch a wild animal like a tiger when you are at the zoo'.

Notable was the skill with which the teacher integrated children's learning in science and literacy, extending children's vocabulary to describe the different textures and colours of skin and helping them note similarities and differences. The children responded well to the challenge of making the visual verbal. Children's spontaneous questions and comments were welcomed as they tried to link their prior knowledge with the new learning.

Selective list of non-narrative non-fiction

Question books

Are You a Snail? Are You a Ladybird?
By Judy Allen and Tudor Humphries
Up the Garden Path series, Kingfisher
The question and answer pattern, which establishes the main physical features and behaviour of the creature, gives the text a rhythmic feel. The illustrations are large, detailed and enormously appealing.

What's under the bed
By Mick Manning and Brita Granstrom
Franklin Watts
A vivid descent from under your bed to the earth's molten core.

Why do Stars Twinkle and other nighttime questions
By Catherine Ripley, illustrated by Scot Ritchie
Oxford University Press
This is a beautifully presented book with entertaining pictures and fascinating questions and answers. The questions are in huge bold print. Answers are speculative when appropriate.

I Wonder Why Triceratops Had Horns and Other Questions About Dinosaurs
By Rod Theodorou, illustrated by Chris Forsey and Tony Kenyon
Kingfisher
This, like the others in the series, is beautifully illustrated with big colourful drawings and smaller cartoons which children will love. A lively text makes it clear that we rely on fossil evidence in finding out about dinosaurs. But there is welcome honesty about the limitations of present knowledge – 'No-one knows what colour dinosaurs were. We have fossils of their skin, but these only show that it was scaly'. Older children would also enjoy this book but from about six years children would enjoy sharing it with an adult or older sibling.

There are many more titles in the series including *Why Camels Have Humps; The Sun Rises; Trees Have Leaves; Soap Makes Bubbles; Mountains Have Snow on Top*

Information picturebooks

Colours
By Barrie Wade, illustrated by Liz Tansley
Collins Pathways, Signpost books
This was one of the books included in the display to support the 'colour' topic in the Castlecombe reception class work. This is a simple, well illustrated book suitable for sharing

with a pre-school child or to support early science in a reception class. Georgia, one of the children, told me she liked the instructions on how to colour a rainbow at the end of the book.

Skin
By Alan Whitaker, Illustrated by DAC/Brian Enting
Wonder Books big books series, Scholastic Canada Limited with Lands End Publishing
This is an attractive book introducing children to the different textures of skin of human beings and animals of different species. The excellent, large photographs invite teacher and children to search their vocabulary to describe the contrasting skin textures and colours shown. For one class's response see case study 7.2.

Creature Hair; Creature Feet; Creature Noses; Creature Tails
By Nicola Whittaker
Creature Feature series, Franklin Watts
These colourful books help children to begin to classify animals by looking at different parts of their body. The creatures are pictured most imaginatively. In *Creature Tails* a large rattlesnake curves its way round the page with its tail held up ready to rattle. A lively text weaves round the pictures. Important words are in larger print. Children will appreciate the witty little touches – for example on the Giraffe page is written 'Some hair makes spots' with the large letters of 'spots' sprinkled with dots.

There is a splendid picture glossary introducing children to encyclopaedia format and indicating the links between a creature's physical characteristics and its lifestyle. These books are likely to inspire much conversation and are an excellent introduction to non-narrative texts for children in the Foundation years.

Fact books

Waste; Firefighters
Pathways to Literacy, Collins
These are two of the 'fact books' in the series. *Waste* introduces children to safe ways of disposing of rubbish and of re-using it. *Firefighters*, in small and big book format, is an introduction to the work of the fire service.

Hearing; Toys; Tasting; Safety First
Collection 2 'Ourselves'
Heinemann Library
This thematic collection of 26 books includes a selection of non-narratively organised 'fact books'.

Oxford Reading Tree
Oxford University Press
One of the first reading scheme publishers to include non-fiction to support the initial teaching of reading, Oxford's 'Fact Finders' provide books on early years topics like *Food*, *People* and *Clothes*.

Oxford Web Non-Fiction
Oxford University Press
'First Words Non-Fiction' is a package of books for children from nursery to reception which are arranged in three stages of increasing difficulty to ensure progression. The titles link with topic themes – for example *The Farm*, *Traffic* and *My School* at the starter stage, *Changes*, *Animal Homes* and *Things that Go* for stage 1 and *Festivals*, *My Pet* and *The Building Site* at stage 2.

Non-book print

Children come to school having had a considerable exposure to non-book kinds of print: advertisements, labels, letters, menus, notices, magazines, leaflets, travel brochures, product lists, posters, flyers and catalogues. Nursery and reception class teachers, knowing how important these are in our society, are skilful in bringing them into the children's work and role play. In the course of my school visits while gathering information for this book I saw a great deal of work drawing on this kind of resource; for example, I joined four-year-olds using menus in the course of their role play in a 'café', six-year-olds using magazines and newspapers in the clinic waiting room and five-year-olds using tickets at a 'railway station'. Children encouraged to use these resources in their work and role play become familiar with some of the features of non-book print. For example, they learn that pages can be very different sizes and on materials from paper to cardboard and plastic. Illustrations and print link closely, each complementing and extending the meaning of the other. Text is often not in sentences but consists of single words and phrases which are slogans, sometimes listed with numbers or bullet points. It is never too soon to learn that advertisements aim to manipulate us and we have to think about the aims and intentions of the person who designed them. The teacher's role is to help children make explicit their observations about these features.

In case study 7.3 children learned about the format and use of a leaflet on pet care in the context of lively work on a 'pet' theme.

Case study 7.3: Leaflets about pet care

I wanted to include this case study because it is such a good example of how teachers of young children build on children's enthusiasms by recognising and taking advantage of opportunities for truly involved learning. Four- to five-year-olds at Corstorphine Primary School in Edinburgh had written 'Caring for Your Cat' booklets as part of work on a 'pets' theme (see Chapter 6). Some weeks later, after a Charity Pet Fair had visited their area, they returned to the pet theme, the emphasis now being on dogs. The teacher decided to use the enthusiasm that had been rekindled by the excitement of the Pet Fair to develop the children's understanding of the format and purpose of informational leaflets.

After the excitement of the Pet Fair, the teacher decided to read her class Walker Books' *The Most Obedient Dog in the World*. This is the story of a dog who waits patiently for his owner, even through snow and rain, and is rewarded by being taken to the beach to play games and enjoy treats. The children also enjoyed some exciting role play about dogs being kept in a puppy pound. At 'choosing time' the children mentioned the 'cat care' booklets they had written some time ago and asked if they could now write about how to care for a pet dog. And so the usual sort of discussion and sharing of anecdotes about pet dogs belonging to the children and to their friends and relatives took place. But of course the teacher wanted to build on the earlier work and she began by displaying pictures, advertisements, posters and leaflets about dog care. She read selectively from a leaflet provided by the local pet shop – 'A Guide to Pets At Home'. It covered some of the aspects of dog care the children had already discussed – how to deal with itchy ears and bad breath and how to clean a dog's teeth. But it also mentioned further issues like travel sickness, vet visits, coughs and dealing with bad behaviour.

The teacher felt that reading from the leaflet, which was aimed at an adult readership, moved the children's thinking up a gear. First, it underlined one of the main uses of print in our society – print to inform and advise about something. Second, the children were exposed, in a sympathetic way, to the style and vocabulary of mature written text of the 'instructional' kind. Third, focused talk in groups made it possible for the children to link their common sense knowledge about dogs and their care with information from a print source. This was reinforced by each child choosing one important aspect of dog care and producing an illustrated page. These pages were shared and displayed.

This case study emphasises how important it is for early years teachers not to be so bound by prescriptive requirements that they lose the flexibility and spontaneity which is so characteristic of successful work with children of this age group. This teacher achieved very good results by taking up a special opportunity to explore an enthusiasm. Building on the 'cat care' work allowed children to resavour a topic and to extend their knowledge and understanding by the new reading and writing tasks. This returning to a previous topic and extending it is very much in the spirit of Jerome Bruner's notion of the 'spiral curriculum' (Bruner, 1975). This whole case study exemplifies the sort of thing we have in mind when we say non-fiction needs to be situated in 'meaningful contexts'.

Further issues

There are some further issues relevant to the provision and use of non-fiction books and resources which seem to me to deserve some explanation. These are the implications of a genre-based approach which is now established in the United Kingdom, the question of bias, and what is known about gender and reading non-fiction.

Genre theory

Teachers, particularly in the United Kingdom and Australia, use the term 'genre' when discussing books and resources to support children's learning. Why is there this new emphasis and what are the implications for lessons with the youngest children?

There is nothing new about the concept of 'genre'. Teachers have always been aware that there are different kinds of texts and that their different forms reflect their different purposes. However, the National Curriculum English programmes and the National Literacy Strategy

Figure 7.5 Front cover of the pet care leaflet.

have brought genre into new prominence (DfEE/QCA 1999a; DfEE 1998a). The assumption is that development in literacy is partly to do with controlling, as readers and writers, the kinds of texts valued in our society. *The Framework for Teaching* which guides the literacy hour requires that we include for shared reading all kinds of fiction and non-fiction in a wider range of media than ever before. (The six non-fiction genres taken over from the EXEL project are discussed in chapter 6.) Not surprisingly, publishers of children's books and reading schemes have started to structure their non-fiction collections round these six non-fiction categories. The best schemes make use of quality authors and some of the titles would make a helpful addition to a school's collection. The reflective practitioner wants to be in control of the school's library and class collections and not to look to any one publisher, however comprehensive their material, to supply all the books and resources!

Underpinning the emphasis on genre in the United Kingdom frameworks is the work of a group of Australian scholars and teachers who are referred to as 'genre theorists'. In a nutshell, they claim that their classroom-based research showed that narrative was the preferred form

Figure 7.6 Jamie's dog care picture and writing

Figure 7.7 Amy's dog care picture and writing. Amy has her own way of indicating this is advice about what not to do: she has placed a cross above the girl pulling her pet's tail!

in school and that other kinds of writing like persuasive and explanatory writing were relatively neglected. As many jobs and professions require good control over these challenging non-fiction forms, the genre theorists believe we should give them systematic attention from the earliest stages in school.

Of course the work and the ideas of the genre theorists have attracted some criticism. Some people feel that they present genre as too static a phenomenon. While the characteristic elements of a genre may be organised fairly predictably, we must remember that language is both socially situated and dynamic. It changes as society's needs change. Think how the e-mail reflects changes in working procedures and resources.

The other main concern is that mature forms may be pressed on young children before they can understand and use them. We should resist this. As I have shown in this chapter, many of the first information books children read are 'transitional' genre with features of format and language to make them more accessible and more interesting. Early writing, too, needs to serve the purposes of young children at the point at which it is done. If you would like to read more about the issues surrounding genre theory you would find useful Wyse and Jones' analysis in chapter 14 of *Teaching English, Language and Literacy.*

Bias

All texts have a bias in the sense that they draw on an author's distinctive view of the world in general and on the story or topic in particular. But when we refer to a text as 'biased' we usually mean that there is an unwelcome favouring of one perspective over another or that important information is missing or distorted.

When it comes to informational material for the very young there are two main kinds of unwelcome bias. The first kind applies to the whole book and resource collection. To put it positively, we would hope to find texts by authors from different parts of the world and which show the variety of human beings, experiences and environments. Teachers find Rosemary Stones' book, *A Multicultural Guide to Children's Books 0–16*, of great help here (Stones, 1999).

The second kind of unwelcome bias is to do with the content of particular texts and with the attitudes expressed. While I think the emphasis is best on including the finest and most interesting texts we can find, no teacher would offer young children a text which in writing or illustration gives a stereotyped view of gender, race or social class or that would offend one of the groups that make up our society.

Even the youngest children are entitled to know that there can be more than one viewpoint on issues. And we should seek books which show not only that knowledge is added to and adjusted in the light of new evidence, but also that our attitudes towards it are not static.

Gender – girls and boys reading non-fiction

There is quite a lot of evidence that, very generally, girls and boys have different learning needs which should be taken account of in the classroom. For a full and interesting overview of gender and language development, including reading development, I recommend Ann Browne's book *Developing Language and Literacy 3–8* (Browne, 2002). As Browne and others have noted, as soon as boys are old enough to make a choice many of them show a preference for information books while girls often favour stories. Baxter observes that girls tend to get more practice at all kinds of reading than boys in nursery school because boys prefer physical play and activity to literacy-based activities. By the time they begin primary school boys show a liking for factual books about how things work and information books about hobbies, computers and sports (Baxter, 2001).[2] One explanation is that boys model their reading behaviour on the male adults in the family who are likely to read sports books and magazines and professional texts (Millard, 1997). Perhaps the recognition of the importance of non-fiction – both print and electronic – in the U.K. National Literacy Strategy will help convince boys that reading is an appropriate activity for both genders. Hopefully also those girls who have a strong preference for fiction will come to realise that non-fiction can also be a source of enjoyment and interest.[3]

Teachers of the very young can help by encouraging boys and girls to enjoy both stories and information books. Several nursery school teachers told me that they found information books on some topics – dinosaurs, pets and wild animals, for example – appealed to boys and girls and this kind of observation is helpful in building class and library collections. The teacher can create an interest in books by showing how they fit into larger learning episodes and serve children's purposes and of course by reading them out loud. The case studies in this book show teachers actively encouraging children to use and enjoy resources.

Summary

Non-fiction texts for children, texts often referred to as 'information books', can be broadly divided into those that are chronologically organised like 'life cycles' and 'day in the life of' books and those non-chronologically organised around the demands of a subject or topic. The least we should expect of books in either category is that they are accurate and well written and illustrated. But the best ones go further: they nourish a child's urge to know and understand and encourage further research. In lively classrooms, books will be complemented by other print forms (as well as electronic resources covered in Chapters 9 and 10) so important in our society.

Providing a range of quality books is important, but it is not enough. Children need their teacher to show how the books can be used to move an area of study forward. Sometimes a book or other resource will provide a dynamic start, sometimes it will give specific information and sometimes it illuminates the big issues in a particular lesson or activity. Once absorbed, children are ready for the teacher's help with library and study skills – the tools to help them in their work as young researchers. Then sharing the fruits of their research helps keep reading, writing, speaking and listening together to promote learning. This learning has two complementary elements: first, children learn more about a topic and, second, they develop their competence in this critical aspect of literacy. Information texts are doing their job if they help children become reflective readers able to evaluate the information and ideas they encounter.

Notes

1   Myra Barrs *et al.* suggest that being able to hear the 'tune' – the pattern and rhythm of different texts – as we read them greatly helps our understanding of them (Barrs and Thomas, 1991).

2   Boys' preference for non-fiction seems to continue in the secondary years. In a small-scale study of one class of 12 year olds, Davies found that 71 per cent of boys' reading was informational compared with 53 per cent of girls' reading. (Davies, 1991) 'Words apart', *Times Educational Supplement.* 19 July, page 18.

3   The National Centre for Research in Children's Literature at The Roehampton Institute is carrying out a funded study, directed by Dr Kimberley Reynolds, into Young People's Reading Interests (tel. 020 8392 3008).

References

Arnold, H. (1992) 'Do the blackbirds sing all day?', in M. Styles, Eve Bearne and Victor Watson (eds) *After Alice*. London: Cassell.

Baker, C. and Freebody, P. (1989) *Children's First School Books*. London: Cassell.

Barrs, M. (1997) *Core Books: The Core Booklist* (See Information Book Collection 1). London: Centre for Language in Primary Education.

Barrs, M. and Thomas, A. (eds) (1991) *The Reading Book*. London: CLPE.

Baxter, J. (2001) *Making Gender Work*. Reading: Reading and Language Information Centre.

Browne, A. (2002, second edition) *Developing Language and Literacy 3–8*. London: Paul Chapman.

Bruner, J. (1975) *Entry Into Early Language: Spiral Curriculum*. Swansea: University College of Swansea.

Butler, D. (1995) *Babies Need Books*. Harmondsworth: Penguin Books.

Chambers, Aidan (2001) *Reading Talk*. Stroud: The Thimble Press.

Dalton-Vinters, J. and Mallett, M. (1995) 'Six year olds read about fire fighters', *Reading UKRA*. April, Vol. 29, no. 1.

DfEE (1998) *The National Literacy Strategy Framework for Teaching*. London: DfEE.

DfEE/QCA (1999) *English: The National Curriculum for England*. London: DfEE.

DfEE (2001) *Early Writing Development*. London: Department for Education and Employment.

Fisher, M. (1972) *Matters of Fact*. Leicester: Brockhampton Press.

Hardy, Barbara (1977) 'Narrative as a primary act of mind', in M. Meek, A. Warlow and G. Barten (eds) *The Cool Web*. London: The Bodley Head.

Mallett, M. (1996/7) 'Engaging heart and mind in reading to learn: the role of illustrations', *Language Matters (CLPE)*, No. 3.

Mallett, M. (1999a) *Young Researchers: Informational Reading and Writing in the Early and Primary Years*. London: Routledge.

Mallett, M. (1999b) 'Life cycles, journeys and historical stories: learning from informational narratives', *Books for Keeps*, July, no. 117.

Mallett, M. (2002) *The Primary English Encyclopaedia: The Heart of the Curriculum*. London: David Fulton.

Meek, M. (1996) *Information and Book Learning*. Stroud: Signal.

Millard, E. (1997) *Differently Literate: Boys, Girls and the Schooling of Literacy*. London: Falmer Press.

Moon, Cliff (revised annually) *Individualised Reading*. Reading: Reading University Reading and Language Information Centre.

Neate, B. (1992) *Finding Out About Finding Out*. Sevenoaks: Hodder & Stoughton with UKRA.

Pappas, C. (1986) 'Exploring the global structure of children's information books', paper presented to the Annual Meeting of the National Reading Conference, Austin, Texas.

QCA (1999) *Early Learning Goals*. London: Department for Education and Employment.

QCA (2000) *Curriculum Guidance for the Foundation Stage*. London: Department for Education and Employment.

Stones, Rosemary (1999) *A Multicultural Guide to Children's Books (0–16)*. London: Books for Keeps.

Wyse, D. and Jones, R. (2001) *English, Language and Literacy*. London: Routledge.

Chapter 8

Early reference books

Dictionaries, thesauruses, encyclopaedias and atlases

Many novice scholars come to familiarity with reference books only when their searches are impelled by a genuine desire to find out … the key to success lies in the origin and nature of the task and the learner's investment in it.

(Meek, 1996: 35)

When young readers meet non-narrative texts, they meet quite different forms of meanings.

(Littlefair, 1993: 126)

Early years practitioners are concerned to remind us not to be too quick to press formal and systematic learning on the very young; after all, many countries do not introduce formal learning until children are six years old. Nevertheless, there are times when even the youngest children feel the need to seek information from secondary sources to answer their questions or tell them more about something which interests them. Some of these sources – dictionaries, encyclopaedias and atlases – are termed 'reference materials' and are often a first port of call. A number of publishers, including Collins, Heinemann, Oxford University Press, Cambridge University Press, Dorling Kindersley, Usborne, Kingfisher and Larousse/Chambers have long been providers of reference books for children of different ages. Reference books, like other information books, need regular updating so the best approach is to have some clear criteria and select from what is currently on the market. Publishers' catalogues and websites help, but before expensive purchases are made, the texts should be examined. The range is greater than ever now that we have electronic books and sites on the internet as well as print reference sources. We benefit from this richer variety but the issues are the same whichever kind of resource we use. It is also true that electronic sources have not replaced books; indeed, different kinds of resource can be combined in our provision for children. I have checked that the reference books I refer to are in print at the time of writing and I have given website addresses to help busy teachers and parents.

This chapter considers how we make sure the first experience of reference sources is positive and enjoyable. This is partly to do with the quality of the materials and partly to do with the teacher's skill in building reference texts into the children's activities and tasks. Above all, as the quotation from Margaret Meek insists, the need and desire to know energises children's research. I will always remember children in a reception class searching an encyclopaedia to find answers to their urgent questions on whales. They insisted the teacher read out the entries to help them discover how many babies a whale gave birth to at one time, how many blue whales were left and what was their size (Doyle and Mallett 1994). Early years teachers, as the Doyle and Mallett case study shows, find they need to have some more advanced reference books intended for adults and older children to respond to the detailed and quite profound questions young children ask.

This chapter looks in turn at the main kinds of reference text – dictionaries, thesauruses, encyclopaedias and atlases – and suggests some broad criteria to help teachers select from what is available. Three things stand out as being important for every work of reference: first, the *design* needs to make using it pleasant and easy; second, the *coverage* – whether headwords in a dictionary or entries in an encyclopaedia – needs to be appropriate for the purpose and for the age of the readers; and third, *clear language* is needed to set out and explain information and ideas. There are also other criteria which are more specific to each kind of text. Just a few texts have, in addition to all the more obvious qualities, that spark of originality, that special imaginative appeal, that marks them out as outstanding.

Finally though, one thing seems clear to anyone who has worked on non-fiction themes with the very young, children are more likely to understand the purpose of reference books if they are helped to make their own simple versions before turning to published texts or as they begin to use them. In chapter 1 the theoretical underpinning to this book presents the young child essentially as an active learner and meaning-maker. From this it follows that the use of reference books is best embedded in the bigger shapes of learning.

First dictionaries

Making their own

The best way to initiate children into how a dictionary works and how to use it is to build some activities round the principle of alphabetic order. Ann Browne suggests that the youngest children might start by making a class alphabet frieze or poster, beginning perhaps by placing the names of members of the class beside the appropriate letters (Browne, 1996). We can then move naturally to ordering beyond the initial letter by asking which would come first amongst, for example, Lawrence, Leon, Leila or Lisa. The thematic approach which is so much a feature of early years work is another context for making simple dictionaries. Themes on animals, people who help us and ourselves, for instance, can all lead to the children, with the teacher's help, making a big class dictionary as a resource to enrich the topic and as a means of reinforcing a sense of alphabetic order. Play can also provide the meaningful situations for activities involving alphabetic ordering, for example writing names on record cards in a baby clinic, on work rotas in a fire station or on customer lists in a plant nursery. By the reception stage teachers often help children to make their own little dictionaries to support spelling development and, since dictionaries do more than give correct spellings, to help them make the meanings of words explicit. We must never forget the motivational aspects: I find most children enjoy adding pictures and drawings to accompany the head words.

Dictionaries on the market: how do we choose?

Experience with alphabetical ordering in the strong contexts suggested above make it much more likely that children will become able to learn from commercially-produced dictionaries. So how do we recognise a good dictionary for the years from about two until six?

We would expect:

- **clear design** so, for example, we would expect to find features like large print and coloured or bold print for the head words. Uncluttered pages make for clarity and aesthetic appeal
- **an appropriate core of words** which children of up to six are likely to meet in and out of school, together with some interesting and challenging words
- **clear language** to provide descriptions and definitions and to explain concepts
- inclusion of 'difficult to define' words which may include prepositions and adverbs as well as nouns and adjectives
- carefully thought out help with verb tenses, with making nouns plural and with synonyms and antonyms
- some gentle humour in sentences and illustrations
- colourful, helpful and dynamic illustrations, sometimes amusing and, where appropriate, labelled. Sometimes the quirkiness of one illustrator appeals more than the predictable efforts of a team of designers and graphics experts
- interesting material to provide a good 'browse' as well as explaining the spelling or meaning of a word. Word games and special pages likely to appeal to this age group with words about animals, space or food help here.

There are a number of dictionaries for the youngest age group that meet at least the first three criteria. These criteria because of their importance are printed in bold.[1] But some reference texts, whether in print or electronic form, while being worthy efforts, just lack that imaginative appeal that makes for an outstandingly good book. I'll be hinting at which books have this spark of originality later.

Let us home in now on the three most important criteria and consider what this might mean for first dictionaries. These apply whether a dictionary is a print resource or an electronic version. A **clear and attractive design** first attracts a young child to a book. *My Very First Oxford Dictionary* has an inviting cover with a child reading this very dictionary with a pet rabbit by her side. Inside, each double spread has a number of words beginning with a letter, each with a contextualising sentence and a jolly picture. A simple approach – but so effective! Other dictionaries with particularly appealing designs are *The Usborne Picture Dictionary* – a large, hardback book with a sky blue cover and uncluttered pages inside – and the brightly coloured Collins *First School Dictionary*.

After being attracted by the design and general format we look next for **a core of words appropriate for the age group**. I like the range of vocabulary in *The Kingfisher First Dictionary* which has some early science vocabulary like 'machine', 'magnet' and 'magnifying glass' and in *The Usborne Picture Dictionary* which does not avoid the words children use every day – both meanings of the word 'bottom' are included. And of course children need to have definitions of words to do with the new technology – 'e-mail', 'internet' and 'computer'. As our culture changes, so does the vocabulary we need to talk about it.

As well as having a good collection of words we also want a dictionary which explains them in **clear language** appropriate for a particular age group. Good compilers can explain words clearly and elegantly. When it is done well it seems easy, but it requires deep thought on the meaning of the word and on the needs of the reader. So, for example, in *The Usborne Picture Dictionary* we have – 'bring' (brought) 'someone or something you take with you. *John brought this letter to post*'. 'E-mail' is succinctly defined as 'a message that you can send from one computer to another'.

There are other features to look out for once we feel sure the three main criteria are met. Illustrations are not usually included in dictionaries for adults or older children, but in the

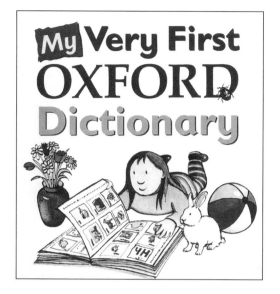

Figure 8.1   My Very First Oxford Dictionary. By permission of Oxford University Press.

early years pictures help clinch and extend the meaning of the definition. So in *My Very First Oxford Dictionary* the definition of date, 'the day something happens', is accompanied by a calendar which shows how a date can be represented in words and figures. Illustrations can also capture children's interest – they like to be entertained as well as taught by books. So the quite hilarious approach in Dr Seuss' *The Cat in the Hat* is much appreciated. Each entry has a witty picture; for example, the 'alphabet' headword shows a rather dour dog holding up blocks with each letter. The final picture shows a nest of deliciously green birds which Seuss claims is a 'nest of zyxuzpf birds'. Have we got any in our garden? he asks. I think he is pulling our legs – teachers and children alike – but it does show that words are created by human beings to refer to the people and things in our world. As well as the fun aspect, this dictionary helps children gain control over alphabetic order and word recognition, and helps with the development of vocabulary.

Dictionaries which do well on most of the criteria discussed here are usually interesting texts to browse through. We have chosen well if, as well as looking up spellings and meanings for a particular need, a child is interested enough to look through a dictionary for pleasure (see Table 8.1).

First thesauruses (thesauri)

Several of the publishers whose dictionaries are described above also publish thesauruses for different ages groups. How soon do children manage to use and understand the purpose of a thesaurus? I think that from around the age of five, with adult help, they can appreciate that there are different words that might have a similar meaning. Making their own lists of synonyms and antonyms would help them understand the purpose of a thesaurus and the way it needs to be designed to do its job. This brings me back to Alison Littlefair's insight at the start of this chapter – that using reference books requires children to understand how particular

Table 8.1   Dictionaries

Title	Design	Content	Comment
My ABC Dictionary Big Book Collins £19.99 pbk 3–5 www.collins.co.uk	large book; animal characters	headwords in simple sentences; colours shapes and number pages	based on the small format dictionary of the same name; good resource for dictionary skills
Collins Rhyming Dictionary Collins £6.99 pbk 5+ www.collins.co.uk	clearly set out headwords	190 words; poems and activities; interesting rhymes – e.g. hind/mind ring/wing	specialised but fun; cartoon pictures; games; helpful alphabetical index
The Cat in the Hat Dictionary Dr Seuss Collins £4.99 hbk 3+ www.collins.co.uk	bright and clear headwords	300 words; e.g. 'zero is too cold for zebras'	has a wonderfully individual flavour
Collins First School Dictionary (Teacher's book is **Collins School Dictionary Skills** by Barry and Anita Scholes) Collins £6.99 pbk 5+ Illustrator S. Strickland www.collinseducation. com	colour headwords inviting dragon cover; strong binding	many photos and pictures; definitions and example sentences; thematic pages	substantial first dictionary with extra information and lively pictures to help
DK Dictionary First reference for young readers and writers Dorling Kindersley £9.99 hbk 5–6 www.dk.com	large cover; bright format	3000 entries; sample sentences; 800 pictures; extended entries on animals, the city; word derivations	useful reference book; good for browsing
Heinemann Library Foundation Maths Dictionary £11.25 hbk 5+ £17.99 Big Book by David Kirkby www.heinemann. co.uk/library	clear format; bright illustrations	48 pages; explains well NLS vocabulary	a good resource for early maths

continued…

Table 8.1 continued

Title	Design	Content	Comment
Kingfisher First Dictionary £9.99 hbk 5+ www.pubeasy.com	clear page layout and headwords	over 1,000 key words; lively pictures	user-friendly
Oxford Reading Tree Dictionary £20 Big Book pbk 4+ Tel. 01536 741171 www.oup.com	clear print; each headword illustrated	300 entries high-frequency words	good for class/group teaching
My Very First Oxford Dictionary £4.99 pbk 4+ Tel. 01536 741171 www.oup.com	clear page layout; lively use of colour in pictures and text; also in big book format	300+ words from 'add' to 'zoo'; picture for each word; topic words at end	more inviting to have one author rather than a team
Oxford First Dictionary £5.99 pbk 5+ Tel. 01536 741171 www.oup.com	clear format	1,500 words plurals and tense endings	useful classroom resource with teacher's help
My Oxford Picture Word Book £4.99 pbk 3+ Tel. 01536 741171 www.oup.com	clear design	first 500 words; word extended to phrase or sentence e.g. 'zooming into space' with picture	visually alive and words well contextualised
Picture Dictionary Ladybird £1.99 mini hbk 2+	clear print; bright pictures	32 pages; picture for each word	a good value first dictionary
The Usborne Picture Dictionary Felicity Brooks, illustrated by Jo Litchfield £8.99 hbk www.usborne.com	large format clear, well spaced headwords	1,000 words; 1,300 pictures; nice games and puzzles; words like 'behind' well explained	appealing illustrations; good range of headwords with helpful explanations

texts make meaning so they can fulfil their purpose. I think there are two purposes for a thesaurus: first, it helps us enrich our vocabulary as talkers and writers; second, it should also encourage an interest in words and in the sheer variety of vocabulary in our language. There are several thesauruses on the market which meet these criteria and which could be used by children from about five years with help from an adult, for example *The Kingfisher First Thesaurus* and *The Collins Junior Thesaurus*.

However, I have found a simply brilliant new thesaurus which is imaginatively designed to appeal to young children. When researching for this book, I visited the children's sections

Figure 8.2   Oxford First Thesaurus by permission of Oxford University Press.

of public libraries, school libraries and many bookshops and sometimes I made a truly exciting find. On one such occasion I discovered an outstandingly good first thesaurus, suitable for children as young as four years, *The Oxford First Thesaurus*. It has 1,000 synonyms and is richly and entertainingly illustrated. Just looking at the writing on the back cover would tell a child about one major purpose of a thesaurus. 'Are you looking for another word for *nice* or *bad*? When you are looking for another way of describing something you need a thesaurus'. This thesaurus helps children extend and refine their vocabularies in a thrilling way. Every page instructs, interests and entertains.

My favourite double spread, on page 98, suggests synonyms for 'sound'. There is a huge picture of a fantasy machine whose different parts are shown moving in interesting and rather noisy ways. Along the top run words to describe sounds more precisely, for example 'bang', 'bleep', 'bubble', 'buzz', 'clang', 'click', 'crackle', 'fizz', 'toot', 'whirr' and 'swish'. This essentially energetic treatment of words would help a teacher encourage interest in vocabulary in the nursery school or reception class.

First encyclopaedias

Some of the early non-fiction writing done by children prepares them for the sort of text used in encyclopaedias and information books. The five- to six-year-olds whose work on caring for a pet (see Chapter 6) led to their writing illustrated booklets thought about what they needed to include to help their readers. Of course encyclopaedias have a distinctive format and children need help to find their way around them, using retrieval devices like contents pages and indexes. Help is also needed in interpreting diagrams and with technical vocabulary, particularly in sections on science and geography. Consulting encyclopaedias is a good start to learning about a topic as they tend to give a basic outline which can be built on by other

Table 8.2   Thesauruses (thesaursi)

Title	Design	Content	Comment
Collins Junior Thesaurus £13.50 hbk 6+ www.collinseducation.com	Large and colourful; clear print	130 key words with clear links to synonyms	a good resource; needs teacher support
Kingfisher First Thesaurus £8.99 hbk 5+ www.pubeasy.com	bright and clear format	144 pages; inviting illustrations	good introduction to antonyms and synonyms
Ladybird Illustrated Thesaurus £4.99 hbk 6+ www.ladybird.co.uk	compact format; headwords in colour	192 pages; sentences to put headwords in context	teacher would need to help; good value
Oxford First Thesaurus £6.99 pbk 5–6 www.oup.com/uk/primary	clear and bright	100 headwords; 1,000+ synonyms; word families	encourages early interest in words; exciting and useful

reading and by other activities and tasks. Using them as resources to research a topic builds them into the bigger purposes and intentions of children's learning.

Early encyclopaedias are organised either alphabetically or thematically. Each approach has advantages and disadvantages. It is often easier to get quickly to what you want in an alphabetically ordered text, but there are problems of overlap and missing out on the unity of bigger topics. In an entry under 'geography' you might want to include information on climate, the continents and occupations which are also under separate entries. So compilers need to organise information between separate entries and main ones. A thematic organisation means you can have some coherence about the main topics of interest to an age group, but getting to the exact information you want is harder. A good index helps here.

Whatever the organisation of an encyclopaedia, whether it is one volume or multi-volumed, print or electronic, there are some helpful criteria to keep in mind. The first three are similar to the most fundamental criteria for all reference books.

- **clear design** so, for example, we would expect print to be clear, with coloured or bold print for entry headings. Uncluttered pages make for clarity and aesthetic appeal. Devices like 'find out more' boxes directing readers to other relevant entries can help children find their way round the text. Fact boxes can also work well but too many or too complicated devices can be counterproductive. An index is essential for thematically organised encyclopaedias.
- **an appropriate core of entries** that children of up to about six years would find of help and interest and some extra entries on things they may not yet have any knowledge but which will be fascinating and thought-provoking.
- **clear language to set out information and ideas**

- an authorial voice which distinguishes between fact and opinion and which approaches knowledge as something which grows and changes as more information is discovered.
- illustrations which work with the written text to explain the topics and ideas accurately and well.
- enough interest and liveliness to encourage children to browse through the text for sheer enjoyment.

The first requirement when choosing an encyclopaedia is that it should have a *clear design.* In other words the print should be easily read, there should be clear headings and subheadings where this would help the young user, and text and illustrations should be arranged on the pages so they look attractive and uncluttered.

Most modern encyclopaedias achieve this. Kingfisher's *First Encyclopaedia* has print of different sizes to indicate the status of information. For example, on the pages presenting the 'insect' entry we have the main defining characteristics of an insect in very large print with smaller print to describe particular creatures. There are also useful 'Find out more' boxes to help young readers extend their research.

The second criterion *coverage of core entries* depends on the scope of the encyclopaedia and the age range it is intended for. *DK Encyclopaedia* has a large number of entries, including the all-important new words to explain technology – 'multi media', 'websites' and 'internet'.

The third essential quality is *clear language to explain* information and ideas. In the *DK Encyclopaedia* we have the following clear simple explanation: 'Grasslands are dusty plains that are too dry for many plants to live'.

Table 8.3   Encyclopaedias

Title	Design	Content	Comment
DK Encyclopaedia First reference for young readers and writers. Anita Ganerit and Chris Oxlade Dorling Kindersley £8.99 hbk 5+	thematic; inviting format; large print; good photos	covers all primary subjects; good illustrations; games	up-to-date comprehensive encyclopaedia; links visual and verbal information; good web links
First Encyclopaedia Kingfisher £12.99 hbk 5+ (in same series – encyclopaedias of human body, animals and science) www.kingfisherpub.com	alphabetic order; bright and clear	1,500 pictures; index, glossary; well-explained text	easy to use
Your World Angela Wilkes Kingfisher £19.99 hbk 4+ www.kingfisherpub.com	thematic; clear format	primary curriculum topics	useful and imaginative first encyclopaedia

Teachers need to be able to consult a resource to help answer some of the quite profound things young children ask. An encyclopaedia aimed at older children, for example Dorling Kindersley's *Children's Illustrated Encyclopaedia*, would be helpful. It is more expensive than the other encyclopaedias mentioned – £29.99 – but it has 450 entries and over 4,000 photographs, art works and maps.

Early map books and atlases

Children greatly enjoy making simple maps, perhaps of their bedroom or classroom and their journey to school. They can be helped to use some simple signs and symbols – rectangles to show tables, beds and chairs, for example. The idea of a key can be introduced by asking how they might indicate a church, a field or a railway station – all structures that might feature in their journey from home to school. While some labelling is helpful, indeed essential, children come to understand, by making their own simple maps, that maps communicate information visually.

The same three criteria that I have used in looking at other reference books are helpful in assessing the quality of published map books and atlases. When it comes to *design* a large-size map is often best for sharing with a group. Print or CD-ROM maps use colour or shading to communicate the size and location of an area. Easy navigation through a CD-ROM atlas is a feature to look for. Good maps for the younger children tend not to include too much detail.

Comprehensiveness is a second main criterion when looking at reference books for any age. When it comes to map books and atlases for the very young it all depends on what is

Figure 8.3 Jamie's map: the way to the park. This is the front cover illustration of a booklet made by six- to seven-year olds. Jamie and the other children had a strong purpose and sense of audience since the booklet was to help the reception class children and parents to find their way from school to the park where the Sports Day was to be held.

Table 8.4   Atlases

Title	Design	Content	Comment
Children's Giant Atlas Heinemann £14.99 6+ www.heinemann. co.uk/library	large format; laminated board	maps of and information about all countries	robust resource; use with adult
First Atlas Heinemann/Philips £6.50 5–7 www.heinemann. co.uk/library	clear organisation	32 maps of UK and countries of the world	has early years topic pages – transport, weather, jobs
First Picture Atlas Anthony Mason Kingfisher £5.99 5+ www.kingfisherpub. com	generous size; clear labelling and headings	maps of all countries; over 2,000 illustrations	has the usual eye appeal of Kingfisher early reference books; a good browse with adult help
The Oxford Infant Atlas Second edition Patrick Wiegand £4.00 pbk 4+ (The enlarged version – **The Oxford Infant Atlas Flopover Book** supports whole-class work. £45)	clear labels; colourful art work	bright maps; UK section; index of place names	a good introduction to maps of countries across the world
The Oxford Talking Infant Atlas CD-ROM £30 4–7 www.oup.com/ uk/primary	multimedia version of *The Oxford Infant Atlas*; fully narrated; easy navigation	satellite images; interactive tasks	introduces young children to geography and ICT
Waylands Big Book of Mapwork 1 4+	large format	map-making skills; simple maps	an active approach for the earliest stages

needed at a particular time. Wayland's *Big Book of Mapwork 1* (unhappily now out of print) is a good one to begin with if you can find it. If not, look for a text that encourages active map-making. The Wayland mapbook includes interesting tasks for the children to try. It starts with some fairy tale inspired maps – Red Riding Hood's journey, for example – then it shows some simple map-making skills and encourages the children to make a map of their own streets. Things become more systematic and later sections teach about following a route, using a grid and understanding signs and symbols.

When children are studying their own or another country there are a number of attractive atlases, but children would need a lot of support to understand and use them. Some of them contain quite a lot of detail even though they are intended for five- to seven-year olds. *The Oxford Infant Atlas* is a useful resource with a special section on the United Kingdom.

The third essential quality, *Clarity of presenting information*, needs to be combined with adult support to make early experience of maps and atlases positive. *First Atlas* (Heinemann/ Philips) has simple maps grouped into sections covering the British Isles, the world and continents. Symbols, keys and co-ordinates are all clearly explained and there are geographical topic pages on transport, weather, work, holidays and wildlife. There is a useful enlarged version, *The Oxford Infant Atlas Flopover Book*, which can support whole-class work and teacher demonstrations of how to use the book. The multi-media version *The Oxford Talking Infant Atlas CD-ROM* has easy navigation through the CD-ROM, colourful maps and some interactive activities with immediate feedback for the children.

Summary

Throughout this book it is argued that children are best treated as active learners, and this applies to their first forays into the world of reference materials. They are more likely to benefit from teaching about study and research strategies if these are harnessed to a genuine wish to find out for purposes that they understand. Making their own versions of early reference material will help them understand the formats and ways of making meaning in the different texts. The quality of the format, language and illustration are all important factors in making early experience of reference works worthwhile. Electronic reference resources need in addition to have good provision for navigation through the CD-ROM.

Note

1   Some early word books have the word 'dictionary' in their title. A dictionary is alphabetically organised and accordingly word books organised round themes are discussed in Chapter 2.

References

Browne, Anne (1996) *Developing Language and Literacy 3–8.* London: Paul Chapman.

Doyle, Cathy and Mallett, Margaret (1994) 'Were dinosaurs bigger than whales?', TACTYC *Early Years Journal.* Vol. 14, no. 2, Spring.

Littlefair, Alison (1993) 'The "good book": non-narrative aspects', in Roger Beard (ed.) *Teaching Literacy, Balancing Perspectives.* London: Hodder & Stoughton.

Meek, Margaret (1996) *Information and Book Learning.* Stroud: The Thimble Press.

Chapter 9

Learning from television and film

Making viewing an active experience

> Children's viewing experiences need to be mediated in order to realise the full educational potential of televisual texts ... watching television with children, talking about what is seen, helping children to make sense of what they see by encouraging them to draw on previous life experiences and experiences of texts (both written and televisual).
>
> (Brown, 1999: 170)

> It is these new literacies that we need to develop alongside print literacy if we want children to be imaginative and flexible thinkers in a technological culture.
>
> (Mallett, 2002: 274)

Technological change has brought ever more use of television, video-film, DVDs, computers and the internet in the home, school and work place. One result of all this is that young children enjoy and use texts that are less linear and more visual than print. This chapter (on children's experience of television and video-film) and the next chapter (on children's use of computers and websites) look at how children can be involved actively and creatively with these new texts and new ways of making meaning.

The analysis in this chapter begins with a look at the issues around watching television at home and school and moves on to a short case study in which young children are helped to understand how television commercials work. The account then considers the uses of video-film and there is another short case study, this time with a teacher and children looking at a video-film on seaside holidays in Victorian times as part of a larger topic on travel. A main argument threading through the analysis is that sensitive adult mediation greatly extends children's response.

Experience of television at home and school

At home

Parents and teachers have long been concerned that watching television is a relatively passive activity. There is still anxiety about the amount of time children spend in front of television at home, time which some feel would be better spent in more active play and reading and listening to stories. However, in her longitudinal study of pre-school children's literacy experiences, Jo Weinberger found that some parents saw television as having a more positive potential. They mentioned that children recognised words on television and Teletext and asked to look in the newspaper to see when their favourite programmes were on. Parents also praised programmes which set out to teach about words and letters, for example *Adventures in Letterland* (Weinberger, 1996). Learning about facts and ideas is also perfectly possible even if programmes – like *Teletubbies, Tweenies* and *Fimbles* – are set in fantasy lands. I spent some time watching children's programmes before writing this chapter; one thing that struck me was that some of the programmes for the very youngest children were curiously lacking in environmental print. The vans and buses in CBBC's *The Story Makers* had no names or advertising material on their sides. We know from four-year-old Orla's picture with a coffee advertisement on the side of a bus that children do notice such things (see Chapter 5). In fairness, the programme showed the word 'Stop' on the lollypop lady's board and we saw clearly the names of the books being read. Such programmes can introduce concepts like number, colour and opposites and therefore can contribute to children's learning about the real world. Programme makers understand this: CBBC produced a five-page statement of criteria when they put out the commission for *Fimbles*. The brief was for a programme for the domestic audience which also had an international appeal but which took account of the United Kingdom's foundation programme with its learning in six areas.

A lot of research studies are now identifying positive aspects of viewing and suggest that reading books and watching television can be mutually supportive. Brown, for example, concludes that the different forms of text – television, books etc. – may support children's development in different ways (Brown,1999). What seems to transform the experience of watching television is the effectiveness of the mediation given by an adult or siblings. Of course children should not be made to feel they are being tested as adults talk to them while they try to enjoy a television programme. The atmosphere should be easy going and friendly and like a genuine conversation. Let us look at some of the things to be borne in mind when intervening with the aim of making watching television as beneficial as possible.

Perhaps the first thing to remember, particularly at home, is to listen to what the child says. All of us who have parented or taught know that very young children often laugh, dance, clap and shout as they watch television. They also make comments and ask questions and these help us to tune into the child's interests and preoccupations so that we can help them make explicit the links between what they already know about something and what they see on television. So we respond to comments linking television with first hand experience, comments like, for example, 'That spider is bigger than the one we saw making its web in the garden'. It is also an encouraging sign if a child links what is seen on television with something in a book. I can remember one of my own children at about age four and a half rushing upstairs to find her Ladybird book on pond creatures during a programme on toads and frogs and asking me to read it when the programme ended. An interest triggered by something on television can lead to buying books – another way in which screen and book link.

A second thing to bear in mind is that children should be allowed, indeed encouraged, to have favourite programmes and have some choice over what they watch. Children will be quick to do this, unless they have been made passive by being put in front of a television set for long periods with no-one to talk to. Just as studies show that very often (although by no means always) girls enjoy fiction in books and in television programmes, so boys quite often prefer non-fiction genres. We can exploit these programme preferences by providing books that extend or build on them. We can also gently nudge children towards a wider viewing range.

A third consideration is that each child, like every viewer, has an individual response to the programmes they watch. This is to be encouraged. After all texts, whether on screen or in print form, are polysemic – capable of different interpretations. Understanding that there are different ways of responding to the same programme represents a considerable step forward. Three-year-old Rosie, treated to a preview of *Fimbles*, remarks that her friend Phoebe will like it. 'But Alexander will say it's rubbish' (Dodd, 2002: 14).

In school

A teacher's television resources fall into two main categories: first, there are the school programmes which can be watched live or pre-recorded for greater flexibility. Second, there are pre-recorded programmes from mainstream television in video-film form. In his book *The Future of Schools Television* Kelly found most teachers preferred to use pre-recorded programmes so that they could stop them to highlight points or invite discussion (Kelly, 1998). Programmes to help with reading are usually interactive; children are invited to call out the names of letters, and to predict and read out short sentences and poems, so the pause button is important to give more time, when needed, than the programme maker has allowed. In the case of television programmes for schools there are usually notes for teachers and booklets for the children and, increasingly software packages. Linking different media to use in lessons takes careful preparation. We have to ask how each text contributes to children's learning about the topic. Like CD-ROMs and computer software, television programmes offer a wide choice of material. We can make good use of programmes about the past, sometimes using historic film as in case study 9.2 or about people and animals in different parts of the world. And, unlike a print source, we can see a process working – speeded up or slowed down film of a flower opening, chicks bursting out of their shells or a hummingbird's wings beating. Technological advances continue to amaze us and expand our experience and understanding. Computer modelling, for instance, can show simulations of how dinosaurs moved, ate and fought each other.

As well as using television programmes to learn about a range of topics and themes, we can carry out work even with quite young children which draws their attention to how meaning is made in this distinctive medium. In the following case study five- to six-year-olds in Australia were helped to take up an analytical approach to television commercials.

Case study 9.1: Children's commercials

Five- to six-year-olds watched television commercials aimed at child viewers recorded by their teacher. The work, which was quite challenging, was spread over several weeks. This case study is based on Carolyn White's account in Callow, 1999.

The children watched a number of television commercials aimed at children and talked about them with the teacher. Then the teacher gave the work a sharper focus. The children were asked to look at a commercial and to comment on a particular aspect with a partner. Each pair of children was given a card headed with one of the following tasks:

- record the colours used
- describe the music
- describe the characters
- record who speaks and what is said

Just beginning to write, the children either asked the teacher to scribe for them or used pictorial representation, for example, using colour pencil to record the colours seen in the commercial. After a number of commercials had been analysed in this way the teacher wrote a summary of the findings in each of the four categories on large pieces of paper for display. The next stage was to talk about the findings and then to make a list on a large chart of the characteristics of a successful commercial for children. The children told the teacher what they wanted her to write. The following characteristics were listed:

- bright colours
- magic and pretending things
- a catchy song or music with a beat

The 'magic and pretending things' ingredient seems to be linked to the children's response to a particular commercial – one advertising McDonalds. This advertisement was set in a fantasy land and showed children following Ronald McDonald along a yellow brick road to find something delicious to eat. White argues that this series of activities taking place over a number of lessons revealed to the children that television commercials are structured in particular ways for particular reasons. As one of the children actually remarked 'somebody made a choice' (Callow, 1999: 45). Becoming a mature reader involves this kind of understanding and, of course, the sooner children know they are being manipulated as well as being entertained by advertisements, the better.

Video-film and DVD

Many of the video-films teachers use are recorded from television programmes so that they can use them flexibly. Most films and video-films for children are fictional, based on picturebooks like *The Snowman* for the under-sixes or stories like *Stig of the Dump* for older ones. These videos can become as precious as storybooks. Three-year-old Tom was found clutching his favourite video and the video control as he hid under the bed – he did not want to go to nursery school that day! But while stories predominate, there are some informational video-films that, with some mediation by the teacher, young children can enjoy. Most teachers have a store of video recordings of factual television programmes both from schools programmes on science, geography and history and from mainstream television programmes. Sometimes just a section of a wildlife film by naturalists like David Attenborough can enthuse young learners. I remember five-year-olds learning about 'creatures of the ocean' enjoying part of a wildlife film on sharks and whales intended for an older audience. The teacher had to fast forward the part where it was made clear that for some whales seals were a source of food, as the children found this upsetting and did not yet have the emotional and intellectual resources to cope.

Other resources are made as video-films, sometimes as part of an educational package as in the case study that follows. Teachers are expected to use all the media important in our culture in school and I was interested to visit a teacher and class working on a project that included print, screen and electronic media.

Case study 9.2: Using the 'Seaside Holiday' video-film

A year 1 class enjoyed a video-film – 'Seaside Holiday with Magic Grandad' – as part of their geography work on travel.

These six- to seven-year-olds had been looking at beaches and seaside resorts, first across Britain and, later, at holiday beaches across the world. The teacher helped them create a large display which featured a map of the British Isles with postcards brought in by the children and some of the teachers showing beaches they had visited. Red lines joined the postcards to the parts of the coastline on the map which they showed.

Having explored beaches in a geographical context, the teacher introduced an historical perspective by showing a BBC video-film to show how people experienced the seaside more than a hundred years ago. The film makers had used the device of a magical character – a grandad who can take his two grandchildren through the screen of an old silent film to explore Victorian life at the seaside. The film sets out to reinforce the children's sense of chronology and concepts of similarity and difference by comparing the experience of the seaside today and more than a hundred years ago. The children particularly enjoyed learning about costume, souvenirs and entertainment now and then. Looking at the past helps children reflect on 'taken for granted aspects' of the present.

There are other benefits from showing a video-film as part of a project like this. The teacher, Norma Fiddler, considered that the strong visual experience together with the explanatory sound track sharpened the children's interest and understanding. She felt it was best to show the video-film with its historical perspective after the children had talked about contemporary experiences of the seaside. This prior reflection on 'what we do now' helped draw attention to some of the differences between past and present. She told me the children continued to think about the video-film: some sought her out when she was on playground duty to talk about the clothes and pastimes of the late Victorian era. So it had made much more than a superficial impact.

The video-film experience seemed to have a payoff in some of the other tasks and activities of the class's travel project. For example, it helped the children understand the sort of timeless features which make for an attractive and sought-after seaside location – not least scenic beauty, entertainments and facilities – and this helped them make convincing travel posters (see Figure 10.3, showing Abbie's poster, in the next chapter).

It is important to stress that Norma chose particular sections of the video-film to show the children. She felt that some of it was too sophisticated for such young children. She had viewed the film and selected the parts to fast forward through and others where she would use the pause button to allow extra explanation to be given.

Using such materials demands skill and sensitivity on the part of the teacher, not least the sensitivity to accommodate children's comments and questions which are such a helpful guide to knowing how to slant our input.

Well chosen and well used, a video-film can add energy and variation to a project. It does not replace books and other print sources, but by showing moving images and by whisking us to different locations it provides a different sort of experience. When evaluating the project the children reflected on what they had learnt from the video-film that would have been more difficult to glean from books. They thought that the music, voices and movement all contributed to providing them with a sense of the distinctive atmosphere of a Victorian seaside.

Annotated list of television programmes and films mentioned

The Fimbles (from CBBC) are Fimbo, Florrie and Baby Pom, half hippo, half mouse-like creatures who live in a fantasyland (Fimble Valley) with a bubble waterfall and a tinkling tree. Other characters are Rockit the frog, Ribble the chick, Bessie the bird and Roly Mo, a bookish mole. There are associated books, videos and soft toys. 2–4 years

The Teletubbies (from CBBC) are Tinky Winky, Dipsy, Laa-Laa and Po, toddlers with a TV in their tummies and an antenna on the top of their heads. They live in sunny Teletubbyland with their friends the live rabbits, the Noo-Noo and a talking periscope. This has been a successful programme in spite of some parents' reservations about the immature speech of the Teletubbies. The programmes have been adopted by 113 countries and have been translated into 44 languages, and there have been £1.2 billion sales from associated videos and books. No new programmes but children can watch the video-films and occasional special programmes. 0–2 years

The Tweenies (from CBBC), Milo, Bella, Fizz and Jake, look like giant soft toys with big boots and beak-like mouths. The set is bright and colourful – reminiscent of a fast food outlet – and their friends are Doodles and Izzles and two adult characters called Judy and Max. The programmes have been sold in 60 countries and translated into 30 languages. Sales of videos, books and the Tweenies Muffin Mix cakes come to £230 million. 3–6 years

The Story Makers (from CBBC)
Shows young children enjoying all sorts of physical activities and provides a lot of spoken vocabulary – push, pull, crash, slow down, and so on. Stories often of the information story type in that they cover everyday things like how to cross the road. There is some environmental print shown – but sparingly.

Seaside Holiday with Magic Grandad
BBC pack of materials with video film. ISBN 0563541660
The package contains information cards, pictures and a 100-minute video-film with three programmes: The Promenade, The Beach and Entertainment. As with all materials, teachers need to edit according to the needs and interests of the children.

Summary

Television, film and video-film are important cultural media and are likely to have a significant influence on children's developing literacy. At home, children benefit from the adult's mediation – warm conversation is best rather than the sort of intervention that gives the impression of a child being instructed and tested. In school, teachers face the challenge of coordinating children's learning from different texts. Those on television, film and video-film complement print sources and provide the energy of the moving image, music and sound and the flexibility of moving swiftly through time and space.

Note

There are a large number of websites giving information to parents and teachers about television programmes and video-films. Three useful ones to start with are:

Film Education's webpage: www.filmeducation.org

www.bbc.co.uk/cbeebies

www.bbc.co.uk/schools

References

Brown, Naima (1999) *Young Children's Literacy Development and the Role of Televisual Texts.* London: Falmer Press.

Callow, Jon (ed.) (1999) *Image Matters: Visual Texts in the Classroom.* Marrickville, Australia: PETA (Primary English Association).

Dodd, Celia (2002) 'Invasion of the Fimbles', *Radio Times*, 21–27 September. www.radiotimes.com

Kelly, P. (1998) *The Future of Schools' Television.* London: Independent Television Commission.

Mallett, M. (2002) *The Primary English Encyclopaedia: The Heart of the Curriculum.* London: David Fulton.

Weinberger, J. (1996) *Literacy Goes to School: The Parents' Role in Young Children's Literacy Learning.* London: Paul Chapman.

White, Carolyn (1999) 'Somebody made a choice', in J. Callow (ed.) *Image Matters: Visual Texts in the Classroom.* Marrickville, Australia: PETA (Primary English Association).

Chapter 10

Information and communication technology

Computers and learning

Children are early adopters of new technology. They always have been.

(Kinnes, 2002: 50)

Children do indeed seem to be early adopters of new technology, as Kinnes remarks, but we still need to think about the quality of the electronic resources we choose from the many now available. And of course reflective practitioners give careful consideration to the ways in which we help young children to use them. Do computer games and software packages stimulate a child's imagination or do they constrain it? This is an important issue as some pre-school software is intended for children as young as two years old. Colwyn Trevarthen doubts whether computer games, however good, are the best way for children under three to learn. He would rather they were encouraged to draw, talk and interact directly with objects and people until the age of about five or six (Kinnes, 2002). We need to ask whether too much visual input at a very young age might lead to less language ability on arrival at school. A survey by The National Literacy Trust suggests that these days some children are less linguistically advanced at five than in the past. While the Trust does not settle on one cause, television and computer games tend to get some of the blame when parents and teachers talk about low concentration abilities (Bourke, 2002).

Others take a more positive view pointing out that we live in a highly technological society and that children are bound to absorb what it has to offer. So children now learn to use computers at an early age as they play with them. As I pointed out when discussing the impact of television on children's learning, the important thing is to mediate between the child and the computer, to talk about the games and programmes. Some of the most well thought of software and sites for the under-threes are listed at the end of this chapter.

While many have reservations about the use of computers by the under-threes, most people accept that the computer is establishing a place in school with every age group. Indeed, the government in the United Kingdom requires that primary teachers use ICT in teaching the core subjects, English, mathematics and science (DfEE, 1998). This chapter considers the ways in which teachers of three- to six-year-olds introduce ICT into lessons and activities to encourage creative language and learning. I consider how talk, reading and writing can be promoted and enriched by using the computer, referring to case studies showing the work of particular classes. Generally the language processes work together in children's activities, but for the sake of clarity I look at speaking and listening, reading, and writing, in turn.

Computers and the development of speaking and listening

Work on the computer in school is often collaborative and so opportunities for developing children's speaking and listening abilities arise. What, then, are some of the best contexts in which children in nursery and reception classes can develop their speaking and listening abilities round the computer? Talking about text on the screen in pairs or in groups of three or four brings reading and talking together to promote learning as we shall see later. Although children can collaborate when they look at a poem or factual account in a print source like a large book, the screen in some ways provides an easier focus for joint attention. Producing a shared written account with an adult or in a small group also generates talk, often about the options and decisions every writer has to make. Contexts involving joint attention to texts or to shared writing encourage the use of a metalanguage – 'word', 'meaning', 'sentence' and 'letter' – to talk about the literacy activities. Talk can also arise from the information on CD-ROMs and websites which teachers help young children to navigate. Some critics of too much work on the computer are concerned that young children may spend long periods without interacting with others. This need not be the case if we talk to children about their activities on the computer, and about what they are learning from a multi-media approach, from text, pictures, music and moving diagrams.

Computers and reading: software, e-books, CD-ROM and the internet

The computer has brought the possibility of acquiring new kinds of literacy, including new forms of visual literacy. Ease of navigation is one criterion to apply to CD-ROMs and computer packages for the youngest children. They also need to be helped to understand the organisation of a medium that uses scrolled and non-linear text and how interactive diagrams help their learning . It will take time and experience for a young learner to know, for example, when all the relevant information on a given topic has been seen and how it relates to the structure of the multi-media document. As Lydia Plowman points out, visualising the mainly invisible structure of the text in its entirety requires some experience and sophistication (Plowman, 1998).

Large amounts of software have been developed to help with the teaching of reading. In assessing its value in the classroom, teachers need to be convinced about the worth of particular products and the precise way in which they contribute to a child's developing literacy. For example, the educational and entertainment aspects need to be balanced. Computer-based reading resources fall into two main groups: first, there are those that help children with the 'smaller shapes' – reading skills relating to initial sounds and sound–symbol relationships – and, second, there are those which support children's understanding of the 'big shapes' – the meaning and context-related aspects of reading. The 'talking books' supporting the 'big shapes' of reading are usually in the form of stories presented on screen using written text, speech and animation. However, there is no reason why some of these texts should not be non-fiction accounts. Indeed the multi-media nature of CD-ROMs – their use of sound and animation as well as text – make them highly motivating and exciting. Children can see moving diagrams showing processes like the digestive system, the working of a machine or the hatching of a chick from an egg. The strategies for interacting with non-fiction discussed

Does the CD-ROM:

- Meet the needs for the age group it is intended for?
- Engage and entertain?
- Make imaginative use of the technology?
- Provide a suitable medium for the subject?
- Enable the user to navigate easily?
- Provide quality search systems and bookmarks?
- Offer quality content-taking account of accuracy, comprehension, creativity and interest?
- Offer quality images and audio experiences?

Figure 10.1   Questions to ask about a CD-ROM (based on BIMA guidelines, 01733 245700).

in this book – taking questions to the text, locating information and reporting orally and in writing on findings – all apply to research using CD-ROMs, software and sites on the internet.

Research so far suggests that the use of 'talking books' is best combined with the use of print resources. Medwell, for example, found that the greatest benefits were achieved when the teacher first heard children read in the traditional way and then set up small groups to use talking books (Medwell, 1998).

Computers and writing

Increasingly, children in nursery schools learn to type alongside learning to handwrite. I agree with Wyse and Jones that, exciting as the new technology is, it is unlikely to replace books, pens and paper (2001). But there are considerable advantages in children controlling word processing from an early stage. Let us look at the main ones in turn.

First, children can start to make marks on screen (perhaps using overlays) from the earliest stages in their development. Of course they will also be making marks on paper, but when they experiment with marks on the screen it is much easier for the adult to scribe to the child's dictation and they can expand an account together. Making adjustments to compositional and secretarial aspects is also easier and the child can feel in control of their writing early on.

A second advantage is the contribution the computer can make to shared writing. By the time a child moves into the reception class the collaboration is with other children as well as with the teacher. Shared writing with three or four children is much more possible when they can see the developing text on the screen together.

Third, the computer offers a large number of options about format and presentation. Young children can be helped to produce professional-looking posters, leaflets and reports using desktop publishing software. These can be brought into their play in motivating ways – making posters for the garden centre in outdoor play, or leaflets for the post office or café in the home corner.

A fourth advantage is that, with the help of a printer, several copies of a piece of writing can be made – one for the class library, one to take home and so on. So much payoff from the initial effort is likely to be motivating!

But finally, and perhaps this is the most significant thing of all, the multi-media authoring made possible by the computer allows teacher and children to combine written text with

Tyrannosaurus means 'tyrant lizard'. It was a carnivore.It lived in Asia and America. It became extinct 65 million years ago. It was a carnivore. Tyrannosaurus was as long as a tennis court. It was as heavy as an elephant It could not chew so swallowed its food whole. Its teeth were 22 centimetres long.

Faith.

Figure 10.2 Faith's dinosaur writing. Faith, at almost five years, enjoyed bringing home from school her word processed dinosaur notes – one outcome of an exciting project which included an outing to the dinosaur rooms of the Natural History Museum. The account is like a list – an early means of organising non-narrative writing – see Chapter 6.

graphics, video and animation to produce on-screen electronic books. Here children develop new kinds of literacy from an early age using the new technology and the innovations which will continue to develop through their lives.

The computer is useful as an information resource for teachers. There are many websites with reviews of books and software for particular age groups, some sites to enable teachers to share good practice, and others with resources for structuring children's writing tasks. Of course, just because a resource or idea is on a computer website does not mean it is appropriate for a particular teaching purpose. We need always to be thoughtful and critical. Publishers are increasingly bringing out combined print and ICT resources. *Spotlight on Facts* (Collins) for instance, presents some core texts for the literacy hour and for lessons across the curriculum in big book and CD-ROM format. These have been carefully thought out and can be helpful in meeting government requirements. But again, teachers should stay in control of their planning and resourcing and not be 'taken over' by even the best commercially-produced programmes.

The following case study brings us into the controversial area of using structured frames which had been downloaded to help children organise their factual writing. It is offered here to trigger reflection.

Case study 10.1: Making travel posters

Six-year-olds in year 1 at Castlecombe Primary School were making a start in geography with some work on travel, concentrating on seaside and water side locations. (Another aspect of this project forms part of my analysis discussing the use of video-film and television to be found in Chapter 9.) Here I look at the use of a resource taken from a website and link it to a wider argument about how we best help children organise their writing.

The teacher asked the children to construct a travel poster promoting a particular location. She downloaded and duplicated a writing frame that could be used to construct a poster from Educate the Children (www.educate.org.uk) to help structure the task. Each child chose a picture postcard, from a selection brought in by teachers and by members of the class, of a place that they had visited or would like to visit and stuck it at the top of the poster-writing frame. The frame was completed using the clues in the picture postcard and, in some cases, their prior knowledge of the location.

There are some issues to think about here. Opinion is divided about when, how often and even whether we should use writing frames to help very young learners. The use of a framework of headings to help children organise particular kinds of writing was revived through the research of David Wray and Maureen Lewis. One outcome of their Exeter University Extending Literacy project (EXEL) was a collection of different writing frames (Lewis and Wray, 1995). Some teachers and educationists consider it is best for children to struggle with the thinking needed to organise the shape and structure of their writing as an important part of learning. However, others believe that the occasional use of a structure provided for them can support less confident young writers in understanding the nature of the task they have been given. Lewis and Wray themselves lean towards the latter view while nevertheless believing writing frames should be sparingly and carefully used. As I thought about it, it seemed to me that the task carried out by the children in this case study involved considerable thought notwithstanding the guidance they got from the frame. After all, their task was to identify from a visual source – the post card – the most attractive features of a location and to decide how best to describe those features in words.

The role of computers in developing visual literacy

The technological age has helped create new kinds of literacy, not least visual literacies. The computer games children play can develop sensitivity to the meaning of images. CD-ROMs can have moving pictures and allow children to see function as well as structure; they can observe the movement of an engine or a machine or see the speeded up process of plant germination or the emergence of a butterfly from a chrysalis.

These new visual experiences are exciting and expand our thinking in ways we are still discovering. But we must make sure that the verbal is not marginalised by the visual – that children's language abilities continue to be developed and refined and that writing is used, as well as illustrations, to create meaning. Indeed, visual literacy is not just to do with 'reading' images, but also with seeing the connections between picture and print (Mallett, 2002). In a most interesting book Jon Callow, an Australian academic, points out that visual images can pass us by if we do not pause to reflect on and evaluate them. The increasingly 'multimodal' nature of classroom texts, drawing as many of them do on spoken, written, visual, spatial and musical modes, can be exhilarating but it can also overwhelm if time is not taken to digest them, perhaps by talking to others (Callow, 1999).

Children enjoy writing non-fiction accounts and stories on the computer, experimenting with different fonts and styles. Programmes like Magic Paintbox make it possible for them to illustrate their writing. Figure 10.4 shows six-year-old Joshua's writing and illustrating using the computer.

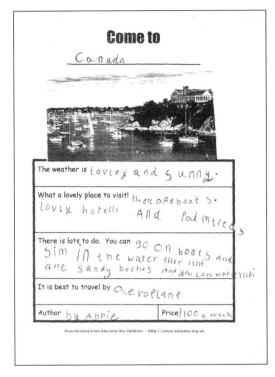

Figure 10.3   Abbie's poster. Abbie, age six, has completed the poster advertisement, choosing Canada as the desirable location.

Annotated list of software, CD-ROMs and websites

Software and CD-ROMs

Jump Ahead Preschool
2–5 years. £19.99
Includes three CD-ROMs; opens with a playroom from which different activities can be selected. Helps with English, maths and logic.

Learning Ladder Preschool
3–5 years £9.99
Interactive screens with activities and animated objects; helps with science, English, maths and logic. Children would need help with navigation.

Infant Video Toolkit
5–7 years
CD-ROM of video-based curriculum activities
There are four programmes – 2Paint, 2Graph, 2Question and 2Investigate – and 'video-ideas' to help children understand how to use the software and carry out further activities.
2Simple Educational Software
www.2simplesoftware.com

One night three baby owls woke up in their
nest. They discovered their mother owl was
gone! Their mummy was hunting for food.
Their mummy owl came back.

Figure 10.4 'The Baby Owls' by Joshua, aged six years. After hearing *Owl Babies* read out in the Shared Reading part of a literacy hour, six-year-olds typed their own 'information stories' about owls and illustrated them using Magic Paintbox.

Spark Island books, CD-ROMs and software for home learning
ABC Learning Adventures 3–5 years (book and CD-ROM)
Number Fun 3–5 years (standalone CD-ROM)
These interactive number and literacy games have simple navigation and good quality sound. Most children will need quite a lot of adult support. Some people may feel there is rather too much emphasis on tests and keeping scores for the younger end of this age-group but there is a playful approach built in.
BBC Learning (a division of BBC Worldwide) and Spark Learning. (www.bbcshop.com)

Scally's World of Verbs
3–10 years
CD-ROM, with handbook, storybook and Intellikeys keyboard for literacy activities.
Scally is a little creature who does what the child types into the computer. So the sentence 'Scally can blow' produces a picture of Scally blowing out a candle. You can opt to use the relevant verbs for reception from The National Literacy Strategy. Children can choose from a number of options, for example Watch and Say or Watch and Write, to build their understanding.
Topologika Software. www.topologika.com

Spotlight on Fact
Big books on 'Toys and Games' and 'The Seaside' for key stage 1 and CD-ROM; writing frames; notes for teachers
Collins
Well tuned in to current requirements in literacy and ICT. CD-ROM includes help with writing texts with different stylistic features.
collins www.CollinsEducation.com

Websites

www.bbc.co.uk/schools/preschool
18 months to 5 years
Pre-school games with favourite TV characters.

www.funbrain.com
18 months to 5 years
American site with games to promote literacy and numeracy.

BECTA
This is the Government lead agency for ICT in Education.
www.becta.org.uk

National Literacy Trust
Initiates and co-ordinates research. The website provides a database of current research projects on children's language development.
www.literacytrust.org.uk

N.B. Teem (Teachers Evaluating Educational Multi-media) – www.teeem.org.uk – offers evaluations by teachers of 200 CD-ROMs and 150 websites.

Summary

Children now grow up in a technological society and this affects their activities at home and school. The under-threes need to talk to adults, friends and siblings about the computer games and software they see and use, so that language abilities as well as visual kinds of literacy are developed. The same active approach is also appropriate in school so that the computer is a tool for learning, something to serve and help extend a child's learning and creativity. Electronic books, software and the internet all bring powerful information sources into the classroom. Three things are worth remembering. First, rather than replacing print resources, the new technology works alongside and complements them. Second, software, CD-ROMs and websites need to be selected and evaluated like any other resource. Third, learning with the computer needs constant mediation by teachers and peers.

References

Bourke, Alison (2002) 'Ways to improve children's ability to concentrate', *Five to Seven*. Vol. 2, no. 3, July.
Callow, J. (ed.) (1999) *Image Matters: Visual Texts in the Classroom*. Marrickville, Australia: PETA (Primary English Association).
DfEE (1998) *Teaching: High Status, High Standards*. London: HMSO (includes details of the ICT competence required by trainees in the use of ICT in the core subjects).
Kinnes, Sally (2002) 'Are you raising a techno tot?', *The Sunday Times Culture*. 8 September, pages 49–50.
Lewis, Maureen and Wray, David (1995) *Developing Children's Non-fiction Writing: Working with Writing Frames*. Leamington Spa: Scholastic.
Mallett, Margaret (2002) *The Primary English Encyclopaedia: The Heart of the Curriculum*. London: David Fulton.

Medwell, Jane (1998) 'The talking book project: some further insights into the use of talking books to develop reading', *Reading.* May.

Plowman, Lydia (1998) 'Reading multi-media texts: learning how CD-ROM texts work', *Language Matters.* Spring.

Wyse, Dominic and Jones, Russell (2001) *Teaching English, Language and Literacy.* London: Routledge (see chapter 28).

Chapter 11

The role of fiction in informational learning

Securing a personal foothold

> We find teachers and children often using fiction and non-fiction flexibly to learn about the world and human experience.
>
> (Mallett, 1999: 112)

This book has concentrated on texts whose function is informational, texts we call non-fiction, and their role in children's learning from the very earliest stages. But children also learn about the world from stories, poems and picturebooks. They do this whenever they read and discuss stories, whether at home or at school. However, while teachers never forget that stories are first and foremost read for sheer pleasure and enjoyment, in this chapter I want to consider the role of fiction when used in the context of informational learning and to explore how stories and information books can be combined in fruitful ways.

I take up three aspects of this that I think are important. First, I argue that fiction helps children gain a personal foothold in new learning right across the curriculum. Second, I suggest that stories sometimes create the passionate involvement that leads young children to ask profound questions and to genuinely care about finding some answers. If this degree of interest can be inspired by fiction, then children may be spurred on to the kind of thinking and researching which leads to constructing an argument much sooner than was previously thought possible. (The National Literacy Strategy, for instance, only introduces argument as a text type for children aged ten years and above). Third, I suggest that illustrations in picturebooks and storybooks may have an important role in integrating children's learning from different kinds of text.

The three case studies show how the contribution of fiction to learning can be realised in imaginative practice. The annotated booklist at the end of the chapter suggests some stories which could help involve children in their work on particular topics and themes.

Fiction to gain a personal foothold in new learning

Children need some inspiration if they are to become truly involved in their learning. There is nothing like a story to invite us into a new topic and show us its human side (Glen, 1987). Reading the story might come as the new work begins or later to energise a series of lessons or even to provide a satisfying end to the work. I have often heard it said that girls in particular find subjects like science and geography more inviting if they are grounded in a personally meaningful context. But in my experience boys are just as likely to benefit from such inviting ways into work as a story or picturebook. Boys and girls in a reception class were inspired to write a variety of non-fiction texts using *Bob the Builder* as a starting point. Their teacher,

Helen Bromley, produced a letter (saying it was from Bob) explaining that he had left the tool shed window open and all the notices from his board had blown away. The children greatly enjoyed writing the shopping lists, receipts for building materials and notes from customers likely to be on a builder's notice board (Bromley, 2002).

In Chapter 1, I set out a simple model of how we might integrate secondary sources (and particularly information books) into a series of lessons and activities on a particular topic. After helping children to talk about their existing or 'prior' knowledge I suggested that some kind of new, shared experience could inspire interest and take the work forward by encouraging children to formulate their own questions. Sometimes listening to a story or poem before turning to information texts can provide just this kind of inspiring new experience. I have observed and talked to a number of teachers and student teachers who have use Diane Sheldon's *The Whales' Song* as an introduction to a study of living things. Children empathise with Lucy – a young girl who visits her grandmother who lives by the sea. Lucy learns from her grandmother that whales are remarkable creatures which communicate with each other in the ocean. Another character in the story, Uncle Frederick, has a contrasting view about the creatures and their relationship with human beings, seeing them as useful 'for their oil and for their blubber'. Following Lucy's experiences, thoughts and feelings provides a personal step into a study of whales and other sea creatures who may be in danger of extinction. I think a story of great imaginative appeal like this one encourages reflection on conservation issues more powerfully than an average children's information book as it shows that people care passionately about their environment. Such stories can encourage children to look at more scientific texts and can inspire their own writing.

Affective and imaginative approaches to learning are just as important as the factual and analytic. Indeed a main theme in this chapter is that they can be complementary. If you would like to read further about the imaginative and affective I recommend the books of Kieron Egan, particularly *Primary Understanding* which argues that story is a powerful tool for understanding the world and our feelings about experience (Egan, 1988).

Bruner's later work also draws attention to the role of story and its contribution to both intellectual and affective aspects of development. In *Actual Minds, Possible Worlds* Bruner explores the implications of fiction as a way of imagining the possible as well as dealing with the actual (Bruner, 1986). If you are interested to read about how the imaginations of five-year-olds learning about sea creatures were fired by *The Whales' Song* and other stories and how this humanised and energised their science work, you can read an analysis in 'Were dinosaurs bigger than whales?' (Doyle and Mallett, 1994).

While stories awaken interest in most subjects, including history and geography, they are particularly valuable in humanising science lessons. Nursery age children in case study 11.1 are drawn into a study of the five senses by a series of picturebooks that use interesting characters and humour to draw in the young learners.

Fiction can stir a passion to find out

Real learning, particularly in the case of the very young, happens when they feel strong interest and fascination. The very best picture and storybooks can generate these feelings. They do not tell of the cosy or bland, but about things as they are. This means some of the rawer kinds of human experience shape the story. Not only did *The Whales' Song* encourage the children to think about endangered species and how human behaviour affects them, they were also inspired to care about the natural world and to ask the sort of questions that they needed to be helped to take to informational sources. 'How big are the biggest whales?'; 'How many babies do they have at a time?'; 'How can we help whales to survive?' The teacher had to read to them from adult reference and information books to find convincing answers to these questions.

The children in case study 11.2 were also motivated to acquire the study skills to find out more from informational sources – in this case after sharing that striking picturebook, Anthony Browne's *Zoo*. This made them think for the first time about how far the routines and the circumstances in which animals are kept in zoos could be construed as 'cruel'. The teacher skilfully used the children's strong feelings aroused by the story not only to find the answers to their questions from information sources, but also to attempt that most challenging of tasks, to construct a powerfully persuasive piece of writing. For me the significance of this case study is that such young children could be helped to do something difficult and not altogether natural: to assemble evidence, to analyse and assess that evidence and then to construct an argument not only in discussion but also in writing. Fiction, skilfully introduced by the teacher, is shown to be amazingly powerful in engaging children's interest and accelerating their intellectual and affective progress.

Illustrations to link fact and fiction

Sometimes the illustrations in a picturebook or storybook provide the spur for turning to information sources. A particular image can intrigue, stimulate or even disturb children as we see in case study 11.2. Here we see the effect on children of the pictures of caged animals and of a caged boy in a dream.

The best picturebooks often show carefully researched landscapes, historical scenes or environments which lead to the sort of questions which can only be answered by non-fiction texts (Graham,1996). A book such as the Ahlbergs' *Peepo!* with its authentic scenes of Edwardian life would be a good starting point for young children to think about how people lived in the past and about the things they used, things like large perambulators and wooden clothes horses. Where stories are used to introduce topics in history, science or geography, information sources can be provided to answer specific questions.

We must remember that today young children bring a high degree of visual literacy to their reading. They will have seen pictures on television, on the computer, in magazines and on posters and vehicles. We should exploit this visual sophistication and awareness by linking image and the written word in their reading and learning. Talking about illustrations extends and sensitises children's use of language. So while the picturebook *Emeka's Gift: An African Counting Story* by Ifeoma Onyefulu presents an interesting narrative – Emeka journeys to give his grandmother a present – the vibrant photographs of children's games, markets and people's occupations encourage discussion. There is much to learn about an African rural environment as well as about the social and cultural aspects of Kenyan village life. Two pictures show the making of a mortar and pestle – crucial equipment for people who grind much of their food. Children can talk about how the wood carver hollows out a piece of wood from a tree to make the mortar, and how the pestle is carefully shaped by special tools.

The role of storybook illustrations in extending children's vocabulary is further explored in case study 11.3 where children, inspired by two picturebooks – *Peace At Last* and *Can't You Sleep, Little Bear* – talk about light sources at night and in daytime.

Case studies

I want to illustrate the points made in this chapter by presenting three case studies. In the first, 11.1, which is in a nursery setting, we see how a number of stories threaded through children's early science work on the five senses greatly enhancing their enjoyment and understanding. The stories with their exciting characters added the human and personal interest needed to keep the children's attention. The second case study, 11.2, shows how six-year-olds in a year 1 class, fired by the image of a caged lion in a picturebook, were helped to present an argument for and against keeping creatures in zoos. In 11.3 we find five-year-olds invited into science work on light sources by the illustrations of night and day in two appealing picturebooks.

Case study 11.1: The five senses. Fiction threads through a science project, supporting a personal foothold and extending vocabulary.

Claire Vickers used stories and poems with three- to four-year-olds in a Deptford nursery school to support five weeks of early science work round the five senses, part of a broader theme, 'ourselves', which over a term included mathematics, history and dance. Two nursery nurses as well as the teacher worked with the class of 27 children. The science activities were carried out in groups of four, but when they listened to stories the whole class came together.

The broad aim was to increase children's awareness of themselves and their environment by developing skills of investigation and description. What is of interest here is the role of story and poetry in inviting children into the topics, in encouraging them to share ideas and in adding human interest. Let us join the class when they began work on the five senses.

A first point to note is Claire's skill in interleaving stories with practical tasks. As all who work with the very young know, young children enjoy, indeed need, a great deal of activity and practical work to keep interested and alert in their learning. The dynamic start to the whole notion of the five senses was the action story *Eyes, nose, fingers and toes* by Judy Hindley. With welcome humour this story helps children think about the their sense organs and how those organs make it possible to experience the world and what is in it. Claire guided a lively discussion: we must never underestimate the role of talk in bringing the insights in stories alive and in sharing them. Then, as touch was the first sense to be investigated, the children (in self-selected groups of four) took turns to take objects from a drawstring bag (a 'feely bag') to describe them to the others and attempt to identify them by touch alone. The children were encouraged to use some of the vocabulary from their discussion inspired by the story – 'hard', 'smooth', 'rough' and to use mathematical language like 'less', 'more', 'on', 'inside' and language of comparison, for example 'this is softer than the first object'.

The mutual enrichment of story and practical task was also evident later when the children tasted and identified crisps of different flavours. They were helped to put the results of a survey of their favourite flavours on a simple computer database using Information Workshop. Claire then made a large graph to show how information – in this case about crisp flavour preferences – can be communicated by diagram. This made a contribution to the children's understanding of the purposes of different kinds of text and illustration. Then, to change the focus and to help think about taste preferences in a different way, they shared the story *What Can Pinky Taste?* This led to using a vocabulary refined by the language they had used while doing the practical tasks to compare their favourite tastes with Pinky's. Reading a carefully chosen story at the end of a series of tasks and activities can serve an integrating role, helping children bring together their insights.

Another thing that occurred to me when thinking about the role of story in Claire's work was how she used the power of humour to bring energy and enjoyment and how she often chose entertaining stories as a way of inviting children to relate their own anecdotes. For example, one of the books used to introduce the sense of sight – *Brown Bear, Brown Bear, What do you see?* by Bill Martin Jr and Eric Carle – teased the children by picturing a startlingly blue horse and a deliciously purple cat alongside more conventionally coloured creatures like a green frog and a yellow duck. Children learn early on that things and events in the inner world of the imagination are not bounded by the rules of the real world. Interestingly, they seem able to step easily from one domain to another and have little difficulty with books which do so. In this case the children were able to enjoy the joke, remarking that their pet cats were not purple, but toy cats could be.[1]

I mentioned earlier that talk with the teacher and other children can help children find personal meaning in a story that then enriches their understanding of a topic. This was certainly the case when the children heard *Brown Bear, Brown Bear, What do you see?* The frontispiece, a blazing pattern of stripes in red, orange, blue, yellow and so on encouraged the children to share their own anecdotes about favourite colours. The discussion moved to more general questions about why animals are the colours they are which led to some talk about the concept of camouflage to protect against predators. The teacher felt the story and pictures and above all the discussion about the story encouraged a more sensitive vocabulary about colour – 'darker than', 'pale', 'bright' and 'match'. Although it did not happen in this case, the children could have moved on to information sources about colour mixing, rainbows and so on.

Another observation is to do with timing, with the placing of the stories in each step of the work programme. Sometimes stories fit best once work is underway. For example, in week 3, when hearing was the theme, the teacher began by taking the children on a listening walk, inviting them to list all the things they heard – birdsong, car engines and so on before reading two stories with a hearing theme. The first story, *What Can Pinky Hear?*, a well loved 'flap' book by Lucy Cousins, gave the children a chance to compare what they had heard with Pinky's experiences. Then *Whose Ears?* by David Bennett brought a chance to use the language of comparison and a welcome touch of humour to exploring ears and the world of sound.

Of course, this short case study cannot do justice to so rich and full a programme. As in other good early years work, the stories were both integrated into the children's other activities and read aloud for sheer pleasure. The shared experience of listening to them gave rise to much talk and use of new vocabulary. Claire noted that in the 'story listening' context, several of the children showed a marked improvement in their ability to listen to the contributions of others. Yu Ying and Katamu, both rather shy children just coming up to age four, began to make links between the story and the activities they had carried out and to make their thoughts explicit. In early science work it seems that stories can place new experiences in a human context and greatly help young children's learning and progress.

Case study 11.2: Should we keep animals in zoos? A picturebook inspires empathy and helps children construct an argument.

In this work, which was part of a larger 'living things' theme, we note how an image in a picturebook, Zoo *by Anthony Browne, awakened the interest and concern of six-year-old children about the ethics of keeping animals in zoos. This led to them becoming passionate enough about the issues to begin to construct arguments in talk and writing, turning to secondary sources for supportive evidence (Riley and Reedy 2000).*

Following the model of reading and writing non-fiction in Mallett (1992), Reedy helped the children to organise their prior knowledge about zoos through discussion, and then capturing the points made on a white board. The children listed zoo animals, described the role of the zoo keeper and mentioned animals were often caged. Nothing controversial emerged. Then, to try to suggest that there were some possible ethical issues, Reedy read *Zoo*, a picturebook by Anthony Browne, which raises issues about how far the animals were 'happy' in the zoo. Two things in the story seemed particularly to disturb the children. First, the mother of the family said 'Poor thing' about the picture of the caged tiger shown pacing up and down. Second, one of the boys was shown having a dream about being caged himself and this brought things to a personal level very sharply. Some of the children commented that they would not like to be put in a cage!

So it seems we may start to respond to and want to learn about things when we are troubled by an issue. Perhaps something does not quite fit with our beliefs about the world and we need to discover more about it to feel comfortable. It was Piaget who saw that children's learning was energised when they experienced this state of discomfort which he calls 'disequilibrium'. As Reedy comments, genuine learning tends to take place when 'a person's current certainties are thrown off balance by new information or by the challenge of a difficult question'. This feeling of disequilibrium can only be eased by finding out more in an effort to understand. Almost every topic has a controversial aspect and it is this which stimulates us to find out more.

I recommend you read the full account of the case study in Riley and Reedy 2000 as here I can only give a brief account of a most interesting series of lessons. Reedy points out that to control the argument genre we have to recognise the likely counter-arguments and have some way of dealing with them. So he scribed the children's comments under the headings 'Good for animals' and 'Bad for animals'. The children constructed their own short accounts setting out some preliminary ideas on good points about zoos, for example 'The animals get fed' and bad things 'they are taken away from their countries'.

To deepen their understanding the children needed to do some research. So, again following the model in Mallett 1992, Reedy helped the children to formulate questions to take to information books from the school and public libraries. Formulating their own questions enabled the children to judge whether the books were likely to illuminate their questions. They did this by being guided to the contents pages and indexes. After their book-based research and, importantly, after a lot of discussion and sharing of views and discoveries, the children were ready to write more detailed accounts presenting an argument. At this stage the children used a writing frame based on the persuasive writing frame of Wray and Lewis set out in their book *Extending Literacy: Children Reading and Writing Non-fiction* (Wray and Lewis, 1997). Pressing a writing frame, a set of headings to guide the structure and content of a piece of writing, on the very young may inhibit their efforts to organise their thinking for themselves. However, Reedy introduced the frame after the children had already done a great deal of thinking, reading and talking and it seemed likely it would be useful in helping children to further control and shape their persuasive writing.

This is a powerful example of how quite young children can be moved on dramatically both intellectually and affectively by fiction. Indeed Reedy's description and analysis of his *Zoo* work shares with us one of the finest examples of exciting early years literacy work that I have encountered in a lifetime of teaching, research and reflection on these issues.

Case Study 11.3: Pictures linking fact and fiction. Five-year-olds begin to learn about light sources by sharing *Peace at Last* and *Can't You Sleep, Little Bear?*

Jane Boyd chose two picturebooks as a starting point for work in science on light sources, both in day time and at night. Pictures and text work together perfectly in each book to inspire thinking and discussion.

Both these picturebooks tell a human story and help children get a personal foothold in thinking about day and night. But in each case it is the illustrations which provide the interesting and detailed information that extends the written text. *Peace At Last* was read first: it begins with a wonderful picture of a night time landscape and, as Jane had hoped, quickly focused the children's discussion and questions. They noticed the different sources of light – the moon and stars and the lights in the houses spilling out onto the lawn. The children 'read' the pictures which provided a huge amount of information to savour and discuss, the kind of information that would take many words to explain. For example the children identified things that were distinctive of night time, things like the baby bear's reassuring night light, the pictures of the family's night time drinks, the tired faces and body language of the family and the nocturnal creatures – bats, owls, hedgehogs and cats – glimpsed through the window. Jane pointed out the contrast between pictures showing the thin quality of the moon's silvery light on the objects in the kitchen giving the mysterious atmosphere of night time, and those at the end of the book showing the bright light of the sun shining into the bedroom and onto morning things like cups of tea and the post.

In the book read second, *Can't You Sleep, Little Bear?*, the children identified a light source which also gives warmth – fire. As in *Peace at Last* there are helpful and appealing pictures of day time and night time landscapes. But, above all, the children got the point that it is difficult to make artificial light as bright as sunshine. They noted that Big Bear brings larger and larger lanterns to illuminate baby bear's sleeping area in the large dark cave with only limited success.

The illustrations in these picturebooks provided a dynamic start to this science project. It was motivating for the children to see the night and day time landscapes and objects in the context of stories where they could identify with the characters. Fiction was a very effective way to introduce the contrast between the atmosphere and sensations of day and night and the very human fear of the dark. The illustrations helped the children to extend their language, using terms like 'darker', 'shadow', 'nocturnal', 'dusk', 'dawn', 'light source', 'glowing' and 'beaming' in their discussion. They also formulated questions which were adapted to take to information sources and were the basis of simple science experiments. For example: 'Where does day light come from?' 'What are the different sources of light at night time?' 'Why is it so dark near Little Bear?' 'What difference will having a bigger lantern make?' 'How are shadows formed?'

Many interesting activities followed – carrying out simple experiments with light beams and candles, putting up displays of objects with labels, going on shadow walks and making collages of the same scene in daylight and at night time. It was significant how well the illustrations in these two fine picturebooks linked with children's research in information sources and with their factual writing. They returned to the picturebook illustrations throughout the work to resavour them and remind themselves of what they had learned.

Here picturebooks were used to enhance work on a science theme but we can find stories to enrich all the other primary curriculum subjects.[2] The list at the end of this chapter makes some suggestions.

Teacher's and children's own imaginative creations as a starting point for all kinds of writing

This chapter has concentrated on using published stories as a starting point for informational learning. But quite often children, with the teacher's help, create their own characters and stories and these can be an extremely powerful impetus into writing – both stories and non-fiction. My visits to many classrooms have shown me what can be achieved when such involving contexts are created. For example, a small dressed bear called William encouraged

Figure 11.1   Cover illustration Barbara Firth. Reproduced from *Can't You Sleep, Little Bear?* By permission of Walker Books Ltd.

reception children to write him letters, make birthday cards and even design a passport. The children's parents took an interest as well and often sent in clothes for William for different seasons and favourite recipes. Bear characters seem particularly well liked by both boys and girls – one named Cocoa in a Scottish reception class was always getting lost and the children made posters and wrote letters to help find him. They wrote down all the things Cocoa enjoyed when it was their turn to take him home for the weekend. The six-years-olds we joined in *Mr Togs the Tailor* had a 'human' context in which to write for a huge range of purposes – burglar alarm instructions, travel brochures, family trees, bills and inventories for the shop. Another character I remember was a panda that needed things to be explained to him very carefully in conversation, pictures and writing if he was to understand. One of the most exciting examples I know of involved a huge blue whale which answered questions by letter. The whale was made out of wire and papier mâché by five-year-olds after a visit to the whale hall in the National History Museum. 'Bluey' directed the children to the information books which would help answer their questions about how many babies whales had, what they ate and how they communicated.

Annotated list of fiction as a starting point for learning

Burglar Bill
By Janet and Allan Ahlberg
Heinemann
Bill and Betty are burglars who decide to change their ways once they have a baby. One of my students dressed up as Burglar Betty after four-year-olds had heard the story read to

them, and invited the children to ask her questions about her change of heart. Then, using a flip chart, the teacher wrote down the children's list of reasons why burglary is wrong. Older children, about age six, enjoy being helped with the following: notices giving a list of things to do to protect your home; letters from burglars apologising for the theft; posters warning of burglar activity in an area; letters to newspapers asking for return of stolen items.

Peepo!
By Janet and Allan Ahlberg
Puffin
A young child, growing up in an Edwardian family, surveys from his cot, pram and highchair his family and his surroundings. Each picture shows objects like the clothes horse, brass bed and coal house, giving the flavour of the period. The texture of life for an ordinary family at this time is brilliantly portrayed and so the book is a perfect introduction to history.

Bringing the Rain to Kapiti Plain
By Verna Aardema
McMillan Children's Books
In this Kenyan folk tale Ki Pat, a young African herd boy, helps to end a terrible drought. The illustrations of plants deprived of water lead easily to discussion about what growing things need to survive and so this book leads easily into a discussion of science concepts.

Whose Ears?
By David Bennett
Mammoth (out of print at present, but obtainable from public libraries)
An amusing book of contrasts which would support work on the senses.

Bob the Builder at www.bobthebuilder.com
Story characters can often provide a context for children's non-narrative kinds of writing. In an inspiring article, Helen Bromley describes how she used *Bob the Builder* to encourage the children in a reception class to write the shopping lists, receipts and notes likely to be found on a builder's notice board (Bromley, 2002).

Zoo
By Anthony Browne
Red Fox
As shown in case study 11.2, this thought-provoking picturebook can lead to profound thinking and discussion about the ethical issues surrounding keeping animals in cages.

Fran's Flowers
By Lisa Bruce and Rosalind Beardshaw
Bloomsbury Children's Books
This simple story about a young child's efforts to get a plant to grow, helped by her pet dog, shows the patience needed to nurture a developing shoot. This would be an appealing story to read to children growing seeds and plants in science lessons.

What Can Pinky Hear?
By Lucy Cousins
Walker Books
An exciting and colourful flap book which helped bring alive the work on hearing in case study 11.1. (There are similar books in the series on taste, smell, touch and sight.)

First Flight: Butterfly
By Sarah Fanelli, illustrated by Chris Biggs
Jonathan Cape
An unusual picturebook with beautiful collage illustrations, this tells the story of a butterfly who struggles to get airborne. Children learn about life cycles, about the interplay between print and image and about travelling. It appeals to young imaginations and may lead to exciting letter-writing or e-mails, to art work and to forays into information books.

Going Shopping
By Sarah Garland
Puffin
Particularly helpful to start discussion about familiar settings, this 'information story' would help children get a personal foothold in geographical ideas about the location of their own nearest shops and making simple maps to get there.

Eyes, nose, fingers, toes
By Judy Hindley
Walker Books
This interactive book is a favourite in nurseries and helped provide a dynamic start to the work on the five senses in case study 11.1.

The Colour of Home
By Mary Hoffman, illustrated by Karin Littlewood
Frances Lincoln
This story about a young refugee child helps children of about six years to understand the human issues involved in adapting to a new country under difficult circumstances. It could also be a starting point for work on different environments and for understanding emotional aspects of colour in the context of work on a 'colour' theme – Hassan paints vibrant pictures of his home in Somalia.

Rosie's Walk
By Pat Hutchins
Puffin
This supports early geographical concepts as it uses directional language to describe a journey round a particular environment – a farmyard. Simple maps and models could follow.

Barnaby Bear Goes to Brittany
By Elaine Jackson
The Geography Association
(www.geographyshop.org.uk)

Figure 11.2   From *The Colour of Home* by Mary Hoffman, illustrated by Karin Littlewood, published by Frances Lincoln Limited 2002. Text © Mary Hoffman, illustrations © Karin Littlewood 2002.

One of a series of books about Barnaby and his travels. Identifying with the experiences of a young animal helps children bridge the gap between the known and the unknown and is an excellent way of helping them develop a concept of place.

Goodbye Mog
By Judith Kerr
Collins
Bereavement is tackled with a light touch here and the book would lead to talk about how we cope when someone dies. Mog leaves happy memories behind as the family get to know a new kitten.

Brown Bear, Brown Bear, What do you see?
By Bill Martin Jr, illustrated by Eric Carle
Puffin
This large brightly coloured picturebook asks the same question throughout – What do you see? – and at the end brings all the children and all the animals together in vibrant double spreads. It approaches seeing and colour with a dollop of humour: children in case study 11.1 loved the blue horse and the purple cat.

Peace At Last
By Jill Murphy
McMillan Children's Books

Based on Father Bear's problems in getting to sleep, this story is a favourite to use in a block of work on 'nocturnal animals', 'night and day' and on 'ourselves' – particularly sound in 'the five senses'. In case study 11.3 the book enriches work on natural and artificial light sources.

Emeka's Gift: An African Counting Story
By Ifeoma Onyefulu
Frances Lincoln
This unusual book is an information story presenting fine photographs of African village life. There is a narrative about a little boy trying to choose a gift to take to his grandmother and information boxes to tell us about the artefacts, culture and lifestyle of the people. As well as being a counting book, this would be a valuable early geography book or, of course, an engaging story for its own sake.

The Whales' Song
By Diane Sheldon and G. Blythe
Hutchinson
Lucy is faced with two starkly different views of the world in general and whales in particular. This favourite picturebook is sometimes used to make children aware of environmental issues in geography and in science.

The Toymaker
By Martin Waddell and Terry Milne
Walker Books
The story in this picturebook has a long time scale. It starts with a toymaker producing toys for his daughter. In the second part of the book we meet the daughter as an old lady with a grand-daughter. She takes the young girl back to the shop where they find the dolls made long ago. This book helps children with historical ideas. They can make a simple chronology of events and also, using the pictures of the toys in the early part of the book, can compare how toys were made and looked when the old lady was young and how toys are made and look now.

Can't You Sleep, Little Bear?
By Martin Waddell and Barbara Firth
Walker Books
When Little Bear is put to bed in the dark part of the cave he is frightened and cannot sleep. Big Bear tries to make the cave lighter with lanterns. This beautifully illustrated picturebook can help start off topics in several different subject areas. For example, it would be an inspiring start to scientific themes like 'night and day' or to design and technology projects like 'making homes for animals' or to PSHE (Personal, social and health education) discussions about caring for others and anticipating their needs.

Summary

This chapter establishes the powerful role of fiction as an initiating and often sustaining force for different kinds of learning. There is nothing like a carefully chosen story to provide the human interest that helps children feel a genuine urge to care and find out about some subject or issue. Sometimes it is the authentic and striking illustrations of a story, particularly of course if it is a picturebook, that encourage children to want to find out more. Sometimes it is the quality of the text and the paradoxes and issues it raises which engage the children's interest and stimulate the questions which can only be answered by turning to informational sources. Once genuine interest is awakened, children are willing to acquire hard-won research and study skills to take their understanding further. They see a point in writing their findings and thoughts down. Talking about their thoughts and research findings with peers and teacher helps young children become able to understand there are different viewpoints about almost every topic. They are entitled to develop their own perspective and, where enough passion and curiosity are generated, construct an argument, first in discussion and then in writing.

Notes

1   This reminds me of a piece of writing by a six-year-old – a short recount of the class visit to a zoo. The brief narrative was structured by a selection of events during the outing but ended dramatically with something like: 'And then I got on my elephant and rode all the way back to school'. The piece is no longer in my possession, but I remember it was accompanied by a delightful illustration of the writer riding the elephant out of the zoo gates. When the writing was read out in circle time another child remarked that the bit at the end 'did not really happen'. The young writer replied 'No, but it happened in my mind.'
2   The Geography Association has produced a series of books using the device of a small bear's travels to different countries. Teachers may have seen episodes from the books on the BBC's *Watch* series for schools. For details of the Barnaby Bear books, big books, puppet and games, for children aged about six to seven years, visit the Geography Association's website www.geographyshop.org.uk or telephone 0114 296 0088. For a reflective article by Paula Richardson on how to use the resources, see *The Primary English Magazine* NATE, Vol. 7, no. 5, June 2002, pages 8–12.

References

Bromley, H. (2002) 'Can you fix it for Bob the Builder?', *The Primary English Magazine*, NATE. Vol. 8, no. 1, October, pages 12–16.

Bruner, Jerome (1986) *Actual Minds, Possible Worlds.* Cambridge, MA: The MIT Press.

Doyle, Kathleen and Mallett, Margaret (1994) 'Were dinosaurs bigger than whales?', *TACTYC Early Years Journal.* Vol. 14, no. 2, Spring.

Egan, Kieron (1988) *Primary Understanding: Education in Early Childhood.* London: Routledge.

Glen, Pat (1987) *Mr Togs the Tailor: A Context for Writing.* Scotland: The Scotland Consultative Council on the Curriculum.

Graham, Judith (1996) 'Using illustration as the bridge between fact and fiction', *English in Education.* Vol. 30, no. 1.

Mallett, Margaret (1992) *Making Facts Matter: Reading Non-fiction 5–11.* London: Paul Chapman.

Mallett, Margaret (1999) *Young Researchers: Informational Reading and Writing in the Early and Primary Years.* London: Routledge.

Riley, Jeni and Reedy, David (2000) *Developing Writing for Different Purposes: Teaching about Genre in the Early Years.* London: Paul Chapman.

Wray, David and Lewis, Maureen (1997) *Extending Literacy: Children Reading and Writing Non-fiction.* London: Routledge.

Glossary of terms relevant to non-fiction reading and writing

Note: Full details of the texts cited in the glossary are included in the Bibliography.

Affective development is to do with the maturing of the emotions and feelings, and complements intellectual or cognitive development. Nearly all learning has an affective aspect which draws on our response as human beings to a topic or an issue. Learning about animals can involve children's concerns about their welfare or perhaps even the survival of a species.

Analytic competence is a term used by J. Bruner in *Towards a Theory of Instruction* to refer to the ability to learn from written texts (Bruner 1967: 284). I rarely see this term used now, but I think it is useful to explain that special concentration we bring when we try to understand something we are reading about. Such effort brings within our range concepts and ideas which are relatively context-free. Discussion around reading with parents and teachers helps children to acquire this mode of thinking (see also 'disembedded' thinking).

Argument is a reasoned analysis for or against a proposition or point of view. Quite young children can begin to think in this way if their interest and concern is engaged (see zoo project, Chapter 11).

Assimilation and accommodation are the central processes in Piaget's adaptive model of learning. When an individual is faced by new learning – in the form of unfamiliar objects, people or events, new situations or ideas in books – two complementary and simultaneous processes are set in motion. These are assimilation, which means the absorption into general schema of a specific piece of new learning, and accommodation, which is to do with the modification of internal structures to fit a changing cognizance of reality. Piaget used the metaphor of the digestive system to explain the processes: food mixes with digestive juices to become capable of assimilation, and the organs of digestion adjust so that accommodation (of the nutrients) is possible.

Piaget believed we have a self-regulatory mechanism which he called 'equilibrium'. Children lose equilibrium when curiosity is aroused and return to a state of equilibrium when new knowledge which satisfies their need is incorporated into their understanding. An adult explaining something is most likely to help a return to equilibrium, but a good information book can play a part too. Piaget's dynamic view of a child constructing their world contrasted with the behaviourist's view of the child as a relatively passive responder to stimuli. Although Piaget never claimed to direct classroom practice, his model of learning has profound implications for practitioners. His work is mentioned less these days probably because he underplayed the role of the adult and of language in children's learning. Yet his model of learning is convincing and useful, particularly if we add more recent insights about the role spoken language can play.

Bias in children's books may refer to an imbalance in the whole collection, one viewpoint or one kind of experience of the world dominating, or to unwelcome stereotyping in individual texts, for example of race, gender or class.

'Big shapes' is a term which refers to the larger textual structures which provide a framework for the reading process. Chapter 7 considers the global features, or 'big shapes' of narrative and non-narrative texts. These overarching textual structures are reflected in the 'rhythms and tunes' of the written text and identify it with a genre (see Barrs and Thomas *The Reading Book* CLPE, 1991: 6). The term 'big shapes' can also be used more generally to refer to larger structures in bodies of knowledge. Information texts need to include enough interpretative writing to relate the small events and details they contain to the larger bodies of knowledge of which they are part (Meek, 1996: chapter 7).

Bilingualism may be used to refer to equal competence in two languages as speakers, readers and writers, to much greater competence in one language or to incomplete competence in either. Gregory suggests the term 'emergent bilinguals' to apply to children beginning on the journey towards competence in a second language (Gregory, 1996: 8).

Blurb is the writing on the back covers of books which tells potential readers about content and style.

Brochures are a significant kind of print in our culture and can explain about travel, products and so on. They can enhance children's role play – for example if the home corner becomes a restaurant, travel agency or pet shop.

Captions are titles or short annotations accompanying drawings, photographs and diagrams in non-fiction texts. It should be clear which illustrations each explanatory caption refers to. Cluttered pages can confuse.

Catalogue refers to a list, often in the form of a booklet, which sets out items for sale or mail order. Bibliographic catalogues provide the contents of a library or libraries.

CD-ROM stands for Compact Disk-Read Only Memory. CD-ROMs are disks which are read by a computer system and often combine a number of media – text, video and sound. They offer a different experience to reading print – short film extracts can demonstrate processes like a machine working or a creature emerging from its egg.

Chart refers to a kind of diagram which usually has a numerical element. Charts found in children's geography books show variations in temperature and population while those in history books might show family tress and timelines.

Chronological non-fiction see **narrative non-fiction** and **information story**

Cognitive development refers to the growth of the intellect and the capacity to know and to perceive. Piaget, Bruner and Vygotsky are three major figures in the history of developmental psychology, writing about the stages of development through which children pass and the competencies they acquire. One major issue in their work is the role they give to language in children's development and meaning-making.

Cognitive frames are structured headings which help to show two or more positions in an argument. There is an example of a simple cognitive frame in *Developing Writing for Different Purposes*: to help the children think of the pros and cons of keeping animals in zoos, the teacher put headings on the chalk board – 'Good for animals' and 'Bad for animals' (Riley and Reedy, 2000).

Cohesion helps create what linguists call 'textuality' – the sense that we have a text, something continuous and linked, rather than a random group of sentences. Cohesive links or ties can be used at sentence level by using conjunctions ('and', 'but') and adverbs ('soon', 'there'). One way of achieving cohesion at text level is by using pronouns such as 'he', 'she', 'they', which help a reader make referential connections to earlier parts of the text. There are a large number of connectives and cohesive ties which are used differently according to the particular kind of text. To give one example, a procedural text like a set of instructions to use machinery might achieve cohesion by numbering or bullet pointing the steps.

Communities of learners occur in classrooms where children are encouraged to share their research into topics with an interested and immediate audience – the teacher and the other children in the class. Co-operation and sharing develops this community spirit which enables children to become young researchers, caring about and sharing what they find out. Children like their teacher to have a hobby, interest or special expertise to share with them. Stephanie Harvey describes how one of her colleagues used 'wonder books', books in which children wrote and illustrated about their interests and passions, as a basis for sharing their enthusiasms and discoveries (Harvey, 1998).

Compositional aspects of writing include getting ideas, selecting vocabulary and grammar. Frank Smith in his book *Writing and the Writer* distinguished these creative aspects of writing from the secretarial or transcriptional aspects (Smith, 1982).

Concept mapping is a way of accessing and organising prior knowledge, particularly when a new topic is being introduced. A teacher might use a chalk board, white board or flip chart to write down all the concepts children can think of about a certain topic. So 'volcanoes' might produce a concept map which includes eruption, extinct, lava, Pompeii, heat, cinders, steam and gases. Concept maps can be lists or set out as webs to show the dynamic relationship between ideas.

Conferencing refers to the planning talk teachers share with one child or a group of children to support a writing task. The notion is associated with the work of Donald Graves who, in his book *Writing: Teachers and Children at Work*, sets out the principles of a process approach to writing (Graves, 1983). This approach values the stages which a writer goes through as well as the end product. Conferencing can go beyond the planning stage to when children are ready to read aloud and to review their first drafts with the teacher. Children may also want to have a conference with their teacher about which writing samples should go in their portfolio.

Constructivism is a theory of learning in which, it is claimed, we form mental representations or 'constructions' from our experience of the world. As we build more and more constructions our mental picture becomes more complex. This is an essentially active notion of learning not unlike Piaget's adaptive model. New experience sometimes demands that we reshape existing ideas and knowledge. I remember young children, learning about whales, being quite upset when they saw them kill seals for food on a video-film. They called this 'cruel' until the teacher explained they had to eat seals to survive.

Core books are those at the centre of a nursery or primary school collection (see Ellis and Barrs' book *The Core Book: a Structured Approach to Reading Books Within the Reading Curriculum* CLPE, 1997).

Critical reading involves reflecting on the ideas in texts and responding to them with heart and mind. This reflective kind of reading, unlike reading to scan a text for a name or date or 'skim reading' to get the gist of the content, requires evaluation of what we read (Lunzer and Gardner 1979). Reading non-fiction demands just as much work from the imagination as does fiction. We need, for example, as Bruner argues in *Actual Minds, Possible Worlds,* to be able to imagine the possible as well as the actual (Bruner, 1986). Young children, even as listeners to text, are able, with some encouragement, to insist it makes sense to them.

Cross-sections are diagrams, usually labelled, showing the inside of a creature, the structure of a building or the workings of an object. The cross-section of an ant colony in Manning and Granstrom's *What's Under the Bed* is a good introduction for the under-eights.

Curiosity kits are the non-fiction version of 'story sacks'. They consist of some children's books on a topic, a book or magazine for an adult on the same topic and a related toy, game, model or puzzle. So a space kit might have information books about space travel and the planets, a magazine with adult-level articles on space and a model of a space ship. The kits were developed by Maureen Lewis and members of the EXEL project based at Exeter University Education Department. Some teachers make their own collections of items for all the children in their class, but very often the kits are used to motivate reluctant boy readers.

DARTs stands for Directed Activities Round Texts. The best of these can help children learn about the structures of texts and the features of print. An activity often used with children aged six years and under is a sequencing game. A text is cut up into sections and children try to assemble the parts in the right order. Teachers often find the activities suggested in *Book-based Reading Games* helpful (Bromley, 2000).

Diagrams in children's books and resources usually show structures like the parts of a machine or vehicle or processes like the water cycle or the digestive system. (Tables and charts are diagrams with a numerical element.) Diagrams, together with other illustrations, provide variety on the pages of a text, whether print or electronic, and explain and extend the writing. Even the visually aware children of today need help in interpreting diagrams and linking the verbal and the visual aspects of text.

Diary (log or journal) can refer to a calendar of engagements or to quite a detailed chrono-logical record of a writer's experiences, observations, feelings and attitudes. In the early years classroom, writing 'news' – a picture and a label or short sentence – is a familiar beginning to the idea of diary writing. Children also enjoy compiling 'nature diaries' which can bring together English and science in helpful and creative ways. Children might record observations of birds that come to the bird table or the development of the classroom tadpoles. Whether the diaries are included on a school internet site or take the form of print booklets, notes can be set out in a format teacher and children have agreed. There are usually headings like 'date' and 'time of observation' and a sketch and comment. Keeping a nature diary reinforces the idea that writing has a clear purpose, that it can be enjoyable and that it makes possible the sharing of interesting information.

Both boys and girls often produce delightful small pictures of plants and animals in their diaries and appreciate being helped to label them. Some of the nature books by Mick Manning and Brita Granstrom combine a story with factual information and drawings. *High tide, low tide* includes the sort of small labelled pictures that encourage children to try their own (Franklin Watts Wonderwise series). Quite a lot of science and nature books give suggestions for observing creatures and recording what is seen, for example *The Amazing Outdoor Activity Book* by Angela Wilkes (Dorling Kindersley).

Discourse refers in a general way to a conversation, dialogue, sermon or lecture. It is used in linguistics to refer to any piece of spoken or written language which is longer than a sentence. Each discourse has a distinctive vocabulary, style and syntax which identifies it with a particular genre. When children begin to learn subjects like history, science, geography and so on, part of their task is to take on the discourse of the subject.

Discussion text, one of the six non-fiction categories identified by *The National Literacy Strategy Framework for Teaching* (DfEE, 1998), presents a case, sometimes setting out competing views. Such a text is used to invite children to discuss different aspects of a topic.

Disembedded thinking helps learning in relatively context-free situations. This kind of thinking is hard for children under seven, who respond best when what they hear and read makes 'human sense'. Margaret Donaldson in her book *Children's Minds* (Donaldson, 1979) believes that spoken language can act as a bridge to thinking that is not centred in immediate experience.

Drafting involves taking ideas from a plan and building them into a written text. In his book *Writing: Teachers and Children at Work,* Donald Graves suggests that children are helped to make drafts at seven different stages from 'pre-composition' to 'publication of the fair copy'. It is helpful for adults and older children to make several drafts of some written work, but most early years writing is 'first draft'. Writing takes much effort for very young children and re-writing could be at best inappropriate and at worst de-motivating.

Egocentrism is Piaget's term for what he considered was the young child's tendency to see things from his or her own viewpoint. However, other developmentalists – Margaret Donaldson, for example – have suggested that, where children have a lot of curiosity and interest invested in solving a problem they seem to be much more flexible in their thinking than Piaget claimed (Donaldson, 1978*)*.

E-mail (electronic mail) – messages and documents prepared on personal computers and delivered electronically, using fixed line or satellite communication links.

Emergent writing refers to the early stages of the journey a young child takes from early mark-making to using the conventions of writing to make meaning.

Emotional literacy refers to a person's understanding of their own motivations and feelings and their appreciation of how to relate to others in a constructive and sensitive way. Many factors are likely to affect a child's developing emotional literacy. For example, stories can provide a window into how people think, feel and behave. Non-fiction books can also help: *Celebration! Children Just Like Me* (Dorling Kindersley, 1997) shows through a sympathetic text and fine photographs what is important to children growing up in 25 different countries.

Enabling adult refers to the support the older person – whether teacher, parent or older sibling – gives to the younger in any learning situation. When it comes to reading, Aidan Chambers argues that all the obstacles faced by learner readers can be overcome if they have the help and example of a trusted, experienced adult reader (Chambers, 1991).

Environmental print describes all the written language a child encounters in their world – shop and restaurant signs, writing on packaging, advertisements and language on television and CD-ROMs. Teachers recognise the power of environmental print in showing the purposes of language in our culture and bring it into the work of the classroom.

Equilibrium is a term used by Piaget to refer to a balanced, stable state of mind. It is contrasted with **disequilibrium** which refers to the instability of mind which accompanies an attempt to solve a problem or deal with difficult new information. A feeling of disequilibrium, a kind of cognitive discomfort, encourages intense learning and problem-solving to help restore the mind to a state of balance.

EXEL project (the Exeter University Extending Reading project) was funded by the Nuffield Foundation. It was led by David Wray and Maureen Lewis who worked with teachers across the country during the 1990s to find ways of supporting non-fiction reading and writing. The project is well known for the EXIT model (see below) and for encouraging two strategies in particular – the use of 'writing frames' to structure children's writing for different purposes and 'genre exchange' which involves a child being given information in one form of writing and responding to it by writing in another form. So children might be asked to find out about Tudor food by reading an encyclopaedia entry and then be asked to construct a noble family's dinner menu.

EXIT model (Extending Interactions with Texts) was an outcome of the EXEL project. The model identifies process stages in integrating texts into learning. These include: 'activation of prior knowledge', 'establishing purposes', 'interacting with the text' and 'monitoring understanding'. The model is set out in detail in *Extending Literacy: Children Reading and Writing Non-fiction* (Wray and Lewis, 1997).

Explanation text is one of the six kinds of non-fiction used in the National Literacy Strategy *Framework for Teaching* (1998). This is the kind of text used to explain a structure like that of a plant, animal or machine or processes like the water cycle and the digestive system or how a lever works. Diagrams are important in showing structures and processes. David Macauley's book *The New Way Things Work* (Dorling Kindersley) has clear, well-annotated diagrams of wheels, levers and all sorts of moving parts. The CD-ROM version is very popular as it shows the parts in motion. This is an inspirational text in both print and electronic form and one which an adult can share with children of different ages.

Expressive language was one of the function categories of the Schools Council 'Development of Writing Abilities' project directed by James Britton in the 1970s. It refers to the fairly unstructured kind of speech and writing we use when we formulate action plans or new ways of construing our experience. Children's first writing is often very like 'written down' speech and more directed towards their own immediate thoughts and preoccupations than the needs of an audience. 'Expressive' writing has those touches that show a child is actively making sense of things; it is one of those useful concepts which we must not allow to slip out of the debate on early writing.

Faction is an emerging term referring to texts, usually for the under-eights, which combine features of both fiction and non-fiction. So we might find talking animals and cartoon characters alongside information boxes and labelled diagrams. An example of this transitional genre is *The Drop Goes Plop* by Sam Godwin (Macdonald Young Books) which introduces the water cycle through a conversation about its stages between a mother and baby seagull.

Field of discourse is an aspect of 'register' and is to do with the topic or content of a spoken or written text. When teachers introduce a new topic they often invite 'brainstorming' to open up the new 'field of discourse'. Here the words and concepts associated with, for example, amphibians, rivers or Edwardian England, can be identified and made into a concept map or web.

First person writing gives one person's viewpoint and response to experience and can take the form of a letter, diary, factual narrative (recount) or a full length autobiography. The 'news' entries young children write are nearly always written in the first person.

Flow chart refers to a kind of diagram which shows the stages involved and the options to choose from in various courses of action.

Fonts The use of different sizes and kinds of print – large, small, bold, italic and coloured – has become more familiar in print books as well as those on the computer. Children can be helped to recognise that variation in the use of fonts can help communicate meaning and significance of information in a text. A good example of this can be seen in Walker's 'Read and Wonder' and 'Wonderwise' series where the narrative is in a different font to the writing in the information boxes.

Format (of books) refers to size and shape.

Functions of language are to do with the purposes for which an individual uses language at a given time and in a particular context.

Genre refers to the features which identify a text with a particular category. So, for example, the recount genre describes some events chronologically.

Genre exchange refers to the reordering of information presented in one genre in another format (see also under EXEL project).

Global structure identifies a text with a particular type or genre of writing (Halliday, 1978: 138). One of the most significant contributions to our understanding of how information books are structured was made by Christine Pappas in her paper 'Exploring the global structure of children's information books' which suggested that the way in which the books were organised greatly affected a child's ability to learn from them. The three obligatory features of an information text are, according to Pappas: topic presentation, description of attributes, and characteristic events (Pappas, 1986).

Hypermedia refers to a computer text which includes words, pictures, video-film, animation and virtual reality.

Hyperstudio is the name of a multi-media authoring tool which enables teachers and children to create interactive books.

Hypertext is a computing term to describe a facility to jump from one page of text to another coming earlier or later.

Iconic representation is a term used to refer to the representation of experience through image. Children begin to think in images in their second year; even after the acquisition of speech, a lot of thinking and learning is achieved by representing experience iconically.

Impersonal language is a formal kind of language often used in textbooks and official reports.

Index refers to the retrieval device which helps the reader locate specific information in a text. If you would like to read recommendations for good indexing of children's books, see Bakewell and Williams (2000) *Occasional Paper on Indexing, no.5.* Sheffield : Society of Indexers.

Inference refers to the ability to work something out from information you already have or are given.

Information books are typically illustrated non-narrative texts on one topic like 'The history of ships' or 'magnets'.

Information stories are texts which follow a time sequence but which also communicate facts and ideas. Some of them are 'experience' stories following typical activities of young children and families; so we might have a narrative about a family's visit to the seaside with some information boxes on each page with pictures and facts about sea creatures and seaside plants. Unlike a conventional story, there may also be a fact file, a glossary, an index and some further reading suggestions.

Instruction (or procedural) refers to texts which tell us how to do something. It is another of the *National Literacy Strategy Framework for Teaching* (DfEE, 1998) text types.

Younger children tend to start with less formal examples of the genre, telling how to look after the classroom tadpoles, carry out a simple science experiment or follow a recipe.

Internet refers to a world wide web linking information sites electronically to provide users with access to a huge database. Children are eager to learn about the resources and opportunities their society provides and even very young learners can be helped to find information on websites.

Intertextuality is to do with finding allusions in one text to other texts. Children's picturebook authors often use this device to intrigue and develop the literacy competence of young readers. The Ahlbergs' *The Jolly Postman* and Anthony Browne's *The Tunnel* are examples of texts that draw on children's cultural knowledge to link ideas in different texts. We associate 'intertextuality' with fiction, but there is no reason why non-fiction texts should not also use the device. I can remember a child's book on fossils – long out of print – that shows, in an illustration, a child taking down a tome with the title *Darwin's Origin of the Species* from a library shelf.

Journals see **diary**

Knowledge telling/knowledge transforming are terms to differentiate between writing which depends simply on the recall of facts and that which transforms, rather than just repeats information. Research carried out by Bereiter and Scardamalia indicated how challenging it is for children to transform information (Bereiter and Scardamalia, 1987). Children are more likely to reflect on information, both first hand and from secondary resources, if we encourage them to take their own questions to their enquiry. This puts them very much in the driving seat as far as their research is concerned.

Library skills include being able to find one's way round the cataloguing system – usually the Dewey system in schools. Children are taught from a young age to look in reference files, often computerised, to find out the identifying number of a particular book so that they can locate it on the shelf. Colour is often used to help children track down different subjects – history, geography and science. I have often seen wall charts with simple instructions on finding a book in school libraries and sometimes these are made by older children for the younger ones.

Literal and inferential comprehension are terms to refer to the depth and subtlety of a person's reading of a text. Literal reading takes what is written at face value while inferential comprehension requires more profound reading and the ability to infer things not actually stated.

Metacognition is an individual's awareness of how they came to know something. It implies some consciousness of the learning strategies we use and how effective they are. Different children find different strategies helpful. An obvious example of this is that some children have predominantly visual memories and others predominantly verbal memories and this has implications, for example, for teaching spelling. This active involvement in one's own learning strategies is very much in the spirit of the constructivist model (see separate entry).

Metalanguage is language used to think and talk about language. Young children soon acquire the vocabulary to talk about their reading and writing – 'letter', 'sound', 'meaning', 'vowel', 'sentence', 'plot', 'character', 'heading', 'index'. They also hear their parents, caregivers and teachers speak of things like 'asking questions', ' interesting new words' and 'lovely opening sentence'. All this contributes to children's 'metalinguistic awareness' or their knowledge about how to discuss their developing understanding of how language works; increasing this awareness leads to greater control over language use and to increasing sensitivity in using syntax and vocabulary.

Metaphor permeates our language; it associates two things with each other so that the qualities of the first thing carry over into the second. Although we think of metaphors as enhancing poetry, they are often helpful in illuminating phenomena in information texts. In her book *Growing Frogs* (Walker Books), Vivien French describes tadpoles just beginning to grow within their frog spawn shells as 'tiny commas'.

Mode is part of 'register', a linguistic concept to do with how we adapt our language use to different situations. 'Mode' refers to the pattern of the text and to the medium in which the spoken or written message is given.

Modelling (of language processes) describes the demonstration of a skill or a means of going about something. Teachers 'model' how to use non-fiction texts, often with the help of big books or enlarged text on a screen, by drawing attention to global aspects like headings or to the way information is set out in particular kinds of writing and illustrating.

Motivation is a psychological term meaning that a person has an urge to do something, usually because they have a clear purpose for doing so. Young children need to find satisfaction in all the activities and tasks that make up their experience at school. Too much prescription from official agencies can make it more difficult for teachers to embed children's reading and writing in the rich experience that can lead to purposeful reading and writing. We know that literacy experience is best linked to other activities, many of them physical – like role play about cafés, post offices and garages – and we have to use our professional skill and judgement to include all this as well as meeting externally imposed requirements.

Multi-media is a term used to describe the many modes of representation and communication used in computer software and CD-ROM. We might have a CD-ROM that shows a steam engine working, the sound of the machine and historic film of the engine and its engineers at work. Reading multi-media texts has led to new kinds of literacy and new challenges (see also visual literacy).

Narrative information books are written in a time sequence and may describe a plant or creature's life cycle, a journey, an experience or a series of historical events. The narrative form does not preclude analysis and comment about events. It may be accompanied by charts, diagrams and some of the other features of non-chronologically ordered information texts.

Non-book print refers to all print not in books, such as posters, charts, labels, letters, advertisements, flyers, catalogues, notices and magazines.

Non-chronological/non-narrative information books (see information books).

Page layout is important in establishing the appeal an information book has for young children. Generally, they have uncluttered pages with inviting illustrations. While we look for some variety on the page, too great a mixture of photographs, drawing and diagrams can confuse the eye. Publishers love to give sub-topics a double spread. However, this approach can be over used as some sub-topics deserve more than a double spread and others need less than a page.

Parable is the term to describe a short story to make a moral point and is often associated with the teachings of Jesus in the New Testament.

Passive voice is a grammatical term used to refer to the form of a verb in which the recipient of an action is the subject of the sentence. So a sentence in the passive voice might be: 'The boy was being praised by the governors for his interesting account of the class outing'. In contrast, in the active voice we would have: 'The governors praised the boy for his interesting account of the class outing'.

Persuasion, one of the six non-fiction categories identified in *The National Literacy Strategy Framework for Teaching* (1998), is a form of language in which someone gives a point of view, usually with supporting evidence. Children are able to express viewpoints orally at quite a young age, given support and encouragement. When children's feelings are engaged they seem more able to step into this quite challenging kind of speaking and writing. In chapter 11 of this book we find six-year-olds arguing the case for and against keeping animals in zoos.

Plenary refers to that part of a lesson, conference or lecture where pupils and students give their responses to what has been offered. The ten-minute literacy hour plenary in school allows teacher and children to reflect on what they have been doing and to share what has been learned.

Portfolios in school are folders or files containing a representative sample of children's work, results of diagnostic tests, teachers' observations and comments about progress. The language section of a portfolio will include evidence about and examples of work showing a child's progress in the non-fiction kinds of reading and writing. As with other writing samples, brief details of context in which the piece was written, date and a qualitative comment are helpful. In their book *Co-ordinating English at key stage 1* Tyrrell and Gill (2000) set out the practicalities of managing portfolios, whether in traditional folders or on a networked computer system to store school data.

Prior knowledge is the existing understanding which we bring to learning about a topic. When teachers introduce something new they talk to the pupils at the start of the work to ascertain where they are conceptually so that they can plan and resource lessons taking into account the needs of particular children.

Procedural or instructional text, one of the six non-fiction text types used in the literacy hour, tells us how to do something. Such a text might be step-by-step instructions about how to cook a cake, carry out a science experiment or build a model. First the text provides a list of ingredients or materials to use and then the steps to follow. The chronological organisation makes this one of the most sympathetic of the informational genres for young children as readers and writers.

Process approaches to writing value the stages a young writer moves through as well as the writing product. The 'process' approach is associated with the work of Donald Graves and especially his book *Writing: Teachers and Children at Work* (Graves, 1983). Here writing is viewed as a task involving much thinking and planning with the teacher in an active role in helping young writers to shape meaning. Graves and others who favour this approach emphasise the importance of the quality of the entire writing environment and of encouraging children to feel part of a writing community. In this spirit, teachers would encourage a 'workshop' approach and often 'model' the writing process by writing themselves alongside the children. This approach has helped children write stories and has also made a significant contribution to children's informational writing, where planning and reflection have paid off.

   In the United Kingdom there is a move towards an emphasis on grammatical aspects of writing, and the English Standard Assessment Tasks assess end products rather than processes like planning, drafting and sharing. Within this more prescribed culture teachers still strive to include some of the motivating aspects of the process approach by emphasising purposes and audiences for writing, encouraging book-making and helping young children talk about their writing.

Reading schemes consist of books and other materials arranged into difficulty levels for teaching reading from about ages five to ten or eleven. In the 1970s and 1980s there was a debate about whether children should be taught to read using books with a controlled vocabulary or whether they should be provided with 'real' books. 'Scheme' books once had a reputation for being linguistically unexciting and for communicating outdated social messages by their choice of words and illustrations. These days the best schemes or reading programmes use quality authors and the characters and settings depicted are more representative of all the groups that make up our society. It is also now more possible to combine strands drawn from different schemes with non-scheme resources in building a reading programme. Non-fiction texts are used in all the main reading schemes and help children experience the six categories required by the National Literacy Strategy. In his book, *Individualised Reading* published annually, Keith Moon includes the non-fiction strands of major schemes. To allow a published scheme, however good, to meet all a school's reading needs risks underestimating and undervaluing of teachers' professional judgement. An alternative to a scheme approach is set out in *Core Books* published by the Centre for Language in Primary Education.

Recount, one of the six non-fiction text types in *The National Literacy Strategy Framework for Teaching* (DfEE, 1998), is one of the first kinds of writing children control. Recount is a chronologically ordered retelling of events.

Reference books include dictionaries, thesauruses, encyclopaedias and atlases.

Reflective reading, in contrast to skimming a text for the gist of a passage or scanning it for a name or date, requires us to read in a profound way and evaluate what we read.

Register is a linguistic term to refer to the way in which language varies according to the context in which it is used. The three aspects of register are 'field' (the topic), 'mode' (the pattern of the text and medium used) and 'tenor' (the way a message is given – how personal or impersonal it is) (see Littlefair, 1991).

Report is one of six non-fiction text types identified in *The National Literacy Strategy Framework for Teaching* (DfEE, 1998). It has a non-chronological organisation and usually begins with a general introduction before moving on to the main characteristics and activities relating to the subject under consideration. Many children's information books are reports on topics like Vikings, volcanoes or voles.

Retrieval devices are those parts of a text, the contents page and index, which help direct readers to the information they need.

Scaffolding is a metaphoric term to explain the teaching support given by an older child or adult to a younger learner. Just as scaffolding on a building provides temporary support, the hope is that scaffolding offered in an educational context will only be needed for a relatively short time until the child is able to work on the task in question independently (see also 'zone of proximal development').

Scan means to check through a written passage to track down a date or name.

Schema theory holds that readers bring important expectations and prior knowledge to their reading. This philosophy shows us an active learner and is compatible with encouraging children to talk through their existing knowledge of a topic and to take their own questions to the texts.

Scribing is a term often used in a teaching context to describe the role of an older child or adult when writing to a young child's dictation. This support helps young children gain experience of composing text even though they still need support with the mechanics of writing.

Simile refers to a comparison made between two things with signal words 'like' and 'as'. Similes create images in poetry but are also used in non-fiction to help understanding. For example, in Nicola Davies' book *Bat Loves the Night* (Walker Books), we read that a bat flaps her wings with a sound 'like a tiny umbrella opening'. Like 'metaphor', 'simile' is a kind of imagery. The difference is that a metaphor tells us something *is* the phenomenon while a simile is always flagged by 'like' and 'as'.

Skim is a word describing the kind of reading we do swiftly to get the 'gist' or main sense of the meaning of a passage.

Spiral curriculum is a term, used by Jerome Bruner (for example in his book *Entry into Early Language: Spiral Curriculum,* 1975) to challenge the view that learning occurs in a simple sequence. He explains how children, once introduced to an idea or concept, revisit it, possibly on several later occasions, as their knowledge and understanding develop and refine. The National Curriculum encourages this kind of building on knowledge by requiring children to revisit different kinds of reading and writing at different stages in the learning programme. For example 'recount' first appears in the third term of year 1 as a genre for children to read and write and is revisited in the first term of year 5.

Spontaneous and scientific concepts are terms first used by Piaget and then taken on and developed by Vygotsky in his book *Thought and Language.* 'Spontaneous' concepts are those like, for example, 'spoon', 'love' and 'sister' that we learn through everyday experience. 'Scientific' or 'non-spontaneous' concepts, for example, 'catalyst', 'feudal' and 'denominator' are usually learnt in the formal context of the school or college. Vygotsky suggests that the teacher's task is to help children make links between the two kinds of concept to facilitate learning. So young children beginning a project on insects would bring to the lesson the experience of finding insects in the garden or park, possibly the knowledge that an insect's body is in parts and that the creatures often start life as eggs. These spontaneous concepts (or 'prior knowledge') could lead to their understanding of related scientific concepts like 'habitat', 'segmented' and 'life cycle'.

Structural guiders are the headings and sub-headings which organise an information book (see Neate, 1992).

Study skills is a term used to refer to all the strategies used by researchers of any age to find out about a topic. English co-ordinators (or the language and literacy co-ordinator) work with colleagues to plan programmes to ensure that children can find their way around the school library and use the cataloguing system – usually the Dewey system. Children also need to learn how to find the information they want from books and other secondary sources by using retrieval devices – the contents and index pages – and how to access material from databases and on internet sites. As they get older, children need to be helped to make notes and summaries from secondary sources to inform their writing. Working from these makes it more likely that children will construct their own account and not stay close to the writing in the texts they have read. The 'shared writing' and 'shared reading' part of the literacy hour, is an opportunity for teachers to 'model' how to find one's way round a reference book or CD-ROM. Study skills are best demonstrated in an interesting learning context about a subject or topic rather than in decontextualised exercises. Finding out is challenging – but should also be enjoyable!

Sub-headings help organise informational texts into discreet manageable sections. Such 'structural guiders' help children to understand the way non-fiction is ordered.

Summary or précis refers to a shortened version of a longer text giving its most important points. Young children can be helped to summarise information orally before coming to written summaries.

Tables see **chart**

Tenor is an aspect of 'register'. Register is a linguistic term which refers to the way in which language varies according to the situation in which it is spoken and written. 'Tenor' refers to the way in which the message is given. So an informal use of tenor might result in a lot of use of the pronouns 'I' and 'you' while a more formal use might avoid the friendlier feel of pronouns by using the passive tense.

Tense applies to verbs and is a grammatical feature which situates in time the events, feelings and so on expressed in a sentence.

Text cues in non-fiction books are common 'signal' words. They may suggest cause and effect – 'since', 'because', 'thus' – or sequence – 'until', before', 'after'. The provision of these words is a feature of the writing frames designed by Wray and Lewis (1997) and there is more on this in *Non-fiction Matters* by Stephanie Harvey, 1998: 211.

Text organiser see **retrieval devices**

Top down approaches to reading emphasise the role of searching for meaning rather than the role of 'code breaking' in the initial teaching of reading.

Transcriptional aspects of writing, are sometimes called 'secretarial aspects' and include spelling, punctuation, legibility, capitalisation and paragraphing.

Transitional genre are texts for children which have some of the features of mature texts but which are modified to appeal to young readers. They may employ story characters to explain new concepts or combine an information story with factual information, often in different print size or style.

Tune (on the page) is to do with the rhythms and patterns in a particular kind of text. When we read out loud to children they hear a mature reader using intonation, expression and pace appropriate to the kind of writing. Teachers have always read stories to their classes, but now there is a welcome trend towards also reading the different kinds of information texts aloud to familiarise children with the particular 'tunes' of non-narrative text. You will find more about this is many of the publications from the Centre for Language in Primary Education.

Visual literacy is to do with 'reading' images of all kinds and seeing the connections between picture and print. Non-fiction books present information through diagrams and photographs as well as through writing.

Voice in non-common sense usage refers to one of three things: the 'voiced' sounds in phonetics (b d g z), the active or passive voice in grammar, and the 'narrative voice' of a narrator or the character who 'speaks' in a story.

Worksheets usually consist of numbered tasks with a space to write answers on a sheet of paper, card or booklet. They were once used a great deal to organise topic work using information books. Often this led to uninvolving and mechanical work and teachers, particularly of the younger age groups, prefer children to research answers to their own questions. However, sometimes the more imaginative kind of worksheet, where one 'right' answer is not expected, can help focus children's activities

Writing frames are frameworks provided by the teacher to help children structure their writing. The EXEL project produced frames for the six non-fiction text types which have been used to inform the non-fiction objectives of the *National Literacy Strategy Framework for Teaching* (DfEE, 1998a). It is not recommended that writing frames are used to teach children about the different genres in decontextualised exercises, but they can sometimes contribute to children's organisation of meaningful writing tasks.

Zone of proximal development, a term associated with the work of L.S. Vygotsky, refers to the area of a child's emerging abilities – to the gap between what a child can achieve on their own and what they can achieve with help.

Official frameworks: their guidance on non-fiction writing and reading

Notes to support Chapter 6 on informational writing and Chapter 7 on informational reading

The foundation stage curriculum for three- to six-year-olds is composed of six areas of learning: personal, social and emotional development; communication, language and literacy; mathematical development; knowledge and understanding about the world; physical development; and creative development. Six early learning 'goals' describe what children are expected to achieve in each area by age six years. 'Stepping stones' of children's progress help teachers track their progress by noting developing skills and understanding in each area. At the end of the reception year teachers provide each child with a foundation stage profile – a record of assessments based on children's ongoing work and teachers' observations.

Nursery practitioners in the United Kingdom have the early learning goals as a framework for the foundation years but teachers of children in reception classes work with three overlapping frameworks in their language and literacy programmes: the early learning goals for the foundation years (three to six years), The National Curriculum, English orders (five to eleven years), and The National Literacy Strategy *Framework for Teaching* (five to eleven). This can seem daunting to a trainee teacher. My own view is that good early years teachers have always done all that is now required and more. Nevertheless the frameworks are designed to help and provide a basic checklist of things to include.

While many of the teachers I spoke to while researching this book had concerns about the pressing down from above of inappropriate approaches for early years work, others felt that calling these important early years 'the foundation stage' and providing a framework of goals placed the age group into the bigger scheme.

I set out below: the early learning goals for communication, language and literacy which are relevant to non-fiction reading and writing; the non-fiction aspects of the literacy hour for children in reception; and the non-fiction requirements for key stage 1 in the National Curriculum English orders.

Early learning goals for communication, language and literacy for children aged three to six years

Early learning goals directed towards language and thinking

Spoken language has a central role in learning, and some of the early learning goals for language and thinking describe opportunities for talk which are important preliminaries to writing and to reading.

We encourage children to:

- use talk to organise, sequence and clarify ideas, feelings and events.

Practitioners also:

- encourage children to talk about how they feel, for example after a disagreement, when they are excited at seeing snow, or at the birth of a sibling
- ask children to give reasons, further explanations, for what they say
- encourage children to explain sometimes how things work in words rather than actions

Early learning goals and non-fiction writing

Children should be helped to:

- attempt writing for different purposes, using features of different forms such as lists, stories and instructions
- write their own names and other things such as labels and captions and begin to form simple sentences, sometimes using punctuation.

Practitioners:

- write non-fiction texts with children
- provide materials and opportunities for children to initiate the use of writing in their play as well as creating purposes for independent and group writing

Early learning goals and non-fiction reading

Children need to:

- show an understanding of how information can be found in non-fiction texts to answer questions about where, who, why and how

Practitioners need to:

- encourage children to add to their first hand experience of the world through the use of books, other texts, and information and communication technology (ICT)
- encourage children to use a range of different reading strategies by modelling different strategies and providing varied texts through which that range can be used

The National Literacy Strategy Framework for Teaching for the reception year – five- to six-year-olds

Non-fiction writing in the literacy hour

In the shared writing part of the literacy hour children should be helped to understand that:

- writing is different from drawing

- writing is used for a range of purposes – to send messages, inform and record

Children also need to:

- experiment with writing in role play situations
- write their own names
- write labels and captions for pictures and drawings
- use writing to communicate – recounting their own experiences, lists, signs, directions, menus, labels, greeting cards, letters

When they move to year 1 children continue to write lists, labels, captions and simple instructions. They write recounts based on their own experience and short non-chronological reports. Children formulate their own questions prior to reading for information and recording the answers in diagrams or a fact file on IT.

Non-fiction reading in the literacy hour

The reading range for children in the reception year covers simple non-fiction texts, including recounts.
Children need to be helped to:

- re-read frequently a variety of familiar texts, e.g. information texts, captions and their own and other children's writing

Moving on to year 1 we help children to read labels around the school and on equipment, and read simple instructions. They begin to understand the differences between fiction and non-fiction, to use retrieval devices and apply their knowledge of alphabetical order to using dictionaries. They are helped to focus their reading by taking their own questions to the texts. Children gain experience of reading recounts and begin to understand their generic structure.

The National Curriculum English orders for key stage 1 – five-to seven-year-olds

Explicit linkage is made between the early learning goals and the National Curriculum English requirements in the left hand margins of the orders.

Non-fiction writing in the National Curriculum

Breadth of study includes writing for different purposes:

- to communicate with others; to explore experience; to organise and explain information.
- to understand the value of writing for remembering and developing ideas

The range of forms of writing include:

- notes, lists, captions, records, messages, instructions

Non-fiction reading in the National Curriculum

Pupils should be taught to:

* use the organisational features of non-fiction texts, including captions, illustrations, contents, index and chapters, to find information
* understand that texts about the same topic may contain different information or present similar information in different ways
* use reference materials for different purposes

The range of non-fiction texts includes:

* print and ICT-based information texts, including those with continuous text and relevant illustrations
* dictionaries, encyclopaedias and other reference materials

References

QCA (1999) *Early Learning Goals.* London: Department for Education and Employment

QCA (2000) *Curriculum Guidance for the Foundation Stage.* London: Department of Education and Employment.

DfEE (1999) *The National Curriculum, English.* London: Department of Education and Employment and Qualifications and Curriculum Authority

DfEE (1998) *The National Literacy Strategy Framework for Teaching.* London: Department for Education and Employment.

DfEE (2001a) *Developing Early Writing.* London: Department for Education and Employment.

DfEE (2001b) *The National Literacy Strategy: Early Literacy Support.* Department of Education and Employment.

Appendix 2

Non-fiction books for under-threes

Twenty-five star books

Anholt, Catherine and Anholt, Laurence, *Here Come the Babies.* Walker Books. 0 7445 6066 7 £4.99.

Ayliffe, Alex, *Boo Barney.* Little Orchard. 184 121 2091 £3.50

Bruce, Lisa and Waterhouse, Stephen, *Engines, Engines.* Bloomsbury. 0747555013 1 £4.99

Bog, Armelle, *Katie and Tom's Busy Day.* Kingfisher. 0753407477 £12.99 (interactive 'lift the flap' book – seasons, colours and time)

Chichester Clark, Emma, *Mimi's Book of Opposites.* Andersen Press. 1 84270 063 4 £5.99

Church, Caroline, Jane, *Bouncy Lamb.* Ladybird. 0 7214 2838 x £3.99 (cloth)

Cousins, Lucy, *Maisy's First Flap Book.* Walker Books. 0 7445 7588 5 £7.99

Dollin, Laura (editor), *Digger Power.* Tough Stuff series. Egmont Books Ltd. 1 4052 0003 0 £3.99

Doyle, Malachy, illustrator Teckentrup, Brita, *Babies like ME!* Frances Lincoln. 07112 17351 £9.99

Elgar, Rebecca, *Jack Rides His Scooter.* Kingfisher Books. 0 7534 0449 4 £6.99

Emmett, Jonathan and Parker, Ant, *10 Little Monsters Counting Book.* Kingfisher Books. 0 75 3404 524 £7.99 (also in box format 07534 0780 9 £12.99)

Falconer, Ian, *Olivia Counts.* Simon & Schuster. 0689836732 £5.99

Henderson, Kathy, illustrator Kerins, Tony, *The Baby Dances.* Walker Books. 0 77445 6360 7 £4.99.

Hill, Eric, *Spot's Noisy Walk.* Penguin. 072324513 4 £7.99 (interactive flap book)

Hughes, Shirley, *Lucy and Tom's abc.* Puffin. 0140 505210 £4.99

Jemima Puddleduck's numbers, illustrated by Beatrix Potter. Beatrix Potter Mini Board Books. Frederick Warne & Co Penguin Books. 0-7232-4091-4 £2.50

Litchfield, Jo, *The Usborne Book of Everyday Words.* Usborne. 07460 22664 £7.99

Lousada, Sandra, *Baby Faces.* Campbell Books (Macmillan). 0 333 903 986 £2.99

Osborne, Martine and Godon, Ingrid, *One Gorgeous Baby.* Macmillan Children's Books. 0 333 90379 x £9.99

Sharratt, Nick, *My Mum and Dad Make me Laugh.* Walker Books. 0 7445 4307 £4.99

Sideri, Simona, illustrator Venus, Pamela, *Let's Go to Playgroup.* Tamarind. 1 870516 56 7. £3.99 (board book)

Watts, Fiona, illustrator Wells, Rachel, *Baby's mealtime.* Usborne bath books. 9 780745041765 £3.99

Watts, Fiona, illustrator Wells, Rachel, *That's not my tractor!* Usborne 0746041918 £4.99 (touch feely book)

Wear, Tim, *I'm a Little Caterpillar.* Buster Books/Michael O'Mara Books. 1 903 840 031 £4.99

Wilson-Max, Ken, *Dexter gets dressed.* Kingfisher/Chambers. 0 7534 02335 £8.99

Non-fiction books for three to fives

Twenty-five star books

Ahlberg, Janet and Ahlberg, Allan, *The Baby's Catalogue.* Puffin Books paperback. 0140 503 854 £4.99

Allen, Judy and Humphries, Tudor, *Are You a Snail?* Up the garden path series. Kingfisher. 0 7534 0421 4 £5.99 (others in the series include spider, ladybird and butterfly)

Asher, Jane, *Round the World Cookbook.* Longman. 0 582 12280 5 £5.99

Collin's Pathways to Literacy series. *Waste* 0 00301061 9 235; *Firefighters* 0 00 301038 4 £3.25 (big book format 0 00301 228, £19.99)

Dodds, D. A., illustrator Lancome, Julie, *The Shape of Things.* Walker Books. 0 7445 4368 1 £4.99

Fajardo, Sara Andrea, *Enrique's Day: From Dawn to Dusk in a Peruvian City.* Child's Day series. Frances Lincoln. 0 7112 1933 8 £10.99 (other countries featured include India, Russia, China, Brazil, Ghana, South Africa, Lapland, Egypt and Vietnam)

French, Vivien, *Let's Go, Anna.* David & Charles. 186233284 3 £4.99

Fridell, Roy and Walsh, Patricia, *Life Cycle of a Spider.* Heinemann Library. 0 431 08464 5 £8.99

Gallimard, Jeunesse and Mettler, Rene, *The Jungle.* Moonlight Publishing/First Discovery 1 85103 183 9 £6.99 (layered pages)

Griffiths, Rose, photographs Millard, Peter, *Boxes.* A&C Black. 0 7136 3626 7 £5.50

Lia, Simone, *Billy Bean's Dream.* David & Charles. 186233 3351 £4.99 (counting book)

My Very First Oxford Dictionary. Oxford University Press. 0 19 910503 0 £4.99.

Milet, Mandy and Milet, Nell, *Hattie's House: A first flap book about Sound.* English/Chinese. Milet Publishing Ltd. 184059 153 6 £5.99 (other books in the series on the senses are in English/Gujurati and English/Bengali)

Mitton, Tony and Parker, Ant, *Flashing Fire Engines.* Kingfisher. 0 7534 0298 x £3.99

My First Numbers and Shapes Pack. Dorling Kindersley. 0 7513 3209 7 £5.99

Ourselves Heinemann Library Collection 2 – selection of non-fiction books on *Taste* 0 431 097 313, *Hearing* 0 431 097 283 £5.50.

Oxford non-fiction, *Traffic* 019 917 4709; *The Farm* 019 917 4687 £1.50

Oxlade, Chris, *Rock.* (0431 1273870); *Soil.* 0 431 12735 20 £8.99. Heinemann Materials series.

Bryant-Mole, *People who Help.* Heinemann 'Let's pretend' series, 0431046530 £5.99

Readman, Jo, illustrator Roberts, Ley Honor, *The World Came to My Place.* Eden Project book. Random House. 1 90 391901 0 £10.99

Stones, Rosemary, illustrator O'Neill, Christopher, *Rosie's First Day at School.* Happy Cat publishers. 1899248 196 £3.99

Walsh, Melanie, *My Nose, Your Nose; My Beak, Your Beak.* 0-385-60292-8; 0-385-60291-x. Doubleday. £10.99 each hbk

Watts, Barry, *Snail.* Franklin Watts. 07496 4431 £10.99

Whittaker, Nicola, *Creature Feet* (0-7496-4025 1); *Creature Noses* (0-7496-4028-6) Creature Feature series, Franklin Watts. £10.99

Wilkes, Angela, *See How I Grow.* Dorling Kindersley 0 7513 513 5127 X £5.99

Non-fiction for five to sixes
Thirty star books

Information stories

Ahlberg, Janet and Ahlberg, Allan, *Starting School.* Puffin. 0140 50737x £4.99
Base, Graeme, *The Waterhole.* Abrams. 0810945681 £12.95
Brown, Ruth, *Lion in the Long Grass.* Andersen Press. I- 84270 048 0 £9.99
Cain, Sheridan and Burgin, Norma, *Little Turtle and the Song of the Sea.* Little Tiger Press. 185430 620 0 £4.99
Davies, Nicola, illustrator Chapman, Jane, *One Tiny Turtle.* Walker Books. 07445 6258 9 £10.99
Davies, Nicola, illustrator Maland, Nick, *The Big Blue Whale.* Walker Books big book. 0 74456300 3 £4.99
French, Vivien, illustrator Bartlett, Alison, *Growing Frogs.* Walker Books. 0 7445 2886 0 £9.99
Garland, Sarah, *Going Shopping.* Puffin. 0140 554009 £4.99
Hill, Eric, *Spot Goes to School.* Puffin. 0140000 506 500 £4.99
Hughes, Shirley, *Lucy and Tom Go to School.* Penguin. 0140 544151 £4.99
Jenkins, Martin, illustrator Chapman, Jane, *The Emperor's Egg.* 0 7445 6237 6 £9.99
Manning, Mick *A Ruined House.* Read and Wonder. Walker Books. 0744562716 £4.99 (science)
Manning, Mick and Granstrom, Brita, *What's Under the Bed.* Franklin Watts big book. 0 7496 32887 £14.99 (science/geography)
Wallace, Karen, illustrator Bostock, Mick, *Think of an Eel.* Walker Books big book. 0 7445 6300 3 £8.99
Meredith Hooper, illustrator Willey, Bee, *River Story.* Walker Books. 0 7445 2893 3 £9.99

Instructions/procedural

Denny, Roz and Waldergrave, Caroline, *The Walker Book of Children's Cookery.* 0744569907 £5.99
Johnson, Paul, *You Can Make Your Own Book!* Pelican Big book. 0582 33388 1 £17.99 (pack of six small format books £19.99)

Concept books

Brown, Ruth, *Ten Seeds.* Andersen Press. 0 86264 849 1 £5.99
Base, Graeme, *Animalia.* Harry N. Abrams, Inc. Publishers
Wilkes, Angela, *My First Book of Time.* Dorling Kindersley. 0 7516 0001 6 £9.99
Yagyu, Genichiro, *The Holes in Your Nose.* Frances Lincoln 011222045X £9.99

Early non-narrative

Delafosse, Claude and Jeunesse, Gallimard, *Let's Look at Animals Underground.* First Discovery/
 Torchlight series, Moonlight Publishing. 1 85103 281 9 £6.99

Llewellyn, Claire, illustrator Lewis, Anthony, *The Earth is like a Roundabout: a first look at night and
 day.* Macdonald Young Books M.Y. Bees. 07500 2645 £4.99

Oxford Web, Stage 2, *My Pet* (019 917 4857); *The Building Site* (019 917 489x) £2.25

Theodorou, Rod, *I Wonder Why Triceratops Had Horns?* Kingfisher. 1 85697 223 2 £4.99

References

First School Dictionary, illustrator Stephanie Strickland. Collins. 0-00 316154 4 £6.99.

My Very first Oxford Dictionary. 0-19-910563-0 £4.99

Oxford First Thesaurus. 0199 910728 9 £6.99

First Picture Atlas. Kingfisher. 075 34 0268 8 £5.99

Oxford Infant Atlas (second edition) advisory editor Patrick Wiegand. 0 19 831 863 4 £4.0 (*The Oxford
 Talking Infant Atlas CD-ROM* (Microsoft Windows and Apple Mac) 0 19 840 519 7 £30.00 + VAT
 – the multimedia version of *Oxford Infant Atlas.*)

Bibliography

Arnold, Helen (1992) '"Do the Blackbirds sing all day?" Literature and Information texts', in M. Styles, E. Bearne and V. Watson (eds) *After Alice: Exploring Children's Literature.* London: Cassell.

Arnold, Helen (1996) '"Penguins never meet polar bears": reading for information in the early years', in D. Whitebread (ed.) *Teaching and Learning in the Early Years.* London: Routledge.

Avery, Gillian (1995) 'Beginnings of Children's Reading', in P. Hunt (ed.) *Children's Literature: An Illustrated History.* Oxford: Oxford University Press.

Baker, C.D. and Freebody, P. (1989) *Children's First School Books.* Oxford: Basil Blackwell.

Bakewell, K. and Williams, P. (2000) *Occasional Paper on Indexing, No. 5.* Sheffield: Society of Indexers.

Barrs, M. (1987) 'Mapping the world', *English in Education NATE.* Vol. 21, no. 3.

Barrs, M. (1996a) Editorial 'information texts', *Language Matters.* No. 3.

Barrs, M. (1996b) 'The primary language record writing scale', *Language Matters.* No. 3. London: Centre for Language in Primary Education.

Barrs, M. (1997) *Core Books; The Core Booklist* (See Information Book Collection 1). London: Centre for Language in Primary Education.

Barrs, M. and Ellis, S. (1997) *The Core Book: A Structured Approach to Reading Books Within the Reading Curriculum* and *The Core Booklist* (Information Collection, Key Stage 1). London: The Centre for Language in Primary Education.

Barrs, M. and Thomas, A. (1991) (eds) *The Reading Book.* London: CLPE.

Barrs, M., Ellis, S., Hester, H. and Thomas, A. (1988) *The Primary Language Record: A Handbook for Teachers.* London: Centre for Literacy in Primary Education.

Bartholomew, L. and Bruce, T. (1993) *Getting to Know You. A Guide to Record Keeping in Early Childhood Education and Care.* London: Hodder & Stoughton.

Baxter, J. (2001) *Making Gender Work.* Reading: Reading University Reading and Language Information Centre.

Bereiter, C. and Scardamalia, M. (1987) *The Psychology of Written Composition.* Hillsdale, NJ: Lawrence Erlbaum.

Bell, Judith (1987) *Doing Your Research Project.* Milton Keynes: Open University Press.

Bissex, G. (1981) *GNYS AT WRK: A Child Learns to Write and Read.* Cambridge. MA: Harvard University Press.

Blenkin, G. and Kelly, V. (eds) (1992) *Assessment in Early Childhood Education.* London: Paul Chapman.

Bourke, Alison (2002) 'Ways to improve children's ability to concentrate', *Five to Seven.* Vol. 2, no. 3, July.

Brabham, E., Boyd, Pamela and Edgington, W.D. (2000) 'Sorting it out: elementary students' responses to fact and fiction in information storybooks as read-alouds for science and social studies', *Reading Research and Instruction.* Vol. 39, no. 4.

Brice Heath, Shirley (1983) *Ways with Words.* Cambridge: Cambridge University Press.

Britton, J.N. (1970) *Language and Learning.* London: Allen Lane, The Penguin Press.

Bromley, H. (2000) *Book-based Reading Games.* London: CLPE.

Bromley, H. (2002) 'Can you fix it for Bob the Builder?', *The Primary English Magazine*, NATE, Vol. 8, no. 1. October, pages 12–16.

Brown, Naima (1999) *Young Children's Literacy Development and the Role of Televisual Texts.* London: Falmer Press.

Browne, Ann (1996) *Developing Language and Literacy 3–8.* London: Paul Chapman.

Browne, A. (2002, second edition) *Developing Language and Literacy 3–8.* London: Paul Chapman.

Bruce, T. (1996) *Helping Young Children to Play.* London: Hodder & Stoughton.

Bruner, J. (1967) *Towards a Theory of Instruction.* Harvard: Belknap Press.

Bruner, J. (1975a) *Entry into Early Language: The Spiral Curriculum.* Swansea: University College of Swansea.

Bruner, J. (1975b) 'Language as an instrument of thought', in A. Davies (ed.) *Problems of Language and Learning.* London: Heinemann.

Bruner, J. (1986) *Actual Minds, Possible Worlds.* Cambridge, MA: MIT Press.

Bruner, J. and Haste, H. (1987) *Making Sense: The Child's Construction of the World.* London: Methuen.

Bruner, J., Jolly, A. and Sylva, K. (1978) *Play: Its Role in Development and Evolution.* London: Routledge.

Butler, D. (1995) *Babies Needs Books.* London: Penguin Books.

Calkins, L. (1986) *The Art of Teaching Writing.* Portsmouth, NH: Heinemann.

Callow, J. (ed.) (1999) *Image Matters: Visual Texts in the Classroom.* Marrickville, Australia: PETA (Primary English Association).

Chambers, A. (1991) *The Reading Environment.* Stroud: The Thimble Press.

Chambers, Aidan (2001) *Reading Talk.* Stroud: The Thimble Press.

Clay, M. *What Did I write?* London: Heinemann Educational Books.

Crompton, R. and Mann, J. (1996) *IT across the Primary Curriculum.* London: Cassell.

Crystal, D. (1987, second edition) *Child Language, Learning and Linguistics.* London: Arnold.

Czerniewska, P. (1992) *Learning About Writing.* Oxford: Blackwell.

Dalton-Vinters, J. and Mallett, M. (1995) 'Six year olds read about fire fighters', *Reading UKRA.* Vol. 29, no. 1, April.

DfEE (1995) *English in the National Curriculum.* London: HMSO.

DfEE (1998) *The National Literacy Strategy Framework for Teaching.* London: DfEE.

DfEE (2001) *Early Writing Development.* London: Department for Education and Employment.

DfEE (2001a) *The National Literacy Strategy: Developing Early Writing.* London: Department for Education and Employment.

DfEE (2001b) *The National Literacy Strategy: Early Literacy Support.* London: Department for Education and Employment.

DfEE/QCA (1999) *English: The National Curriculum for England.* London: DfEE.

Dodd, Celia (2002) 'Invasion of the Fimbles', *Radio Times*, 21–27 September.

Donaldson, M. (1978) *Children's Minds.* London: Fontana Press.

Doyle, K. and Mallett, M. (1994) 'Were dinosaurs bigger than whales?', TACTYC *Early Years Journal.* Vol. 14, no. 2, Spring.

Egan, K. (1988) *Primary Understanding: Education in Early Childhood.* New York and London: Routledge.

Evans, Janet (2001) 'Four little dollies jumping on the bed – learning about mathematics through talk', in P. Godwin (ed.) *The Articulate Classroom.* London: David Fulton.

Find That Book: Making Links Between Literacy and the Broader Curriculum (1999) London: Lewisham Professional Development Centre.

Fisher, M. (1972) *Matters of Fact.* Leicester: Brockhampton Press.

Fox, Carol (1993) *At the very Edge of the Forest: The Influence of Literature on Story Telling by Children.* London: Cassell.

Godwin, D. and Perkins, M. (2002, second edition) *Teaching Language and Literacy in the Early Years.* London: David Fulton.

Gopnik, A., Meltzoff, A. and Kuhl, P. (1999) *How Babies Think.* London: Weidenfeld & Nicholson.

Gorman, T. (1996) *Assessing Young Children's Writing.* London: The Basic Skills Agency NFER.

Gould, Terry (2002) 'Language and literacy through outdoor play at the foundation stage', *English 4–11 (The English Association).* No. 15, Summer.

Graham, J. (1996) 'Using illustration as the bridge between fact and fiction', *English in Education.* Vol. 30, no. 1.

Graham, J. and Kelly, A. (2000, second edition) *Reading Under Control.* London: David Fulton.

Grainger, T., Goouch, Kathy and Lambirth, Andrew (2002) 'Research in progress: the voice of the child, *"We're Writers"* Project', *Reading, literacy and language* UKRA. Vol. 36, no. 3, November.

Graves, D. (1983) *Writing: Teachers and Children at Work.* London: Heinemann Educational Books.

Gregory, Eve (1996) *Making Sense of a New World: Learning to Read in a Second Language.* London: Paul Chapman.

Gregory, E. (2000) *City Literacies: Reading Across the Generations and Cultures.* London: Routledge.

Griffiths, H. (2001) 'Babies and Books', *Books For Keeps.* No. 129, July, pages 4–5.

Halliday, M.A.K. (1975) *Learning how to Mean: Explorations in the Development of Language.* London: Edward Arnold.

Hancock, R. and Cox, Alison (2002) '"I would have worried about her being a nuisance": workshops for children under three and their parents at Tate Britain', *Early Years, TACTYC.* Vol. 22, no. 2.

Hardy, B. (1977) 'Narrative as a primary act of mind', in M. Meek, A. Warlow, and G. Barten (eds) *The Cool Web.* London: The Bodley Head.

Harrett, J. (2002) 'Young Children Talking: an investigation into the personal stories of Key Stage 1 infants', *Early Years: International Journal of Research and Development.* Vol. 22, no. 1, March.

Harste, J., Woodward, V. and Burke, C. (1984) *Language Stories and Literacy Lessons.* Portsmouth: Heinemann.

Harvey, Stephanie (1998) *Non-fiction Matters.* York, ME: Stenhouse Publishers.

Hurst, V. (1992) 'Assessment and the nursery curriculum', in G. Blenkin and V. Kelly (eds) *Assessment in Early Childhood.* London: Paul Chapman.

Hurst, V. (1997, second edition) *Planning for Early Learning: Educating Young Children* London: Paul Chapman.

Hurst, V. and Joseph, J. (1998) *Supporting Early Learning: The Way Forward.* Milton Keynes: Open University Press.

Jessel, J. (1997) 'Children writing words and building thoughts: does the word processor really help?', in B. Somekh and N. Davis (eds) *Using Information Technology Effectively in Teaching and Learning.* London: Routledge.

Jessell, J. and Matthews, J. (1993) 'Very young children and electronic paint: the beginning of drawing with traditional media and computer paintbox', TACTYC *Early Years Journal.* Vol. 13, no. 2.

Johnson, P. (1997) *Children Making Books.* Reading: Reading University, Reading and Language Information Centre.

Kelly, P. (1998) *The Future of Schools' Television.* London: Independent Television Commission.

Kenyon, Pauline (2002) *Nursery Education.* September, No. 53, page 4.

Kinnes, Sally (2002) 'Are you raising a techno tot?', *The Sunday Times Culture*, 8 September, pages 49–50.

Lewis, M. and Wray, D. (1995) *Developing Children's Non-fiction Writing: Working with Writing Frames.* Leamington Spa: Scholastic.

Lewis, M. and Wray, D. (1996) *Writing Frames: Scaffolding Children's Non-fiction Writing in a Range of Genres.* Reading: Reading University, Reading and Language Information Centre.

Littlefair, A. (1991) *Reading All Types of Writing.* Milton Keynes/Philadelphia: Open University Press.

Littlefair, Alison (1993) 'The "good book": non-narrative aspects', in Roger Beard (ed.) *Teaching Literacy, Balancing Perspectives.* London: Hodder & Stoughton.

Lunzer, E. and Gardner, K. (1979) *The Effective Use of Reading*. London: Heinemann.

Mallett, M. (1992) *Making Facts Matter: Reading Non-fiction 5–11*. London: Paul Chapman.

Mallett, M. (1996/7) 'Engaging heart and mind in reading to learn: the role of illustrations', *Language Matters*. CLPE, No. 3.

Mallett, M. (1999a) *Young Researchers: Informational Reading and Writing in the Early and Primary Years*. London: Routledge.

Mallett, M (1999b) 'Life cycles, journeys and historical stories: learning from informational narrative', *Books for Keeps*. No. 117, July.

Mallett, M. (2002) 'Mathematics and English', in *The Primary English Encyclopaedia: the Heart of the Curriculum*. London: David Fulton.

Medwell, Jane (1998) 'The talking book project: some further insights into the use of talking books to develop reading', *Reading*. May.

Meek, M. (1991) *On Being Literate*. London: The Bodley Head.

Meek, M. (1996) *Information and Book Learning*. Stroud: The Thimble Press.

Millard, Elaine (1997) *Differently Literate: Boys, Girls and the Schooling of Literacy*. London: Falmer Press.

Millard, E. and Marsh, J. (2001) 'Words and pictures: the role of visual literacy in writing and its implication for schooling', *Reading, Literacy and Language*. UKRA. Vol. 23, no. 2, pages 54–61.

Mills, Roger (2002) 'Hal's Reading Diary' *Books for Keeps*. March, no.133, page 9 and 'Hal's Reading Diary', *Books for Keeps*. July, no.135, page 7.

Minns, H. (1997, second edition) *Read it to Me Now! Learning at Home and at School*. Buckingham: Open University Press.

Moon, C. (published annually) *Individualised Reading*. Reading; Reading University Reading and Language Information Centre.

Moore, P.J. and Scevak, J.J. (1998) 'Learning from texts and visual aids: a developmental perspective', *Journal of Research in Reading*. Vol. 20, no. 3, October.

Navarra, J.G. (1955) *The Growth of Scientific Concepts in the Young Child*. New York: Teachers College, Columbia University.

Neate, B. (1992) *Finding Out About Finding Out: a Practical Guide to Children's Information Books*. Sevenoaks: Hodder & Stoughton with UKRA.

Pagett, L. (1997) 'Look! Here's a new idea! Using information technology to facilitate the use of expository text', *Reading UKRA*. Vol. 31, no. 2, July.

Pahl, K. (1999) *Transformations: Making Meaning in Nursery Education*. Stoke on Trent: Trentham Books.

Pappas, C. (1986) 'Exploring the global structure of children's information books', paper presented to the Annual Meeting of the National Reading Conference, Austin, Texas.

Plowman, Lydia (1998) 'Reading multi-media texts: Learning how CD-ROM texts work', *Language Matters*. Spring.

QCA (1999) *Early Learning Goals*. London: Department for Education and Employment.

QCA (2000) *Curriculum Guidance for the Foundation Stage*. London: Department for Education and Employment.

Redfern, A. and Edwards, V. (1997) *Practical Ways to Inspire Young Authors*. Reading: Reading University Reading and Language Information Centre.

Riley, J. (1996) *The Teaching of Reading*. London: Paul Chapman.

Riley, Jeni and Reedy, David (2000) *Developing Writing for Different Purposes: Teaching about Genre in the Early Years*. London: Paul Chapman Publishing.

Robertson, L.H. (2002) 'Parallel literacy classes and hidden strengths: learning to read in English, Urdu and classical Arabic', *Reading, Language and literacy*. UKRA. Vol. 36, no. 3, November.

Sassoon, Rosemary (1990) *Handwriting: The Way to Teach it*. Cheltenham: Stanley Thornes.

Sealey, A. (1996) *Learning About Language: Issues for Primary Teachers*. Milton Keynes/Philadelphia: Open University Press.

Smith, F. (1982) *Writing and the Writer.* New York: Holt, Rinehart & Winston.

Stones, R. (ed.) (1999, second edition) *A Multicultural Guide to Children's Books, 0–12.* London: Books for Keeps.

Taylor, D. (1983) *Family Literacy: Young Children Learning to Read and Write.* London: Heinemann Educational.

Temple, C., Nathan, R., Burris, N. and Temple, F. (1988, second edition) *The Beginnings of Writing.* London: Allyn & Bacon.

Townsend, J. Rowe (1995, definitive edition) *Written for Children: An outline of English language children's literature.* London: The Bodley Head.

Tucker, N. (2001) *The Rough Guide to Children's Books, 0–5 years.* London: Rough Guides Ltd.

Tyrrell, J. and Gill, N. (2000) *Co-ordinating English at Key Stage 1.* London: Falmer Press.

Vygotsky, L.S. (1978) *Mind and Society: The Development of Higher Psychological Processes.* Cambridge MA: Harvard University Press.

Vygotsky, L.S. (1986) *Thought and Language* (edited by A. Kozulin). Cambridge, MA: MIT Press.

Wade, B. and Moore, M. (1996) 'Home activities: the advent of literacy', *European Early Childhood Educational Research Journal.* Vol. 4, no. 2, pages 63–76.

Watson, Victor (2001) *The Cambridge Guide to Children's Books in English.* Cambridge: Cambridge University Press.

Weinberger, J. (1996) *Literacy Goes to School: The Parents' Role in Young Children's Literacy Learning.* London: Paul Chapman.

Wells, Gordon (1981) *Learning Through Interaction: The Study of Language Development.* Cambridge: Cambridge University Press.

Wells, G. (1987) *The Meaning Makers: Children Learning Language and Using Language to Learn.* London: Hodder & Stoughton.

White, Carolyn (1999) 'Somebody made a choice', in J. Callow (ed.) *Image Matters: Visual Texts in the Classroom.* Marrickville, Australia: PETA (Primary English Association).

Whitehead, M. (1997) *Language and Literacy in the Early Years.* London: Paul Chapman.

Whitehead, M. (1999) *Supporting Language and Literacy Development in the Early Years.* Milton Keynes: Open University Press.

Whitehead, M. (2002, second edition) *Developing Language and Literacy with Young Children.* London: Paul Chapman (chapter 4).

Winnicott, Donald (1965) *Playing and Reality.* Harmondsworth: Penguin Books.

Wood, Peter (1988) *How Children Think and Learn.* Oxford: Blackwell.

Wray, D. and Lewis, M. (1997) *Extending Literacy: Children Reading and Writing Non-fiction.* London: Routledge.

Wyse, D. and Jones, R. (2001) *English, Language and Literacy.* London: Routledge.

Index